Vegetarianism and Animal Ethics in Contemporary Buddhism

Buddhism is widely known to advocate a stance of total pacifism towards all sentient beings, and because of this, it is often thought that Buddhist doctrine would stipulate that non-violent food practices, such as vegetarianism, be mandatory. However, the Pāli source materials do not encourage vegetarianism and most Buddhists do not practice it. Using research based on ethnographic evidence and interviews, this book discusses this issue by presenting an investigation of vegetarianism and animal ethics within a Buddhist cultural domain.

Focusing on Sri Lanka, a place of great historical significance to Buddhism, the book looks at how lay Buddhists and the clergy came to understand the role of vegetarianism and animal ethics in Buddhism. It analyses whether the Buddha preached a view that encouraged vegetarianism, and how this squares with his pacifism towards animals. The book goes on to question how Buddhist food practices intersect with other secular activities such as traditional medicine, as well as discussing the wider implications of Buddhist animal pacifism including vegetarian political movements and animal rights groups.

Shedding light on a subject that, until now, has only been tangentially treated by scholars, this interdisciplinary study will be of interest to those working in the fields of Buddhist Studies, Religion and Philosophy, as well as South Asian Studies.

James John Stewart is Research Associate at the University of Tasmania, Australia.

Routledge Studies in Asian Religion and Philosophy

1 **Deconstruction and the Ethical in Asian Thought**
   Edited by Youru Wang

2 **An Introduction to Daoist Thought**
   Action, language, and ethics in Zhuangzi
   Eske Møllgaard

3 **Religious Commodifications in Asia**
   Marketing gods
   Edited by Pattana Kitiarsa

4 **Christianity and the State in Asia**
   Complicity and conflict
   Edited by Julius Bautista and Francis Khek Gee Lim

5 **Christianity in Contemporary China**
   Socio-cultural perspectives
   Edited by Francis Khek Gee Lim

6 **The Buddha and Religious Diversity**
   J. Abraham Velez de Cea

7 **Japanese Religions and Globalization**
   Ugo Dessi

8 **Religion and the Subtle Body in Asia and the West**
   Between mind and body
   Geoffrey Samuel and Jay Johnston

9 **'Yogini' in South Asia**
   Interdisciplinary approaches
   Edited by Istvan Keul

10 **The Confucian Philosophy of Harmony**
    Chenyang Li

11 **Postcolonial Resistance and Asian Theology**
    Simon Shui-Man Kwa

12 **Asian Perspectives on Animal Ethics**
    Edited by Neil Dalal and Chloe Taylor

13 **Objects of Worship in South Asian Religions**
    Forms, practices and meanings
    Edited by Knut A. Jacobsen, Mikael Aktor and Kristina Myrvold

14 **Disease, Religion and Healing in Asia**
    Collaborations and Collisions
    Ivette Vargas-O'Bryan and Zhou Xun

15 **Asian Religions, Technology and Science**
    Edited by István Keul

16 **Vegetarianism and Animal Ethics in Contemporary Buddhism**
    James John Stewart

Vegetarianism and Animal Ethics in Contemporary Buddhism

James John Stewart

LONDON AND NEW YORK

First published 2016
by Routledge
2 Park Square, Milton Park, Abingdon, Oxon OX14 4RN

and by Routledge
711 Third Avenue, New York, NY 10017

First issued in paperback 2017

Routledge is an imprint of the Taylor & Francis Group, an informa business

© 2016 James John Stewart

The right of James John Stewart to be identified as author of this work has been asserted by him in accordance with sections 77 and 78 of the Copyright, Designs and Patents Act 1988.

All rights reserved. No part of this book may be reprinted or reproduced or utilised in any form or by any electronic, mechanical, or other means, now known or hereafter invented, including photocopying and recording, or in any information storage or retrieval system, without permission in writing from the publishers.

Trademark notice: Product or corporate names may be trademarks or registered trademarks, and are used only for identification and explanation without intent to infringe.

British Library Cataloguing in Publication Data
A catalogue record for this book is available from the British Library

Library of Congress Cataloging in Publication Data
Stewart, James John, author.
　Vegetarianism and animal ethics in contemporary Buddhism / James John Stewart.
　　pages cm. -- (Routledge studies in Asian religion and philosophy)
　1. Vegetarianism--Religious aspects--Buddhism. 2. Buddhist ethics--Sri Lanka. I. Title.
　BQ4570.V43S85 2015
　294.3'5693--dc23
　　　　　　　2015003899

ISBN 13: 978-1-138-49336-0 (pbk)
ISBN 13: 978-1-138-80216-2 (hbk)

Typeset in Times New Roman
by Taylor & Francis Books

For my mother, Suzanne Hutchison, and father, David Stewart.

මගේ අම්මා සහ තාත්තා වෙත ආදරයෙන් පිරිනමමි
ඇයගේ සෙනෙහෙබර දෝත මගේ මෙම පොත බැතියෙන් පිරිනමමි

Contents

Acknowledgement		viii
Abbreviations		ix
	Introduction: vegetarianism and dietary ethics in Sri Lanka	1
1	The lion and the cow	11
2	Eating, drinking, killing: vegetarianism and animal welfare in Sinhala literature	41
3	Food of compassion	73
4	The disciple's diet	98
5	Milk of life	122
6	Meat aversions: vegetarianism, health food and medicine in Sinhala society	148
7	Food politics	175
8	Conclusion	200
	Bibliography	203
	Index	210

Acknowledgement

I would like to first of all thank my wife, Kumudu Stewart, for her many years of support and encouragement in this project. She has spent countless hours helping me with difficult texts and has taught me everything I know about the Sinhala language. She routinely provided me with insightful observations and comments that have helped shape this work.

Shihara Fernando has also been enormously helpful and has spent a great deal of time checking all the translations. Several audio interviews were also carefully translated by him. His work has been absolutely indispensible.

Kumudu Stewart and Bishma Jayathilaka both spent their valuable time helping me conduct the interviews in Sri Lanka and ensured that the fieldwork was conducted in a smooth manner.

Others have also helped me gather many useful documents that have assisted me with my work. Chitra Jayathilaka has helped collect a large amount of material not all of which I was able to use in this work. Her husband, J.M. Jayathilaka Banda, has also been extremely supportive of my work and has helped resolve a number of logistical problems.

A number of academics in Australia have frequently helped encourage me in pursuing this project. They have often provided excellent advice and suggestions that have vastly improved this work. I would therefore like to thank Professor Jeff Malpas (University of Tasmania), Dr Sonam Thakchoe (University of Tasmania) and Chris Clark (University of Sydney).

Finally, I would like to thank my parents for their constant and unwavering support throughout the development of this project. This book is dedicated to both of them.

Abbreviations

AN	Aṅguttara Nikāya
Atth	Atthasālinī
DN	Dīgha Nikāya
Iti	Itivuttaka
Jat	Jātaka Tales
MN	Majjhima Nikāya
SN	Saṃyutta Nikāya
S	Sutta Nipāta
Vin-CV	Vinaya: Cūlavaṃsa
Vin-MV	Vinaya Mahāvaṃsa

Introduction
Vegetarianism and dietary ethics in Sri Lanka

Buddhism and vegetarianism

The famous golden rule – treat others as you would like yourself to be treated – is a principle of morality that appears in numerous religious systems. Buddhism numbers amongst them.

The Buddha says, 'Since I am one who wishes to live, who does not wish to die; I desire happiness and am averse to suffering, if someone were to take my life, that would not be pleasing and agreeable to me. Now if I were to take the life of another – of one who wishes to live, who does not want to die [etc.] – that would not be pleasing and agreeable to the other either.'[1] From this reasoning, the Buddha produces the following maxim, a maxim that arguably forms the cornerstone of Buddhist ethics. He says that the good Buddhist, 'having reflected thus, abstains from the destruction of life, *exhorts others to abstain* from the destruction of life, and *speaks in praise of abstinence* from the destruction of life. Thus bodily conduct of his is purified in three respects' (my italics).[2]

It is clear that a good Buddhist should not kill, but more than that a good Buddhist *should encourage others* not to kill. There is therefore a proselytizing aspect to right Buddhist conduct. The Buddha insists that a good Buddhist should try and persuade others to give up acts of violence and help build a society free of conflict. Notice that the basis of this persuasion is not grounded in rhetoric or religious dogma, but on a rational argument that harming others contradicts our own desires and beliefs. I am not claiming that Buddhism is absolutely free of dogma and rhetoric, but at least the Buddha's principle of non-violence does find its origins in a rational argumentation. In addition, this principle is not obviously anthropocentric. There is no claim here that only human beings should be considered morally relevant. Instead, the destruction of life *as such* is the point of reference. Animals, and perhaps even other more basic life forms, are clearly encompassed within this rubric.

It is one thing to say that a good Buddhist should not kill, however, and quite another thing to also define a good Buddhist as someone who encourages others not to kill. This suggests a range of other implications. For example, the canonical Pāli texts – a body of ancient scripts that are said to document the sayings of the Buddha – make it clear that Buddhists must not participate in industries that depend upon killing. The Buddha, for example, questions whether it is right for a Buddhist to become a soldier.[3] But more importantly for our purposes, he condemns occupations that are concerned with animal slaughter. It therefore seems to be a virtual requirement of the principle of non-violence that programmes involving the purposeful destruction of life be boycotted.

There are other subtle moral implications that follow from the Buddha's teachings. The *Vinaya* – the Buddha's instruction manual for monks –requires that monks not build their huts from mud due to the fear that insects might be killed in the construction process.[4] Monks are similarly required to avoid wearing animal skins.[5] Examples of this type multiple and monks and nuns are expected to be completely scrupulous in their engagement with living creatures. Consequently, the principle of non-violence has direct implications not only over what one's chosen occupation should be, but also over how one should engage in even minute day-to-day affairs.

Later Theravāda commentators have drawn even more radical conclusions from these general principles. Buddhaghosa – a fifth-century Indian Buddhist monk who resided for some time in Sri Lanka – wrote in his *Atthasālinī (The Expositor)* that a good Buddhist is required to engage in acts of protest that might even end in the destruction of private property. He says that a good Buddhist has, 'The (fish) net destroyed, the fish-trap broken, the bird-cage spoiled, [and] effects the release of the fettered...' and that the good Buddhist, 'prescribes by beat of drum the non-taking of life and does such other acts to protect life...'[6] These radical acts of protest are reminiscent of contemporary animal rights organizations who engage in criminal acts for the betterment of animals. But for Buddhaghosa, and other Buddhists who interpret the Buddha's exhortation against violence as a clarion call for animal liberation, such acts are unremarkable. This interpretation of the Buddha's teaching demands more than just a meek attempt to persuade others not to kill but instead requires direct intervention that ends with the destruction of the very instruments that entrap and hurt animals.

We see that the Buddha outright calls for the total boycott of the slaughter industries. Meanwhile, Buddhaghosa practically requires that we engage in acts of civil disobedience. As we shall also see, the Buddha also asks that his monks not take meat that they know has been killed for them.

Taken together, there is a strong implication that the good Buddhist should not purchase animal flesh from institutions in which animals are killed. This implication seems even more apparent in context to the Buddha's demand that the good Buddhist encourage others not to kill. What better way to achieve this than by boycotting the purchase of meat altogether? From such a boycott, vegetarianism seems to follow naturally.

Indeed, a number of Buddhists have interpreted the Buddha's teaching in precisely this way and regard this argument as obvious. Even if the Buddha doesn't explicitly endorse this argument, some Buddhists believe that the principle of non-violence, and its various associated rules, all implicitly suggest an endorsement of vegetarianism.

This book is a study of those Buddhists and their arguments in favour of why Buddhism encourages vegetarianism.

But this book does not restrict itself by discussing only these pro-vegetarian Buddhists. The question of vegetarianism in Buddhism is controversial even within the Buddhist community and many Buddhists argue that there is no doctrinal justification for vegetarianism. Some Buddhists and Buddhist Studies scholars point towards the Buddha's ambivalent attitude towards vegetarianism in the canonical texts. The Buddha restricted the consumption of meat but he did not ban it outright. Vegetarianism is allowed, but it is not mandatory. Some Buddhists believe that ethical vegetarianism motivated from Buddhist views is a flagrant misinterpretation of doctrine. Some even think it is downright heretical. Therefore, this book also studies the conflict that originates from the question of vegetarianism and the way in which Buddhist anti-vegetarian proponents deal with those who speak in favour of vegetarianism.

While there are very few Buddhists that would argue that we are allowed to hurt animals, there are a number who do not see the Buddha's first precept as a justification of vegetarianism. How these Buddhists address the tension between the first precept of non-violence and the implication of direct and indirect action, including the adoption of vegetarianism, remains a vital question that has not been adequately addressed in previous literature.

The Buddhist reputation for vegetarianism

In the West, Buddhism has a reputation for kindness towards animals. This reputation is, in my view, generally justified. Historically, however, it is this supposed kindness towards animals that has also earned Buddhism rebuke. Take, for example, this public statement made by Robert Moncrief to an assembled crowd of British Christians in 1879. Moncrief is making comment on the recently released book *The Light of Asia* by Edwin Arnold. Moncrief says:

'Sirs and ladies, I venture to ask you if any people on the face of the earth seem to be more utterly indifferent to the shedding of blood and to human suffering than the followers of Buddhism. At the same time, with all this wretched, horrible disregard for human suffering and human life, they show the greatest care for animal life. ...These contradictions are parts of the darkness proceeding out of the *Light of Asia* which we are asked to accept in preference to the Light of the World (applause).'[7]

Moncrief's complaint is that the religion of Buddhism seems to cares more for animals than humans. This is, quite obviously, a misinterpretation of Buddhism as the Buddha praises the importance of protecting all life, not just animal life. But in the context of Moncrief's period there is a way in which his statement demonstrates just how shocking and foreign the Buddha's pacifistic sentiments were to Victorian-era Europeans. Moncrief saw Buddhism as a threat to the orthodox Christian tradition of his time, a tradition that did not view animals as particularly morally relevant.

But Moncrief's statement also shows how animal welfarism can become politicized and used to polarise debates between 'us' and the 'other'. As we shall see, despite the seemingly innocuous subject matter of non-violence towards animals and vegetarianism, the animal welfare movement is easily co-opted into nationalist and xenophobic narratives. Moncrief did this in 1879, and in 2014 the same strategy is used in the country of Sri Lanka.

While Moncrief gets things wrong by misinterpreting the first precept and disregarding the Buddhist world's concern for *all life*, not just animals, it is possible to fall into the opposite error by uncritically accepting Buddhism as a force only for good. Buddhism's reputation for animal welfare and vegetarianism is sometimes assumed in an uncritical manner in the West. The Western association between vegetarianism and Buddhism is rooted in the history of European scholarship. For example, in discussing the growing popularity of Buddhism in Germany during the 1890s, Douglas McGetchin notes that Buddhist societies often met in vegetarian restaurants.[8] It was in the context of these restaurants that the meaning and significance of Buddhist philosophy was discussed by budding German Buddhologists. There was an expectation amongst European enthusiasts of Buddhism that Buddhists would be vegetarians. And if they were not already vegetarians then they ought to be.

This connection between vegetarianism and Buddhism was also strongly made in Victorian England. Indology and Buddhology was in its infancy and many of those who studied it were already on the fringes of conventional society. They were already interested in investigating ethical views that were at odds with the prevailing – primarily Christian - status quo.

Leela Gandhi puts this as follows: 'Thus leavened in its originary moments by civilizational contestation well in excess of its basic theme of dietetic reform, English vegetarianism by the time it entered the nineteenth century was primed, we might conjecture, for anticolonial polemic. Certainly vegetarianism, most scholars and historians of the subject agree, mixed in as it was in its transmission with the intellectual and political matter of positive romantic orientalism, millennialism, and indigenous traditions of dissent, was already the preserve of radical counterculture, already possessed of excessive revolutionary aspirations.'[9] A vegetarian diet was already associated with non-conformity. Thus it was easy for renegade Buddhist enthusiasts to adopt such a practice and connect it to their interest in the heathen religion of Buddhism.

The assumption that vegetarianism was an automatic feature of 'Indic civilization' was also obvious in the case of Europeans engaged in the study of Sri Lanka. Henry Steel Olcott, an individual we will examine in Chapter 1, was convinced that the Sinhalese habit of eating meat was evidence that Buddhism had been significantly degraded in Sri Lanka. This attitude is typical of what is now known as Orientalism: Asian practitioners are typically wrong about their own religion and need instruction from European scholars. This patronising outlook is a danger in any assessment of Asian religious practices.

This romanticism about the ethical propriety of Buddhists has therefore been a historical problem. Nonetheless, today a number of books and articles have been written in the West that support the idea that Buddhism maintains a favourable attitude towards animals and even vegetarianism. Authors such as Roshi Kapleau (1981), Norm Phelps (2004) and Bodhipaksa (2009) have all written books in defence of Buddhist animal welfarism and animal rights. These authors have also mounted a vigorous defence of the idea that Buddhism should – and even does – endorse vegetarianism. Websites, such as Shabkar.org maintain repositories of English language literature that are intended to demonstrate the connection between Buddhism and vegetarianism. There is therefore a strong idea in the West that Buddhism supports vegetarianism and the better treatment of animals more generally.

A number of scholars have been at pains to point out, however, that many Buddhists in a number of Buddhist countries are pointedly *not* vegetarians and cultivate a considerable affection for meat foods.[10] In fact, the rule tends to be that Buddhist countries are typically meat-eating countries and there are only a few exceptions to this. Vegetarianism is popular within Taiwanese Buddhist communities, for example, due to the influence of pro-vegetarian texts like the *Laṅkāvatāra Sūtra*. But in the majority of Theravāda countries – countries like Myanmar, Thailand, Cambodia and Sri Lanka – meat-eating of one form or another seems to be a sociological fact. Some writers, such as Paul Waldau (2001), have actively maintained that this reputation for animal welfare is completely wrong-headed. He maintains that Buddhism is a speciesist religion that adopts a bigoted position towards animals.[11]

The historical expectation that Buddhists are vegetarians, therefore, may not always be consistent with the lived reality.

Western expectations about ethical vegetarianism in Buddhist countries may even be just another example of Western cultural neo-colonialism or Orientalism. Such expectations may, in fact, say more about the West and how Western academics, writers and Buddhist enthusiasts, have co-opted Buddhism and re-appropriated it for their own purposes. In the process of this Western re-appropriation, the meaning of Buddhism, as it is understood by Buddhist communities in Buddhist nations, may be ignored.

It may also be an example of Westerners dictating to the non-West as to what constitutes 'proper' Buddhism, that is, a Buddhism bereft of supposedly non-Buddhist accretions. Overly simplistic interpretations of Buddhism that were developed during the earliest days of European Buddhist Studies in the nineteenth century continue to germinate even today. The view that Buddhism is a 'philosophy' and 'not a religion' is a prime example of nineteenth-century Orientalist scholarship entering into the Western public consciousness that persists even now.[12] This question originated during a period of scholarship in the late 1800s, a period where European thinkers were looking for alternative non-Christian spiritualities that were simultaneously compatible with scientific developments. Buddhism seemed to fit this criterion. Such a view also emerged as a way of criticizing Buddhism because of its atheistic tendencies. Scholars and commentators of the period could not accept that a particular religious tradition could be atheistic.[13]

Under such views it was not appropriate to view Buddhism as a religion. It was better to regard it as a rational philosophy that, depending on one's assumptions, may or may not have spiritual benefits. But such a view is overly reductionist. It was an interpretation that served European concerns but did not necessarily reflect the lived reality of Buddhists in Buddhist countries.

The reputation that Buddhism has earned as a tradition that advocates vegetarianism may very well be another overly simplistic interpretation. In fact, it is virtually indisputable that from a doctrinal perspective such an interpretation is false. But what constitutes Buddhism is not determined only by the texts, nor by what the traditional interpretation may say. The lived Buddhist tradition is a complex and organic entity that contains a wide range of opinions and voices and it is important to listen closely to these different views.

In this book I endeavour to avoid making these types of faulty assumptions. Instead, I have tried to let Sri Lankan Buddhists speak for themselves about the question of vegetarianism. As one might expect, there is a range of views about the question of vegetarianism. Some of these views justify the traditional reputation Buddhism has for animal welfare and vegetarianism. Sometimes these views contradict that reputation.

I have made a point of putting many of these comments into doctrinal context. In doing so I have sometimes noted that certain authors or informants have views that contradict the textual materials. I do not make these comments with the intention of saying that these individuals are wrong about Buddhism *per se*. Indeed, I do not believe there is a correct way to characterize 'authentic' or 'original' Buddhism and I believe any attempt to do so is wrong-headed. My comments are instead simply statements of fact about such contradictions and this in itself is interesting simply because it shows that there are a multiplicity of ways to interpret and understand the Buddhist tradition.

Sri Lanka

This study is primarily an ethnography that attempts to capture the views and opinions that Sri Lankan Sinhalese Buddhists have of the issue of animal welfare and dietary ethics.

Sri Lanka is an ideal starting point for such a study for a range of reasons: (1) Sri Lanka plays a culturally significant role in modern Theravāda Buddhism. It has been historically influential in developing and sustaining Buddhism in surrounding nations such as Myanmar and Thailand; (2) as a Theravāda nation, there is considerable focus on the Pāli canonical texts, a body of texts that discuss the issue of vegetarianism and animal welfare in some detail; (3) unlike Mahāyāna nations like Taiwan, a nation where vegetarianism has been widely adopted, Sri Lanka is noteworthy precisely because there is dispute over the veracity of vegetarianism as a diet and the limits of animal welfare. Because there is dispute there is a multiplicity of opinion. This therefore makes Sri Lanka an intrinsically interesting place to study these questions.

Sri Lanka is an ethnically and religiously divided nation. Nearly 75% of the population are ethnic Sinhalese. The remaining population are comprised of Sri Lankan Tamils (11%), Sri Lankan Moors (9%), Indian Tamils (4%), and other tiny minority groups including Malays and Burghers. The Sinhalese typically view themselves as the original and true inhabitants of the island, though historically Tamil Sri Lankans have also lived in Sri Lanka for an equally long period of time and the indigenous Veddahs predate the Sinhalese and Tamils respectively. Sri Lankan Moors, descendants of Arab traders, have also lived in Sri Lanka for a very long time – at least since the ninth century. Meanwhile, Indian Tamils have lived in Sri Lanka since the British colonial period where they were transported to Sri Lanka by colonial authorities to work on the up-country tea and coffee plantations. Sri Lanka is an island that has been long inhabited by a range of different ethnicities and religious persuasions.

Nonetheless, this melting pot of cultures and religions has not always been a place of harmony and mutual tolerance. Disputes over who has a rightful place on the island have led to violence and even civil war. In 2009, a nearly thirty year civil war – a war preceded by decades of hostility – came to a bloody end when the Sri Lankan military, composed primarily of the Sinhala majority, crushed the severely diminished Tamil separatist militia known as the Tamil Tigers. Tensions between the Sinhalese and Tamil communities continue to run high, as do tensions with other minority communities, notably the Muslim community.

Ethnic conflict therefore dovetails with religious conflict. Buddhism is the majority religion in Sri Lanka (70%) and Buddhism is almost exclusively practiced by Sinhalese. Hinduism is the second most popular religion (12.6%) though it should be noted that many Buddhists also participate in Hindu activities. As a total religious identity, however, Hinduism is mostly practiced by Tamils. Islam (9.7%) is typically associated with the Sri Lankan Moors while Christianity (7.45%), a religion that has its origins in European colonization, finds favour with a number of different ethnicities mostly Sinhalese and Tamil.

This study focuses on Sri Lankan Sinhala Buddhists. This is because my study is first of all about Buddhism and, inevitably, Buddhism is almost entirely practiced by ethnic Sinhalese. Nonetheless, towards the end of the book I begin to broach the issue of how vegetarianism and animal welfarism intersects with ethnic and religious politics. Consequently, I will also be looking at the role Muslims have played recently in the Buddhist animal welfare movement.

Methodology

In discussing these issues I will be using a combination of historical and textual analysis, as well as utilizing social data in the form of interviews, newspaper articles, pamphlets, books and other literary materials. This analysis is done in the context of participant observation and draws upon several years of cumulative work in Sri Lanka.

The ethnographic component of the study relies heavily on interviews. This qualitative aspect of the study was undertaken using purposive sampling. As is clear from the above discussion, the sampling criteria was that the participant be Sinhalese and a Buddhist. Of course, how people identify as Buddhists can be complicated and various studies have shown that many Sinhalese Buddhists nonetheless believe in deities of Hindu origin and engage in acts of worship commensurate with those beliefs.[14] Nonetheless, it is clear that Sinhalese Buddhists are individuals who identify first of all as Buddhists and simply incorporate Hindu rituals and beliefs into their own Buddhist worldview.

Lay informants were initially recruited through several cultural insiders who were able to provide contact with potential participants. Subsequent participants were recruited through further recommendations and snowball recruitment. Monastic informants were gathered in a similar manner. Cultural insiders would introduce us to temples that they believed would be willing to participate in the research. Some refused and others agreed. This led to further introductions and wider participation.

This qualitative research is obviously not intended to be statistically significant, particularly in light of the small number of research participants. Nor is the research intended to be free of statistical bias. As an ethnographic study the project's aim is to capture the opinions of a number of different Buddhists in order to shed light on some Sinhalese Buddhist views on the issue of animal welfare and dietary ethics. Some bias has been eliminated by seeking out a range of different Sinhalese Buddhists who have a number of competing views on this issue. I have also examined different perspectives on the topic by investigating not only the ethical motivations behind vegetarianism, but also the health or prudential motivations.

The two areas this sampling took place were Colombo and Kegalle. A few interviews also took place in Kandy and Kurunegala (though the Kurunegala informants were affiliated with the Kegalle informants and the interviews took place in Kegalle in any case). The need to interview monks in Kandy will be made clear in the subsequent study but, in short, it was to gain greater understanding of issues to do with the Srī Daḷadā Māligāva otherwise known as the Temple of the Tooth. The reason for this divide between Colombo and Kegalle is partly a matter of convenience, but there are also some advantages to this division in sampling insofar that the Colombo informants helped provide an urban perspective while the Kegalle informants provided a more rural context.

Apart from the interviews, I have heavily utilized a range of Sinhala language written sources. Again, the use of these different materials helps support conclusions that are drawn from the interview data and helps avoid the work being contaminated by a one-sided viewpoint. For example, much of the written material – though independent of the informants who were interviewed – helps corroborate the conclusions that are drawn from that data. So despite there being a relatively small informant sample size, it is possible to form some meaningful conclusions from the information available.

Setting the scene

Sri Lanka is an island nation located off the southeast coast of the Indian subcontinent. It has a long history, some of which will be examined in the forthcoming study. It has also been subject to extensive European colonization from the 1500s onwards.

The areas in Sri Lanka primarily of concern for this study are Colombo and Kegalle. Colombo is the largest city in Sri Lanka and is home to around 1.5 million people. Colombo is not officially the capital of Sri Lanka, but instead one of its suburbs is: Sri Jayawardanapura Kotte. Despite this, Colombo is casually referred to as the capital in day-to-day affairs. It is the economic and political powerhouse of Sri Lanka and is also a major centre of educational and cultural affairs. Of course, there is a rivalry between long time inhabitants of Colombo and residents of the so-called up-country and its major centre of Kandy. Kandy (Nuwara in Sinhala) was formerly the seat of power for the Kandyan Kingdom and many Sinhalese identify this area as being the seat of Sinhala sovereignty. Colombo, on the other hand, is sometimes dismissed as an urbane metropolis that has a tendency to fetishize Western decadence and other foreign intrusions.

Kegalle is part of the up-country and is considered a satellite of Kandy. Kegalle is the capital of the Sabaragamuwa district. The elite of Colombo might hold the stereotype – however unfair – that people from the area of the Kegalle area are simple country folk. Kegalle is very much a market-orientated town that acts as a hub for an area rich in agricultural production. Despite the fact that Kegalle is situated in a rural area, urban sprawl leads one to label Kegalle as peri-urban. Unlike Colombo it is difficult to definitively refer to Kegalle as urban, but it is also not obviously rural and the two classifications tend to blur together. However, unlike Colombo district, the wider Sabaragamuwa district can probably be confidently regarded as rural.

Colombo and Kegalle therefore represent two different worlds within the country of Sri Lanka. One is a coastal low country metropolis; the other is an up-country quasi-rural market town. As we shall see, however, the differences between these regions matters less than one might expect and there is remarkable synergy and agreement in how informants responded to the issue of animal welfare and vegetarianism.

Terminology and diacritics

Wherever possible I have attempted to avoid the unnecessary use of Buddhist jargon and terminology. In accordance with this I have translated terms, whenever feasible, into their appropriate English meaning. Some terms are not easily translatable and so I have kept them in their original Sinhala or Pāli but with an appropriate explanation of their meaning.

In terms of diacritics I have followed, as much as possible, the UN Romanisation framework for the Sinhala language. Some common terms (for example, Nirvana, Buddha, Bodhisattva and so on) I have left without diacritics as these terms are now common in English.

Similarly, I have not used diacritics for many Sinhala names be they the names of informants, Sinhala authors, or the names of temples to avoid cluttering the page. It is also the convention in Sri Lanka that these names generally be spelled without diacritics. Sinhala text is, however, fully Romanised. For the most part, Sinhala text has been relegated to the endnotes.

Notes

1 SN 55.7, 1797.
2 Ibid.
3 It is suggested that a soldier who 'exerts himself in battle', believing that he will be reborn in glory, will in fact be reborn in the animal realms or in hell (SN 42.3, 1335).
4 Vin-Pat, 2, 65.
5 Vin-MV, 5, 267.
6 Atth, 106.
7 Almond, 2.
8 McGetchin, 138.
9 Gandhi, 76.
10 These authors will be discussed in later chapters.
11 See my article *Violence and Nonviolence to Buddhist Animal Ethics* (2014) for my reply to Waldau's claim here (644–645).
12 King, 7–35.
13 Almond, 93–100.
14 For further details on this see: Holt, 2004; Obeyesekere, 1977; and Obeyesekere and Gombrich, 1988: 96–132.

1 The lion and the cow

Non-violence towards animals in Sinhala myth and history

There is a myth in Sinhala society that the Sinhala people are the product of a union between a human princess and a lion. Indeed, the very name 'Sinhala' means 'the lion people'.[1] This stems from the mythic origins of the Sinhala people: a people created from the union of a lion and a princess. This union is supposed to have originally taken place in north India in a mythic place called Sinhapura or 'Lion City'.[2]

Lion imagery is common throughout the island and the lion has become a symbol of the Sinhala ethnicity. King Kashyapa (ruled 473–495 CE) moved his capital to Sigiriya which means 'Lion's Rock'. Today you can see the remains of an enormous lion shaped entranceway that is located near the start of the ascent to the top of the rock. Parakramabahu IX of Kotte (ruled 1508–1528 CE) reportedly had a throne built in the image of a lion.[3] Many Sinhalese continue to believe that the traditional traits of the lion are evident in their cultural disposition: proud, beautiful, intelligent, powerful and, when challenged, able to respond with a confidence that guarantees success.

The image of the lion continues to be a basic symbol of the Sinhalese. For example, it features prominently on the Sri Lankan flag and pointedly represents the Sinhala people. Simple green and orange bands serve as a modest representation of the two main ethnic minorities: the Tamils and the (mostly Moorish) Muslims. The use of the lion even extends to trivial matters such as the national beer. Its slogan reads, 'Is there a lion in you?'

When considering the question of food and animal ethics, the fact that the lion is a symbol of the Sinhalese is instructive on a number of levels. First of all, the lion is a carnivore – he cannot survive on vegetables but must eat meat. In keeping with that, the lion is a hunter who must prey upon other animals. Furthermore, the lion is the best of all hunters in the animal kingdom. The lion symbol is therefore a bloodthirsty symbol. It would therefore seem that the legitimacy of vegetarianism and animal non-violence as an ordinary Sinhala cultural activity is already called into question.

Yet although the Sinhalese cherish the lion, they also cherish another animal that – although not explicitly symbolic of the Sinhalese – is perhaps of more practical significance and celebration: the cow. As will become very apparent in Chapter 5, the cow is a pre-eminently favoured animal within Sinhala Buddhist society. The cow is a protected animal, more so, perhaps, than the widely respected elephant. Indeed, an entire movement has developed around the defence of the cow. The cow represents, for many Sinhala Buddhists, the nurturing and love expressed by one's own mother. It is also the locus of discourse about the importance of the Buddhist view of non-violence (ahiṃsavādiyo). The killing of the cow is used as a mechanism to expose the barbarity of other cultures and their religions and this is contrasted with the intrinsic peacefulness of the Buddhist religion and its arch adherents, the Sinhalese.

The cow is regarded as an innocent and gentle creature that generously supplies the Sri Lankan people with nutritious food that sustains the entire nation. It is the opposite of the fierce lion: it is not an animal that is on the offense, but is a helpless creature that needs protection. If anything, it is the aggressive lion-like quality of the Sinhalese that must be called upon to defend this creature against the barbaric 'other' that wants to kill the cow.

This duality between the lion and the cow lies at the heart of the complicated attitude Sinhalese have towards animals, animal welfare and the attitudes they have about food ethics. On the one hand, there is the aggressive, militaristic and meat-eating aspect of Sinhala culture. On the other hand, there is the pacific, non-violent, vegetarian side that wants to protect animals and cherish Buddhist principles.

These two sides are at once incompatible and at the same time mutually dependent. One of the key arguments made during the civil war was that Buddhism, which represents non-violence and peace, was to be defended through an aggressive military.[4] This ethos is apparent in some aspects of the modern Sinhala Buddhist animal welfare movement where bloody protest and retaliatory violence is justified as a necessary way to defend animals from being slaughtered by certain minority groups.

This tension between violence and non-violence is one of the most interesting aspects of Sinhala Buddhism not only now, but throughout Sinhala history. Authors like Bartholomeusz[5] and Tambiah[6] have long commented on this peculiar tension. Here we will look at some of these tensions. At the same time, we will also be looking at the origins of Sinhala attitudes towards food and animal ethics. This chapter is a preparatory chapter to lay the groundwork for future ethnographical discussions.

Animal protectionism in India

In considering animal welfare in Sri Lanka, and therefore its food ethics, it is vital that the antecedent ancient Indian traditions are also examined. To begin with, Sinhala Buddhists often look to ancient India for moral guidance primarily because the Buddha himself had his origins in India. But it is not just the Buddha who is a source of moral guidance here. King Aśoka

(304–233 BCE), the great king of the Aśokan Empire, is celebrated amongst the Sinhalese as a benevolent ruler, but also a ruler who was guided by Buddhist principles. These two historic figures are therefore widely recognised as authorities on matters to do with animal welfare and vegetarianism.

The Buddha's views on these matters are complicated and will be examined in Chapter 2. That chapter focuses on literary sources that argue in favour of vegetarianism and animal welfare. Instead, in this chapter I will focus primarily on King Aśoka as well as aspects of the Vedic and Hindu religions that support vegetarianism.

In terms of heterodox religions, both Buddhism and Jainism famously promote non-violence as a central tenet. Of these two religious movements, only Mahāvīra of the Jains enforced vegetarianism as a religious ideal. As we shall see in the next chapter, the Buddha only made vegetarianism optional. As a general rule, Jainism seems to have little influence in Sinhala Buddhist culture and society. This is perhaps owed to the received view (which originated with the Buddha himself) that the Jain religion represents an 'extreme' view that is anathema to the moderate doctrine prescribed by the Buddha. This was made clear by one of our monastic informants who insisted that vegetarianism had no doctrinal basis in Buddhism because it was associated with the Jains and was therefore fundamentally an ascetic practice.

Despite the fact that Buddhism arose as a doctrine that, in many ways, challenged the prevailing orthodox Vedic view (in part because of how the Vedic tradition treated animals) Sinhalese in Sri Lanka have been deeply influenced by the Hindu tradition. If any outside force to have had an influence on Sinhala vegetarianism it is the Hindu tradition. One of the traditional medical doctors complimented Hindu practitioners on their vegetarianism since they carried it out authentically and, furthermore, did so in a healthy way.

India is famous for being a nation in which vegetarianism is favoured. This perception is also maintained in Sri Lanka. In the West, we are familiar with one famous Hindu exponent of vegetarianism: Gandhi. In Sri Lanka too, Gandhi is also recognised as a great vegetarian.[7] Worldwide, the idea that Hindus are vegetarians is so integrated into the public perception that it is now understood to be a traditional dietary requirement of the Brahman caste.[8]

There is some basis for this perception. As will become apparent in a later chapter on cow protectionism, the Vedic and Brahmanical texts sometimes condemn animal slaughter and this tendency towards animal protection often results in the adoption of vegetarianism as a dietary ideal. Christopher Fuller points out that vegetarianism is widespread amongst Brahmans in South India and even amongst some non-Brahman castes.[9] Fuller observes that the adoption of vegetarianism is controlled to a large extent by caste: caste purity is generally maintained through a strict adherence to a vegetarian diet the contravention of which requires the implementation of complex purification rituals.[10]

Pollution is therefore a key factor in food ethics in Hindu religious practices. Vegetarianism in these contexts has a great deal less to do with the avoidance of animal suffering and more to do with separation from other castes. Mary Douglas makes this clear as follows: 'A Havik, working with his Untouchable servant in his garden, may become severely defiled by touching a rope of bamboo at the same time as the servant.'[11] She adds that, 'Pollution lingers in cotton cloth, metal cooking vessels, cooked food'[12] and it is this reason, as Orenstein points out, that food represents a particular threat of contamination.[13] Things are made worse by the fact that the pollutant is not merely touched, but also ingested. Fuller notes that castes are differentiated from one another in part through the dietary practices that they undertake. This state of affairs can be compared with the vegetarian movement amongst the Sinhala Buddhists. As we shall see, caste pollution has nothing to do with vegetarianism and only two issues impact the adoption of vegetarianism: (1) health, and (2) animal welfare.

The Hindu motive for vegetarianism has little to do with animal welfare, but in addition to that there is also a tendency to overstate the extent of Hindu vegetarianism or even its general association with the Brahman caste. For example, vegetarianism is practised not only by the elite Brahmans but is sometimes also practised by the Vaiśyas and even the lowly Śudras.[14] Moreover, vegetarianism is not always diligently practiced even by the Brahmans themselves. As R. S. Khare indicates, for example, a high sub-caste within the Kanya-Kabja Brahmans community (a community of Brahmans located in central India), the Katyayan clan, frequently consume meat.[15]

This, of course, contradicts the received wisdom that Brahmans must, and therefore do, universally practice vegetarianism. Khare explains that meat is considered legitimate for several reasons. For one thing, he observes that historically some Brahmans had consumed meat reluctantly as a way to improve martial skills so that they could defeat colonial powers.[16] Fuller also observes that the Ksatriya caste historically consumed meat using the same justification: improved martial skill.[17] Ritual pollution, in these circumstances, is therefore acceptable provided that there is a serious prudential justification for its use. We will see presently that, just as in India, Sinhalese also recognise that meat consumption has the power to bestow power on its wielder. Like in the Indian case, but for different reasons, meat is considered evil but sometimes necessary to achieve a higher goal.

Khare also argues that an increased interest in tantricism amongst Brahmans may have led to meat consumption. The ritual slaughter and consumption of animals is sometimes necessary in Hindu tantric activities.[18] In fact, tantricism in both the Hindu and Buddhist tradition are associated with the 'charnel ground' and tantric texts in both traditions recommend ritual meat consumption as a way to achieve elevated levels of spiritual development.[19] The acknowledgement that meat is morally impure, but nonetheless almost irresistible, is a common theme in Sinhala Buddhism.

A final point that Khare makes is that Hindu meat eating amongst these Brahman groups may have been a consequence of influence from traditional meat eating communities that settled in India – in particular the Muslims.[20]

Again, this theme of outside influence shaping food consumption practices is something that also troubles some Sinhalese vegetarian authors. As will be illustrated in Chapter 6, some of these authors blame various non-Sinhala groups for the introduction of foreign food practices. This is especially obvious with the case of beef eating but also extends to other purportedly 'foreign' foods such as the eating of unhealthy Western fast foods.

Meat eating is therefore present in India, even amongst castes that we would expect to abstain completely from meat. But there is still a view that vegetarianism is a morally pure diet – if for no other reason that it is a good way to avoid caste pollution. Of course, this pro-attitude towards vegetarianism is enshrined in growing expectation that the Hindu gods also practice vegetarianism.[21] After all, if it is good to be vegetarian then surely the most morally pure of all, the gods themselves, should also be vegetarian. This logic is also present in Sri Lanka where Sinhala Buddhist worshippers of Hindu-Lankan gods, such as Kataragama, dither over the virtues of giving meat as an offering. The details of this complex affair will be discussed presently.

The Case of King Aśoka

It would seem that traditional pro-attitudes towards vegetarianism in India often have little to with animal protection. Nonetheless, there have been moves to protect animals for their own sake and it is this impulse that Sinhala Buddhists sometimes refer to. They do this in part because this non-violent impulse is often attributed to King Aśoka himself and is in turn further attributed to his perceived Buddhist tendencies.

The Aśokan rock edicts are the main source for claims that Aśoka was a good Buddhist king who instituted state policies that legislated for animal protection. The rock edicts, erected during his rule in ancient India, appear to condemn the slaughter of animals and indirectly encourage vegetarianism. I. B. Horner says that, 'Aśoka, who became exceedingly sensitive to the taking of human life, abolished ... communal feeding [on animal flesh], first of all by reducing the number of animals slain daily to three, and for the use only at the royal table itself, and then decreed on the rock that "even these three living creatures shall not be slain in the future".'[22] Vegetarianism was therefore ostensibly mandatory in the Aśokan Mauryan Kingdom simply because of the illegality of animal slaughter.

Before we address the historical reality of Aśoka's apparent pacifism and concern over animal welfare, it's also interesting to note another element of Aśoka's legend within the Buddhist community. In his earlier life Aśoka was regarded as a cruel and violent warmonger. This charge is supposed to be demonstrated by his prosecution of the Kalinga campaign (262–261 BCE).

The Kalinga campaign was essentially a war of expansion in which Aśoka was the principle antagonist. He invaded the Kalinga state and the ensuing war reportedly resulted in 100,000 dead on the Mauryan side and 200,000 (or more) dead on the Kalinga side. But it is thought that these figures are almost certainly inflated, probably by Aśoka himself.[23] The traditional narrative has it that Aśoka had a change of heart after the Kalinga campaign, adopted Buddhism and renounced all forms violence. His inflating of the Kalinga casualties was to illustrate the barbarity and incivility of war and to further amplify the significance of his conversion to Buddhism.

This move from violence towards non-violence, and therefore his transformation from evil ruler into a righteous *cakravartin* – a righteous Buddhist king – is a narrative one routinely finds throughout Buddhadom. In Sri Lanka this transformation is thought to illustrate the restorative power of the Buddha's dharma.[24] This transformation also illustrates, for our purposes, the tension between the violent impulse to kill (people and animals) and the more difficult resolution to abstain from such activities and also adopt behaviours commensurate with that (such as vegetarianism).

This is how Aśoka is portrayed by many Buddhists including those in Sri Lanka. Scholars, however, have challenged this romantic account in a number of ways. To begin with, Basham suggests that Aśoka himself recognised that his animal conservation policy was a failure and inscriptions imply that people went on killing regardless of them.[25] Furthermore, it seems that some of the restrictions enacted were limited and hunters and fishermen were restricted in their killing of fish and birds only on particular dates.[26] This suggests that Aśoka was not completely committed to universal non-violence. This is highlighted by the fact that Aśoka allowed for some game to be killed for the royal banquet hall. In other words, he barred others from hunting and eating animals, but not himself or his fellow royals. Furthermore, these animal welfare edicts seem to have come much later in his life well after his purported conversion to Buddhism. Aśoka was in no hurry to institute policies of non-violence towards animals.

On top of this, Ludwig Alsdorf has argued that, at the time, pro-attitudes towards animal protectionism was common to all major Indian religious movements in some form or another and therefore Aśoka policies may have been generic rather than specific to Buddhism. Alsdorf writes, 'In the emperor Aśoka's edicts too, ahiṃsā is evidenced as non-Buddhist. Aśoka participates in a common Indian movement of thought and is a religiously tolerant monarch; his Buddhism only favours his ahiṃsā.'[27] These regulations may have been instituted regardless of his Buddhist leanings.

As part of his argument that this pro-animal sentiment was not necessarily Buddhist, Alsdorf suggests that *realpolitik* may have been a factor in the adoption of this policy. Aśoka's non-violent sentiment may have been a strategy to bring together the diverse religions under one common banner – in some form or another nearly all the pan-Indian religions agreed that harming animals was not good. Adding credence to these ideas Alsdorf notes that a number of the Aśokan rock edicts contain inscriptions borrowed directly from Brahmanical textual sources and not Buddhist ones.[28] K. M. Norman has also argued that many of the prohibited animals listed in the fifth edict are similar to lists of protected animals produced by Jains, thus implying that the inspiration here is not Buddhism but rather Jainism.[29]

In addition, Alsdorf argues that Aśoka did not even specifically mention anything Buddhist in any of his edicts and that subsequent interpreters have simply projected Buddhist intentions into the regulations in a *post hoc* fashion.[30] Alsdorf therefore cautions us against over-attributing his benevolent attitude towards animals to Buddhism. From a food ethics point of view, it is clear from the edicts that Aśoka still ate meat irrespective of the fact that he implemented policies that limited hunting. The presumption that Aśoka was a strict vegetarian and animal lover because of his Buddhist predilections is consistent with the presumption that the Buddha himself was a vegetarian – in both instances these assumptions turn out to be false.

Just as the case with Hindu vegetarianism, we can see that this myth that Aśoka was a great animal welfarist can be problematised. But it is interesting to note that the authority of Aśoka as a great Buddhist ruler still presides over Sinhala Buddhist political reality and Sinhala Buddhists refer to Aśoka affectionately in part because of these legends. Yet this also illustrates an impulse within some Sinhala Buddhist circles to feel the need to justify animal welfarism and they do this by invoking the name of Aśoka.

Non-violence towards animals in Sinhala myth

Indian vegetarianism and animal welfarism is influential in the development of Sinhala Buddhist attitudes towards these issues. But there are also indigenous influences. Native Sinhala myths and legends sometimes have an unexpected focus on animal welfare and animal welfare related issues.

Take, for example, the attitude the *Mahāvaṃsa* has towards hunting. The *Mahāvaṃsa* is perhaps one of the most important texts in Sinhala Buddhism. It chronicles the rise and development of Buddhism on the island. It is treated by Sinhala Buddhists not only as an authentic historical text but also as a religious and political treatise. Religious because it includes canonical material that claims the Buddha visited Sri Lanka on several occasions. Political because the text provides an account of the political decisions made by past Sinhala rulers and condones their actions in dealing with Tamil outsiders.

However, the historical veracity of much of the *Mahāvaṃsa* is extremely questionable and at least some of it is downright false (the Buddha did not visit Sri Lanka). Yet the *Mahāvaṃsa* has had a huge impact on Sinhala Buddhist attitudes so in considering Sinhala Buddhist views on animals it is prudent to think about what the *Mahāvaṃsa* says on such matters.

The text discusses how the true history of Sri Lanka only really begins with the arrival of Buddhism (the indigenous inhabitants of Sri Lanka are treated as demonic). One interesting feature of this arrival is that it interrupts the slaughter of a deer. The *Mahāvaṃsa* describes the arrival of Mahinda – the emissary sent by King Aśoka – who, after entering the island, immediately meets the island's king – Devānaṃpiyatissa. King Devānaṃpiyatissa is engaged in a hunting expedition when he is first approached by Mahinda and, after a discussion, Devānaṃpiyatissa abandons his hunt and converts to Buddhism.[31]

These events are illustrative of the power of Buddhism to disrupt acts of violence. Often it disrupts mundane violence such as conventional violence towards animals. Buddhism is also transformative in that it has the capacity to cure unhealthy habits – in this case hunting. The *Mahāvaṃsa* here is reminiscent of the Buddhist *Jātaka* tales since a number of *Jātakas* are explicitly anti-hunting. This will be discussed more in Chapter 2. There is therefore a pervasive narrative that opposes hunting and animal killing in Buddhist literature.

The origins of Buddhism on the island indirectly condemn animal killing. But there is a Sinhala myth reported by Gombrich that highlights the connection between violence (in general), animal violence (in particular), and the end of the world. When it comes to violence towards animals, the stakes are so high that the very fate of the world is tied up with it. The myth, which is timeless and can be construed either as a premonition of things to come or as a tale set in the distant past (or both), is relayed by Gombrich as follows: as materialism and greed increases Buddhism also declines.[32] As a result of this decline people become increasingly driven by baser desires and this, in turn, leads to greater wickedness. The more evil people become the shorter their lives become.[33] Finally, a great king warns the people that, due to their degeneration, a great monsoon is coming. 'Do not get wet,' he warns them. Ignoring this, the majority of the degenerate people become drenched. But the water is magical and the people that are wetted are immediately turned into wild animals. All those unaffected are overcome by bloodlust and a great slaughter ensues. Gombrich writes, 'In this way all the wicked kill each other till nothing is left but a great pool of blood.'[34]

After the slaughter is finally concluded a very few remaining humans emerge from their hiding places. Upon seeing the vast slaughter in front of them they are overwhelmed by compassion for the dead. This good thought (*hoñda adahasa*) leads to the cultivation of a small amount of good karma. This merit is enough to germinate the possibility of a bodhisattva (a future Buddha) at some time in the distant future. Incredibly, then, the Sinhala idea of Buddhism itself finds its origin in a single thought of compassion towards animal kind.

The above demonstrates a connection between kindness towards animals and the genesis of Buddhism and, contrariwise, the end of humanity with evil deeds towards animals.

The genesis of the Sinhala race itself, however, is also loaded with implications about the treatment of animals. The Sinhala people themselves are traditionally regarded as having come from noble animal stock. As mentioned at the start of this chapter, the origin myth of the Sinhala people states that they are the result of a union between a lion and a human princess. The myth itself is found in the seventeenth-century Sinhala text, the *Rajāvaliya (The Chronicle of Kings)*.

The story reads: 'Hereby know the royal race who came to illustrious Lanka. The king of the Kaliñgu country, who was a Sakviti monarch, gave his daughter to said king. On ascertaining the aspect of the natal star of the said princess, it was discovered that even if she were put in an iron room she should have connection with a lion and bear him children. When these indications of the star were told to the king he placed her in a seven-storied palace, set guards around it, and brought her up. But when the said princess had attained to years of maturity, maddened by lust, she descended privily at night from the upper story, and without knowledge of the guards fell in with a party of merchants: going with them she was seized by a lion in the wilds of the country called Láḍa. having cohabited with [the lion] she bore twins, one a son, and the other a daughter.'[35]

A few observations about this passage: (1) it illustrates the absolute necessity of the horoscope (*kendara*) in Sinhala society (even in instances of coupling with animals); (2) it is a strangely irreligious passage in that it openly celebrates bestiality and this is the case in spite of the fact that the *Vinaya* explicitly repudiates bestiality and regards it as an act that will lead to expulsion from the order. Of course, no one really believes that the Sinhala people exist as a result of such a union, but the story is illustrative of the power and vibrancy of the Sinhala people and this power and vibrancy is reflected in the gloriousness of the lion.

The conclusion of the above tale also leads to another anti-animal hunting discourse. The father of the princess (the King) is enraged to learn of his daughter's bestial affair and orders the lion to be killed. In a typical poetic twist, the lion's own son (the lion–human hybrid) is sent as the King's champion. It becomes quickly apparent, however, that the lion cannot be easily slain. Every time the son fires at the lion each arrow, 'turned and fell to the ground.'[36] The lion is only killed when he finally allows himself to be struck by the arrow on purpose and thus dies in an act of martyrdom. Not only does this indicate an anti-hunting sentiment in the text, it also paints the lion as a noble and peaceful creature that only volunteers to dies as a way to improve the lot of his children and descendants (the Sinhala people). It also harks back to the *Jātaka* tales where the animal Bodhisattva routinely sacrifices himself for the betterment of his followers.

Furthermore, the lion restrains himself from violence. This furthers the Sinhala trope that the Sinhalese are a peaceful people that, although powerful, restrain themselves out of virtue.

Note, of course, that the boy slays his own father in an act of violence. Yet he was driven to do this only out of revenge by another person – the boy was an innocent actor. This misdirected act of violence can be construed as a comment on justifications of violence during the civil war: even in instances where violence occurs, it is an act of violence born from the failure of the Other. For example, according to some nationalist narratives, the civil war is the result of violence not brought on by the Sinhalese people's own choosing. Finally, this boy turns out to be none other than Vijaya, the mythic founder of the Sinhala people who helped colonise the island of Lanka.[37]

One of the things we can observe from the above case is the fluidity between humankind and animalkind. Animals are treated as being on the same continuum as humans. As we shall see later, there is a critical fear amongst animal welfarists that one might inadvertently kill a human who is merely inhabiting an animal's body. These concerns are a natural product of reincarnation. This fluidity between animal and human has important animal welfare implications and there are, of course, numerous examples that illustrate this fluidity.

Throughout the *Rajāvaliya* we find that humans are constantly moving between the human and non-human realm. Take for example the case of Kuvēṇi – a demoness who later marries prince Vijaya who is the legendary first ruler of Sri Lanka. At two points in the tale told in the *Rajāvaliya* Kuvēṇi transforms herself into a dog and then a mare.[38] The deity Rahu similarly transforms into a wild boar.[39] In the course of this these animals are depicted as being governed by human concerns and urges. We have also seen that this occurs in the case of the lion story. The lion is also described in human terms: we find that it is 'missing its wife and child' and that it is 'greatly distressed.' In this way animals are routinely attributed human qualities. In this way, not only is there a concern about killing animals because they might contain a human spirit, there is the implicit matter that some animals convey respected human qualities. These similarities therefore govern decisions to harm some animals but not others. Animal slaughter is therefore implicitly questioned in these tales. Another story in the *Rajāvaliya* helps cement the association between animal slaughter and evil deeds. As a result of various contrivances, King Keḷaṇitissa inadvertently confuses his own brother with a known criminal and sentences his brother to death by boiling. His brother, who also happens to be a monk, is sitting in the cauldron as he is about to be executed and, at that moment, realises the cause of this situation. The *Rajāvaliya* states, 'the Elder perceiv[ed] with his divine eyes that retribution was overtaking him for the sin of killing an insect when he was boiling milk in a previous state of existence as a shepherd.'[40]

The story concludes with the monk declaring that the killing of this insect was a 'stain on Buddhahood' and thus he deserved to die and was thus 'burnt up and turned to ashes.'[41] It was the fault of his past evil deed that led him to be in this position and the apparent injustice of the situation was actually a charade. Not only is this an interesting story that illustrates the power of karma, it also shows that the mere killing of an insect was considered – at least in theory – a great crime in the seventeenth century.

This same level of concern is conveyed in a moving Sinhala story this time found in Buddhaghosa's *Atthasālanī* (*c.* fifth century).[42] In this text Buddhaghosa discusses the case of a young Ceylonese layman called Cakkana. Cakkana's mother is gravely ill so a doctor recommends 'hare flesh' as a curative.[43] With this advice in mind Cakkana leaves to hunt for hare and finally finds one caught in a bramble bush.

Cakkana is on the verge of slaying the animal when he realises that, 'it is not proper that I, for the sake of my mother's life, should take the life of another.'[44] He thereafter frees the hare from the brambles, but when he returned home he is admonished by his brother for returning empty handed and consequently condemning their mother to illness and death.

Still, Cakkana is committed to non-violence and tells his mother he will never intentionally, 'take the life of any creature.'[45] This good thought alone cures his mother of her illness.[46] In Sinhala myth, kindness towards animals cures illness or, as we saw in the eschatological drama, revive the very basis of society and trigger the beginnings of the Buddhist religion.

Caste and animal killing

Kindness towards animals has a revivifying effect, but evil deeds towards animals casts one into a lower realm. As reported by Bryce Ryan, historical Sinhala sources sometimes attribute the existence of low castes to immoral occupations. For example, he states that, 'One version of the *Janavaṃsa* attributes a low position to the fishing people on the grounds that they sinned, "in the taking of life without mercy".'[47]

The *Janavaṃsa* is a fifteenth century poem, possibly written by a monk, and provides a detailed account of the Sinhala caste system.[48] We can see here that the organisation of the caste system, and the relative placement of castes within that schema, is in part governed by how those castes purportedly treat animals. It should be pointed out that the fishing people singled out here are the *karāva* caste and in modern day Sri Lanka these people are almost entirely Christian. So there is an added religious complication in the modern day case (it is difficult to know whether this would hold at the time of the composition of the *Janavaṃsa*). The *karāva* are morally impure because they kill fish, but that in itself is governed by their decision to convert to Christianity, i.e. a foreign religion antithetical to the basic moral and metaphysical principles of Buddhism. The role of foreign religion and culture as a corrupting force on Sri Lankan food and animal practices will resurface again and again throughout this study.

In discussing the origin of the *karāva* caste, the *Janavaṃsa* is also instructive as it adds credence to the Buddhist notion that killing *in general* (whether human or animal) is the root of moral imperfection and leads to a downward spiral that can only be recovered from if one first seriously adopts the Buddhist attitude of absolute non-violence. For example, the *Janavaṃsa* discusses the case of a king 'at the commencement of this *kalpa* (our human epoch)' who, due to a bought of rage, killed the prince Dharmapāla and 'ate his flesh'.[49]

What follows is essentially an origin myth concerning the advent of meat eating. The *Janavaṃsa* then says that after this action, 'killing living things [and] the eating of flesh became general'.[50] The connection between these mythic actions and the origin myth cited by Gombrich are obvious. Unlike the Gombrich story, however, what follows is not a great flood, but rather a great drought brought on as a consequence of the king's evil actions. Out of desperation, the people began to eat dogs and crows.

But even after the drought ends and corn and grain are able to be harvested once again, the people continue to eat meat as they had grown accustomed to flesh. Before long these people were hunting and catching fish. The *Janavaṃsa* states, 'Thus making a means to kill animals, engaged in killing fish, they were sinning. Seeing people so doing, some who had eaten and become accustomed to it in the former famine season, not themselves sinning, gave hire to those who killed fish and took them. Therefore, those more and more endeavouring to kill fish, killing them, both ate and gave them away.'[51] These fish killers, who were born ultimately from the people who grew used to animal killing *in general*, are, of course, none other than the *karāva* caste.

The *Janavaṃsa* is somewhat even-handed in that it also tarnishes those who support the *karāva*. In the modern context, this is essentially most Sinhalese since the majority of Sinhalese eat fish. For example, the *Janavaṃsa* points out that even those who did not sin went to the *karāva* to secure their stock of fish.

In contrast to the *karāva* caste and their customers, another caste – called the *sakuro* – are mentioned in glowing terms due to their sinlessness. The *Janavaṃsa* associates this sinlessness with forest renunciation and vegetarianism. The text reads: 'At the beginning, among the seven hundred men who came to Lakdiva [Sri Lanka] with Wijaya Raja, pure in both lines on ancestry, after much time had elapsed, the injustice and power of kings and ministers enjoying rule in Sri Lanka increasing, some among the Raja, Bamuna and Grahapati [i.e. some of the most important people in Sri Lanka – the kings and farmers] who went to the forest from fear of robbers and enemies, *committing no sin, possessed of modesty and fear, eating yams, roots, vegetables and fruits lived staying in the forest*' (my italics).[52]

The *Janavaṃsa* is therefore an excellent example of Sinhalese historical literature that distinguishes between those who undertake and support actions that deprive animals of life and those who repudiate such actions. This repudiation seems to involve living 'without sin,' caring for animals and undertaking a vegetarian diet.

These various myths and stories illustrate a number of things. First, they show just how critical animals are in Sinhala legend. Second, they illustrate the moral significance that animals have and, most importantly, the role that animals have in the revival of not only Buddhism on the island, but also in the resurrection of Buddhism more generally. Furthermore, we find that the killing of animals is viewed with enormous hostility whether that be in the form of hunting or even the accidental killing of animals. Yet this opposition to animal killing transcends myth and begins to enter historical reality.

Food and the Portuguese period

It is clear from various historical sources that meat eating was not necessarily celebrated amongst the Sinhalese. The first case is *The Carpenter Prēta Tale*. This Sinhala folktale originated during the period of the Portuguese occupation (1505–1658) and it indicates both a respect for vegetarianism and a repudiation of meat eating – the latter being especially associated with foreigners. This view also relates to later proto-nationalists, such as Anāgārika Dharmapāla, who viewed vegetarianism as a suitable Buddhist diet and regarded meat eating as a decadent Christian interpolation that displaced proper Sinhala Buddhist values. Dharmapāla will be discussed presently but this attitude already has antecedent causes in the form of, for example, *The Carpenter Prēta Tale*.

The Carpenter Prēta Tale, translated by Robert Fox Young, is essentially a piece of Buddhist propaganda aimed at undermining the Christian religion that was beginning to make substantial in-roads in Sri Lanka at the time of the tales composition in the 1700s. The *Carpenter Prēta Tale* is therefore a very early example of anti-Christian propaganda. During the Buddhist Revivalist period proto-nationalists like Migettuwatte Gunananda Thēra and Anāgārika Dharmapāla reproduced and extended this type of propaganda.

The Carpenter Prēta Tale targets Christianity by reappropriating the Christ legend. It depicts Jesus as a *prēta*, a so-called hungry ghost, who craves flesh. *Prētas* are beings that failed to follow the Buddhist path and gave into their base hedonistic desires. As a result they are condemned to an afterlife solely governed by these desires. The cause of Jesus' rebirth as a *prēta* is made clear in the Tale. During his life, Jesus is described as a rascal and thief who, 'drinks liquor, eats flesh, and calls himself god.'[53]

Jesus is further described as, 'propagating the false doctrine that animals have no soul and may therefore be eaten.'[54] Jesus and his followers' obsession with animal flesh is so severe that he, 'breaks into the city and steals goats and cattle from [the] pens. They eat the meat and wash it down with toddy stolen from somewhere or other.'[55]

It is this craving of flesh that leads to his downfall – a group of merchants trick Jesus' followers into betraying him (i.e. a reimagining of the Judas story). Jesus is consequently executed and his body is buried deep underground (the crucifixion and consequent burial in the tomb). Jesus is thereafter reborn as a hungry ghost because of his worldly desires.

From this story we can already get a sense of the Buddhist ideal regarding animals that existed in the 1700s. Meat eating is not good and the killing of animals is similarly immoral. *The Carpenter Prēta Tale* is a fascinating reimaging of the Christ legend where Jesus is recast as a villain who hungers after worldly desires especially animal flesh and alcohol. The idiosyncratic focus on Jesus' diet only highlights the oddity of his meat and alcohol consumption in the eyes of the author(s) of *The Carpenter Prēta Tale*.

Some accounts suggest that from the very start of the Portuguese occupation European meat consumption was regarded as being unusual. Young recounts an early Sinhala report of Portuguese colonists that reads: 'There is in our harbour in Colombo a race of people fair of skin and comely withal. They don jackets of iron and hats of iron; they rest not a minute in one place; they walk here and there; they eat hunks of stone and drink blood; they give two or three pieces of gold and silver and one fish for a lime; the report of their canon is louder than thunder when it bursts upon the rock Yugandhara. Their cannon balls fly many *gawwa* and shatter fortresses of granite.'[56] The accuracy of this report can be questioned, however.[57]

Young argues that the phrase 'eating stone and drinking blood' refers to the practice of eating meat and drinking alcohol. He suggests that, 'eating stone is a synonym for 'eating meat' in old Sinhala.[58] Young adds, 'In the Sinhala imagination a craving for flesh and blood is characterised [with] demons and or wandering ghosts (*prētas*).'[59]

As we shall see, this supposition is entirely correct – flesh eating is frequently associated with evil and the supernatural. Young also observes that the 'stone and blood' formula could refer to sacramental bread and wine consumed by Catholics (the Portuguese were primarily Roman Catholic). Young does question the veracity of the notion that the term 'stone' refers here to 'bread'. For Young, the 'stone and blood' formula is a comment about flesh and alcohol *sui generis* and is an implicit criticism of foreign food ethics. This can be contrasted with local food which is associated with the consumption of milk and rice: milk and rice are considered morally pure foods while meat and alcohol are immoral – and, more importantly, un-Buddhist.

This discussion also shows how food comes to produce national identities. Foreigners are associated with immoral foods while the Sinhalese are associated with morally unproblematic foods. As we shall see throughout the following ethnographic study this dyadic structure of the Sinhalese and the 'other' – and their associated foods – is still apparent even in modern times.

Attitudes towards vegetarianism during this period appear to be positive. Writing on this period of Portuguese occupation, P. E. Pieris says, 'The Oriental[60], moreover, realised that meat was not essential for strength, for the strongest beast on earth, the elephant, eats no meat. The teachings of the Buddha against the taking of life had made the Sinhalese almost a race of vegetarians, and such little meat as they did use was so prepared as entirely to remove the suggestion of blood.'[61] Pieris quotes Father Morales writing in 1552: 'According to the exaggerated notions of their religion, they do not kill anything that has life, not even venomous snakes. *They eat no meat of any kind, neither flesh meat nor fish, even if they happen to be ravenously hungry*' (my italics).[62] These comments by Father Morales are almost certainly an exaggeration.

Pieris adds that 'fishing was carried out along the coast' but that the 'occupation itself was regarded with disfavour.'[63] Not much has changed since then, it would seem, and fishing is now relegated mainly to the karāva caste, who are a lower caste and mostly Christian (and therefore Buddhist rules of non-violence do not apply to them).

Food and the Kandyan Kingdom

I will treat the Kandyan Kingdom separately from the above and following discussion that are primarily concerned with Sinhalese living on the coast.

Robert Knox (1641–1720) was a captain in the British East India Company who became a prisoner of the Kandyan Kingdom from 1659 to 1679. After fleeing King Rājasiṃha II's kingdom in 1659 he wrote a memoir that detailed his experiences and this document appeared in 1681. The text, *A Historical Relation of Ceylon*, is an influential and important book that not only inspired the fictional *Robinson Crusoe*, it also offers an insight into medieval Sri Lanka. *A Historical Relation of Ceylon* proved so influential that John Locke even mentions the memoir in his own philosophical work *Two Treatises of Government* and uses the example of King Rājasiṃha as an example of an evil tyrant.[64]

Though a prisoner of the King, Knox was nonetheless able to wander widely and consequently observed the Kandyan people's diet and hunting habits. He noted that the Sinhalese had an appetite for almost every type of animal. Hogs were hunted for food using pit traps[65] and fowl were widely killed except, of course, for birds used to ornament the King's gardens.[66] The rivers surrounding Kandy were full of fish and Knox reports that fish comprised a significant portion of the interior Sinhaleses' diet.[67] None of these animals are especially uncommon on the average plate even today, but Knox also reports that more obscure animals were consumed: *kabara-goya* (water monitor lizard) were considered aggressive and inedible, but the flesh of a *thala-goya* (land monitor lizard) were considered delicacies.[68] Knox even states that monkeys were sometimes eaten.[69] Needless to say, none of these animals are eaten today.

On the topic of deer, Knox observes that they were hunted and killed by blinding them with large torches and then shooting them with arrows.[70] Obviously, these practices go against the fair chase principles advocated for in the *Mahāvaṃsa* where it states that one should, 'not shoot an animal while it is inattentive'[71] but it does demonstrate a theme that will continue to rise again and again throughout this study – the tension between religious advice not to act in a certain way towards animals and the commonplace practical violation of that rule.

These philosophical tensions present in the act of hunting and killing animals in the Kandyan Kingdom are further illustrated by the anti-hunting discourse of the *Mahāvaṃsa*, but also the eschatological myth discussed by Gombrich. Then there are, of course, the anti-hunting arguments of the Pāli texts which will be discussed in the next chapter.

Despite the widespread hunting and killing of animals Knox nonetheless reported many acts of great compassion towards animals. These actions point towards the more sympathetic side of Kandyan society. One example here is the extraordinary care people took in avoiding hurting leeches. Because villagers often went barelegged leeches would routinely attach themselves to people's limbs. Knox writes that people tried to remove the leeches but, 'this is some trouble, and they [the leeches] come on again so fast and so numerous, that it is not worth their while [to remove them]: and generally they suffer them to bite and remain on their legs during the journey; and they *do the more patiently permit them, because it is wholesome for them*' (my italics).[72]

We see here an interesting combination of prudence and compassion. On the one hand, villagers didn't bother to remove the creatures because it was not worth the trouble; on the other hand, villagers explained that this was also an act of compassion towards the animal because they benefited from the blood. The phrase 'more wholesome for them' has a double meaning, of course. It is wholesome for the animal, but it is also, in a roundabout way, wholesome for the host. By allowing the animal to feed the person is doing a good deed and therefore accrues merit. So even in cases of seeming genuine compassion there is sometimes the presence of ancillary motives again prudence, personal benefit and self interest will be major factors in the following ethnographic analysis.

During this period in the Kandyan Kingdom it seems that vegetarianism and abstinence from animal violence was regarded favourably. Knox writes, 'they reckon the chief poynts of goodness to consist in giving to the Priests, in making Pudigahs [doing *pūjā*, donation ceremonies], sacrifices to their Gods, [and] *forbearing shedding the blood of any creature*' (my italics).[73] Knox ranks not hurting any creature to be of equal importance to performing *pūjā* and donating to the clergy. Knox even states that it is considered, 'Pou boi, a great sin.'[74] He adds that, 'abstaining from eating flesh at all, because they would not have a hand, or anything to do with, [the] killing [of] any living thing.' He concludes from this that vegetarianism is popular saying, 'they reckon that Herbs and Plants [are the] more innocent food.'[75] Clearly non-violence towards animals, and even vegetarianism, was a religious ideal – and yet people still readily consumed meat and hunted animals. As will become apparent, this complicated attitude will become a signature of the question of vegetarianism in Sri Lanka even in the modern case.

Knox reports another view that is continuous with modern Sri Lanka and that is the attitude clergy have towards animals. Knox states that while monks do not kill or harm animals they will readily consume animal flesh if it is supplied to them by the laity. As I will illustrate in Chapter 3 it seems that little has changed between the Kandyan Kingdom in Knox's period and modern Sri Lanka (at least as far as my research is concerned).

Finally, again in continuation with modern attitudes, it seems that the Kandyan's of the seventeenth century were influenced especially by anti-beef eating norms. Knox writes, 'beef here may not be eaten, it is abominable.'[76] We also discover that the Kandyans viewed beef-eaters with special disdain. White foreigners were subject to a unique insult – they were called 'beef eating slaves.'[77] Sapramadu, editor of the 1958 edition of Knox's book. Observes that Buddhism in Kandyan society was not as we know it today and was much more influenced by Indian-Hindu norms. But as I will argue in Chapter 5, attitudes towards cow protectionism are rooted in a range of complicated internal religious views only some of which are to do with the Indian mainland. Regardless, the consumption of cows is considered especially immoral and heartless.

Knox's description of these Kandyan attitudes is confirmed by other sources too. As with the *Carpenter Prēta Tale* described earlier we also find resistance to meat consumption on the basis that it is non-Buddhist and a Christian corruption (specifically Catholic corruption).

Of special note here is the reign of the Kandyan King Kīri Śrī Rājasiṃha (reigned 1747–1782), who was influenced by Catholic political factions. Catholics took a special interest in the Thēravāda Buddhist view on meat consumption and saw that this represented a specific break between Buddhism and Catholicism. Monks who resisted Catholic expansion exploited this difference to promote Buddhism as a religion of non-violence. Young reports that Catholic orator Jacome Gonçalves was particularly opposed to Buddhist vegetarianism. Young writes of Gonçalves anti-vegetarian propaganda that, 'In tract upon tract in mellifluous Sinhalese he drew distinctions between spirit, soul, and anima, thereby justifying meat consumption.'[78] The purpose of this discourse was to inculcate Buddhists into a more sympathetic view of Catholicism.

These propaganda attempts were opposed by monks such as Vælivita Saranaṃkara who petitioned King Rājasiṃha to enforce the Buddhist prohibition against the consumption of wine and meat (recall the immoral dyad of meat and wine mentioned in the report on the Portuguese occupation).[79] In response to this a Catholic missionary group's report read, '[Vælivita Saranamkara] called upon [the King] to issue an edict...that all pigs and hens should be set free and that there should be no breeding of animals for food.'[80] Young adds that, 'no other monarch [referring to King Rajasiṃha] is considered to have been so as he in promoting abstinence, vegetarianism, and the protection of animals.'[81] Vælivita Saranamkara was therefore ultimately successful in his effort to persuade the King to adopt an animal welfare agenda within the Kandyan kingdom and this helped drive away unwanted Catholic influence.

This propaganda war is one of the first instances where animal welfare is used as a device to advance national and religious interests. As we shall see later this same basic rhetorical strategy is used by contemporary nationalist groups to target Muslims. These Muslims are perceived of as threats and interlopers just as the Catholics were during this early period. They argue, as Vælivita Saranamkara did, that Buddhism is a non-violent religion and the Muslim religion is violent and cruel to animals. Vælivita Saranamkara's animal welfare propaganda, and even his attempt to influence the political establishment, should therefore be viewed as continuous with modern day propaganda activities Sri Lanka.

Food and the British period

During the period of Portuguese and Dutch occupation, it seems that vegetarianism was considered a moral ideal. This was also the case in the Kandyan Kingdom. Coastal Sinhalese under British rule also seemed to favour vegetarianism and denounced animal violence. Robert Percival writes the following observation of Sinhalese food practices in his book *An Account of the Island of Ceylon* (1803), 'In their diet they are exceedingly abstemious: fruits and rice constitute the chief part of their food. In some places where fish abounds they make it a portion of their meals but scarcely any where is flesh in common use.'[82]

Elsewhere Percival is astounded by the Sinhalese non-violent attitude: 'Their tenderness is at times extended even to the brute creation; and it is customary for them to bind themselves during the continuance of certain festivals or seasons of devotion, to refrain from killing any living creature, but subsist entirely on herbs and fruits.'[83] Here Percival is clearly referring to the practice some devout Buddhists undertake during *poya* (full moon days) where meat is abstained from as an act of piety. In any case, despite this positive attitude towards vegetarianism, Percival – as others before him have also noted – observes that the Sinhalese routinely ate fish.[84]

But this pro-attitude towards vegetarianism – as we have seen time and again – was used as a way to mark off difference between the Sinhalese Buddhists and foreign occupying forces. It was used as a device to repudiate the character of foreigners in the Kandyan Kingdom and, through Vælivita Saranamkara, became an important propaganda weapon.

Animal welfare, and food ethics as a propaganda device, reached an apex of importance during the Buddhist Revivalist period of later British rule. The Buddhist revivalist period (spanning from the 1870s until the 1890s) was characterised by a heightened anti-British, anti-Christian, sentiment that was based on a desire to revitalise Buddhist institutions in the country. The view amongst many Sinhalese at the time was that Buddhism was waning in part due to foreign attempts to stamp out Buddhism and replace it with foreign religions, especially various types of Christianity.

Important monastic figures began to appear that championed Buddhism and denounced the virtue of Christianity. These figures included individuals such as Migettuwatte Gunananda Thêra (1823–1890), Hikkaduwe Sri Sumangala Thero (1827–1911) and Anāgārika Dharmapāla (1864–1933). But some of the earliest progenitors of Buddhist revivalism in Sri Lanka were not Sinhalese at all but were, oddly enough, European. Namely, Henry Steel Olcott (1832–1907) and Madame Blatavsky (1831–1891).

These last two individuals arrived in Ceylon with the notion that they would help wrest Buddhism away from the clutches of Christian missionaries. On arrival in Sri Lanka in 1880 they immediately 'converted' to Buddhism and set about repairing Buddhism which they believed had decayed under foreign rule. It should not be thought, however, that Olcott and Blatavsky were necessarily enlightened anti-colonials who championed the oppressed foreign Other. They still maintained conventional Orientalist attitudes and believed that the Sinhalese were indolent and had helped corrupt their own religion. Foreign powers had simply stepped into finish the job.

Olcott and Blatavsky maintained a romantic idea of Buddhism and reproduced the popular view at the time that (then) contemporary Buddhists had lost the 'true' spirit of Buddhism. Olcott wrote, for example, tracts that argued for a return to 'original Buddhism' and Olcott hoped that his writings would cure the Sinhalese of their moral and religious laziness. On this topic, Stephen Prothero writes that, 'Like his *Buddhist Catechism*, which aimed to eradicate mass ignorance, these compilations sought to uplift the Asians out of their supposed moral degradation.'[85]

In his *Golden Rules of Buddhism* (1887) Olcott aimed to rectify this apparent moral degradation in part by encouraging vegetarianism. Prothero writes, 'Olcott enjoined vegetarianism ('One who buys butcher's meat or poultry violates the Buddhist scriptures').'[86] Of course, Olcott is referring in his passage here to the Buddha's own claim that one should not harm any living creature. Olcott extrapolates from this that this would entail the non-buying of flesh, but not all Sinhalese Buddhists agree with this logic (though some do as we shall also see). Prothero notes that Olcott held a range of progressive ideals such as 'women's rights ... caste reform, vegetarianism ...' and so on.[87] Regardless, Olcott's attitude here is the very definition of Orientalist: an Occidental studying a religion in the Orient and then telling the native practitioners that he knows the meaning of their religious texts better than they do.

Although Olcott and Blatavsky were early players in the Buddhist revivalist period, and although they encouraged vegetarianism as a proper expression of Buddhism, their positive relationship with indigenous revivalists was short lived. Their supposed 'scientific' outlook clashed with some of the traditional views of some Sinhalese. Anāgārika Dharmapāla, an early supporter of the Olcott-Blatavsky duo, eventually shunned them when Olcott claimed that the tooth relic in Kandy was just an animal bone.[88]

In fact it is Anāgārika Dharmapāla who is perhaps one of the most influential thinkers in Sri Lankan history. He has certainly shaped, to a large extent, how Buddhism is understood in contemporary Sri Lanka. He is revered by many Buddhists and, even now, some have his picture hanging in their homes. Dharmapāla was a lay Buddhist who helped found the so-called Protestant Buddhist movement in Sri Lanka.

Protestant Buddhism is not a term coined by the Buddhist revivalists, but is a later term applied to the movement by some Buddhist scholars. This movement was an attempt to purify the Buddhist religion of foreign accretions – including, to an extent, the well-meaning, but flawed, efforts of people like Olcott. In this regard Dharmapāla was anti-Christian and, like others before him, used vegetarianism as a way to differentiate Buddhism from Christianity.

Dharmapāla attitude towards meat eating and animal killing is clear, He writes in his autobiography that he hated his Christian schoolmasters because they ate meat and shot bird for game.[89] In his *Daily Code for the Laity (Gihi Vinaya)* (1898) Dharmapāla argued that a proper interpretation of the Buddhist dharma demanded a strict vegetarian diet.[90] Dharmapāla writes that, 'the first principle of the Religion of the Buddha was prevention of cruelty to animals...'[91] Lay Buddhists should not 'trade in flesh'[92] and the Buddha 'prohibits the sale of...animals for slaughter.'[93] He was against the killing of animals.

In his autobiographical writings Dharmapāla laments the indolence of the local monks and contrasts their passivity with the active and violent pastimes of the local missionaries: 'In contrast to my wine-drinking, meat-eating and pleasure-loving missionary teachers, the Bhikkhus were meek and abstemious.'[94] Like others before him, Dharmapāla was struck by the dietary practices of his Christian rivals. The following passage from another of Dharmapāla's tracts illustrates his disdain for animal slaughter and meat eating: 'No Buddhist can hate gods...But gods who murder, and get angry, set fire to cities, kill innocent men, women and children, send tornadoes, typhoons, cyclones, earthquakes, thunderstorms, plagues, pestilences, and create blind, deaf, dumb, the Buddhist rejects. *Some gods want wine and bread and meat for their food. Some gods without the blood of cows are not happy. Some gods get the worship of muddle-headed by giving them the liberty to kill animals and eat their flesh*' (my italics).[95]

He specifically attacks Christians and Hindus for their consumption of animal flesh in the following savage passage: 'Sinful Christians preached their religion to the filthy and low *chaṇḍālas* of India because they consumed beef and pork. Muslims[96] don't eat pork. And in certain areas Brahman priests offer goat flesh to the Kali she-devil.'[97] Dharmapāla's violent dislike of non-Buddhist eating habits is most apparent in these passages. The *chaṇḍāla* in India are a particular group of very low caste and marginalized people who are responsible for the disposal of corpses. The association with meat eating, being of a low caste and corpse disposal is a very heady and telling mix.

Dharmapāla goes on to celebrate King Aśoka for becoming a vegetarian as a consequence of his Buddhist convictions.[98] As we already know, Dharmapāla is perhaps mistaken here, but we can see from this, and his other comments, just how important animal welfare and vegetarianism is for him. But his reference to the myth of King Aśoka, and the associated mythic notion that he was a great animal welfarist, is a rich node for Buddhists to tap into. Dharmapāla, and his revivalist associates, maintained and propagated dietary ethics as an important part of what it means to be a good Buddhist. Modern Buddhists have inherited these revivalist impulses and efforts to abstain from certain foods continue to characterise contemporary Sinhala Buddhism.

Diet in the twentieth century

Vegetarianism in modern Sri Lanka has been discussed by only a few ethnographers. The general view is that of scepticism and it is felt by the bulk of these scholars that vegetarianism in Sri Lanka is not widely practiced. Gombrich notes that vegetarianism, while being viewed at morally laudable, is nonetheless rarely practiced.[99] This observation also relates back to Knox's reports in the 1700s. Recall that he reported that while vegetarianism was considered pious it was not widely followed.

Gombrich and Obeyesekere both believe that the non-practice of vegetarianism stems from the notion that Sinhalese Buddhists see no connection between the first precept of non-violence and the consumption of meat. They write that the precept not to kill, 'has not generally been so interpreted as to impose [vegetarianism].'[100] Although not speaking strictly about Sri Lanka Ruegg writes, 'Although the idea of *ahiṃsā*, 'non-harming' is generally proclaimed and respected in Buddhist thought and practice, what might seem to be its logical corollary, namely abstention from the eating of the flesh of animals killed for their meat is ... far from practiced in most parts of the Buddhist world.'[101] Gombrich and Obeyesekere, and Ruegg, all agree that, while the principle of non-violence is widely respected, it is not widely interpreted that this demands a diet of non-violence and vegetarianism.

In the next chapter I will begin to make a case that the connection between non-violence and vegetarianism is certainly present amongst some Sinhala Buddhists. In fact, one of the core reasons why meat-eaters and vegetarians alike justify vegetarianism is the first principle of non-violence. Even Obeyesekere accepts that the first precept is relevant to vegetarianism. Obeyesekere states that, 'In Ceylon, although meat eating is common, all castes recognise that such an act is a violation of *ahiṃsā*. Thus, everyone subscribes to an ideal of vegetarianism, but the fulfilments of the ideal does not depend on one's caste affiliations but on one's religious affiliations.'[102] Obeyesekere goes on to argue that animal killing is always perceived of as wrong further implying the necessity of vegetarianism. He also reports that even hunters occasionally regard hunting as being improper and thus condemn their own occupation.[103]

Animal killing is routinely condemned in Sri Lanka. This is especially the case with the slaughter of large animals, in particular cattle. Gombrich reports that butchers' shops are frequently boycotted because their business is based on the slaughter of animals.[104] As we saw above, moral entrepreneurs like Dharmapāla urge such actions. Today acts of violence are not unheard of and butcheries are sometimes the targets of arson. Again, the violence associated with animal welfare groups will be addressed in Chapter 7.

Apart from these general cases of the promotion of vegetarianism there are also organisations that specifically promote vegetarianism. George Bond has called this general movement 'neo-traditional' and to a certain extent, as we have seen, it is correct that traditionally Sinhalese have idealised practices that restrict certain foods. Bond discusses two relevant groups here: the All Ceylon Buddhist Congress and the Young Man's Buddhist Association, both of whom are groups who seek to extend the revivalist aspirations of individuals like Dharmapāla.

Bond writes that in 1985 the All Ceylon Buddhist Congress, 'adopted a resolution urging all Buddhists to refrain from eating beef.' He adds that, 'On the one hand they argued on grounds of non-harming, Buddhists should not eat the animals that help the rice farmer, and on the other hand they contended that a vegetarian diet is to be preferred because it is healthier.'[105] This connection between diet, health and even nationalism is supported and developed further in the following chapters.

The extent of this support of vegetarianism has sometimes taken on a more sinister tone. There is, first of all, the nationalism and xenophobia that sometimes taints the animal welfare movement in Sri Lanka and this will be discussed in Chapter 7. Another sinister element is the way in which vegetarianism has sometimes been enforced as a mechanism by the state to control renegade monks. Ananda Abeyesekere has pointed out that, during the 1980s, monks involved with the Janathā Vimukti Pĕramuṇa (People's Liberation Front) movement were arrested and then subject to 'rediscipling'. This 'rediscipling' entailed that the monks were reprogrammed to engage in behaviours that were viewed by the state to be appropriate for clergy. Not only did this involve not being involved in political agitation, and the violence associated with the JVP, it also involved the adoption of passive non-violent activities like vegetarianism.[106] Vegetarianism is therefore considered a moral ideal, but as a moral ideal it can be used as a weapon to reshape the order for the political benefit of the state.

Meat consumption and the demonic

The previous discussion has been primarily historical, but there is also a general matter of some importance and that is the issue of meat and the supernatural. Sinhalese routinely associate meat with violence. The violence that imbues meat can be contained in certain ways to create personal advantage and this is possible through the harnessing of the supernatural world.

This general principle should be born in mind throughout the following discussions of meat eating and vegetarianism. After all, while vegetarianism is in strict keeping with the principles of non-violence and Buddhism, and therefore offers various long-term advantages to do with merit cultivation, meat consumption provides immediate benefits in the form of the hexing of enemies, exorcism practices and also brute physical power. This tension between the good of abstention from meat and the attraction of meat eating as a force of power is symbolic of the general problem facing many Sinhalese Buddhists. As we shall see, meat consumption is something that many know they should avoid and yet they do it anyway.

The supernatural is an important part of the Sinhalese cultural ethos. It is something that operates in the background of many Sinhalese Buddhists' lives and generally goes unquestioned except by the very few who adopt highly sophisticated rationalist outlooks. Magic, horoscopes, curses, deity worship and exorcisms are all routine features in the life of many Sinhalese. The use of flesh in these activities and rites is also fundamental.

Yet even in these activities vegetarianism and non-violence is implicitly required. Again, the queer tension between violence and non-violence arises here. Traditionally, it is understood that blood sacrifice is critical for many of these rites and yet Sinhalese Buddhists habitually use meat surrogates as a way to avoid actually using dead animals. It is a subtle way to by pass the more bloodthirsty elements of these rituals. For example, in exorcism rituals a cock is called for to be slaughtered. But rather than actually slaughtered, the cock is only subject to a mock execution.[107] Demons are regarded as stupid and therefore unable to tell the difference between a real sacrifice and a fake one.[108]

Meat, though regarded as necessary, is also repudiated in part because it is associated with morally questionable, or even evil, creatures such as demons (*yakṣa*). This is where exorcism (*yakṣabhūta vidhyāva* or the science of demons or demonology) becomes important. These Sinhala exorcism rituals that are most often practiced along the Southern coastal areas of Sri Lanka.

Gombrich states that meat offerings are associated heavily with the demonic. He writes, 'But the Buddhist values of compassion and non-violence have dictated that no god can receive blood-sacrifice: any supernatural being who demands an animal victim is *ipso facto* a devil, inherently cruel and therefore below man in the scale of being.'[109] Being 'below man' is important here because it implies that meat consumption is itself a demonic influence and that human beings are intended for a higher non-violent ideal. Meat eating is a base pleasure that weighs them down and is a corruption of the human spirit. Gombrich and Obeyesekere observe that, for these reasons, Kāli can never be regarded as a benevolent deity because she requires a blood sacrifice (*bili*).[110]

Meat is offered by Sinhala Buddhists in sacrificial contexts to demons, but only out of a motive of disrespect. In his detailed study of Sinhala exorcism rituals, Bruce Kapferer notes that demons are treated with contempt by exorcists and observers alike. One of Kapferer's key observations about exorcism rites is that the demon is to be reduced in power and finally expelled through ridicule and humiliation (this can be contrasted with Christian exorcisms where the demon is usually banished through a command). This illustrates the low status that demons hold in Sinhala consciousness. The food they are given is associated with this. Obeyesekere says, 'The food given to them is *pulata*, or burnt meat, fish or egg. Often some blood from a chicken is offered to them also.'[111] Kapferer confirms this notion when he says, 'The lowest (ghosts, demons) receive fragmented flower petals roasted grains, *curries with meat*, and pollutants such as fecal matter and stimulants.'[112]

The theoretical importance of meat in exorcism is clear from the following poem said through the mouth of the demon itself:

I am going having raised the pyre of wood,
Having requested blood and flesh of the body as food,
I am giving the flesh, cooked, to the Yaka,
Deign to take, sparing the sufferer.[114]

On the other hand, Obeyesekere notes that pure celestial beings, such as virtuous gods, are offered pure foods such as vegetarian food.[113] In this way there is a supernatural hierarchy established that is based around diet. Evil and mischievous creatures crave flesh while pure and virtuous beings accept vegetarian food. Even higher ranking demons are considered pure enough to take vegetarian food – only the most base and violent demon is given meat.

Kapferer writes, 'Unlike Riri Yaksa and Mahasona, Kalu Yaka receives relatively pure vegetables and grains and no meats.'[115] He adds that offerings given to Riri Yaksa are similar to that of Kalu Yaka but, 'with the addition of roasted meats from land and water creatures (*godadiyamas*) and blood (*le*) drawn from the comb of a cock.'[116]

Again even though, 'a cock is an indispensible part of every exorcism' it is only symbolically slaughtered.[117] Exorcists are careful to avoid using actual meat lest they be corrupted by the evil influence of the demonic. The goal is not to appease the demon, after all, but to banish it through trickery and deception. It should also be recognised here that actual animal sacrifice is considered very wrong by Sinhala Buddhists because the Buddha explicitly rejected it. The importance of animal non-violence is even consecrated in the very songs performed during the anointment of the victim. One song tells of the Buddha's sacrifice in a former life so that the death of another animal can be avoided.[118]

Other purportedly immoral foods are supplied to other vicious supernatural creatures. Meats are associated with violence and brutality. So-called sweetmeats – i.e. cakes, buns and deep fried foods – are associated with unhealthiness and largesse. These foods are sometimes given to so-called *prēta* or 'Hungry Ghosts'.[119]

As discussed during the analysis of *The Carpenter Prēta Tale, prēta* are maligned beings governed by greed and extreme desire. They live in a limbo where they constantly seek to satisfy desires (most often food orientated desires) but their gluttony can never be realised. For example, a *prēta* may be condemned to a scenario where they are surrounded by delicious food but they mouth is too small for it to fit in. In this way they are tormented by their desires. Regardless, people sometimes donate sweetmeats to *prēta* out of sympathy and with the goal of doing a good deed so that they may gain merit (though this means that they also add to the creatures torment, but no matter). As we shall see, this repudiation of sweetmeats, and the associated concern over unhealthiness, is also a part of our story of food ethics in Sri Lanka.

Dining with the Gods

There are other ritual spaces where animal sacrifice is replaced by more sanitised rituals. Take, for example, the practice of black magic. In such instances, violent gods like Kāli are invoked with the goal of cursing an enemy. As mentioned, Kāli is considered an evil deity because of her bloodlust, but it also this bloodlust that makes her attractive. It is the bloodlust that gives her power so those who want an effective way to target their enemies are sometimes forced to see her. But that does not always mean that one needs to give her animal flesh – other means are available.

The temple at Sīnigama near Hikkaduwa is a good example of this. The temple is a popular site for black magic and it is believed that Devol Dēviyo is a particularly effective medium for curses. Devol Dēviyo is a local deity and, like Kāli, has a violent aspect. When we visited the temple it was extremely busy despite the fact that the temple is practically inaccessible as it is located on a tiny island and can only be approached by banana boat.[120] The cursee approaches the *kapurāla* (religious officiant). We observed the *kapurāla* crush a number of limes and chilli in a pestle whilst muttering the curse under his breath.

Kapferer provides an accurate description of this process: 'At Sinigama, on the south coast near the large town of Galle, people come to curse at the main shrine to Devol Deviyo, often grinding chillies and mustard seed mixed with broken glass as they make their curses.'[121] The *kapurāla* informs the cursee that 'something bad' will happen to the cursed within a specified period of time. The cursee still has to do work, however, and they are required to maintain a shrine to Devol Dēviyo at their home and they are often required to return to the temple to boost the potency of the curse. Needless to say, there is a booming industry in Sri Lanka concerned with black magic and cursing.

The interesting aspect of this procedure is that meat is substituted for lime and chilli. In Kapferer's account the materials used were chilli, mustard and even glass. Regardless, all these items are considered aggressive foods (the glass is just aggressive *simplicitor*) and therefore they are considered appropriate replacements for meat.

Meat, of course, is itself considered aggressive and violent. Lime and chilli therefore have a similar practical effect as meat but is a non-violent alternative. The inconsistency of this arrangement should be obvious however. The cursee and officiant want to avoid using animal flesh on the basis that it would violate a bevy of religious principles. Yet at the same time they aim to bring harm to another person through the intermediary power of Devol Dēviyo. Again, the tension between violence and non-violence here is clear. Despite the fact that there is considerable awareness over what constitutes appropriate religious behaviour, baser human desires for vengeance are still strong.

Kataragama (also known as Murugan or Skandha) is another deity that is relevant here. Kataragama is perhaps the most important Hindu deity worshipped by Sinhala Buddhists in Sri Lanka. This may be considered odd for two reasons: (1) because Kataragama is a Hindu deity and may be expected that Buddhists would not worship Hindu deities; and (2) because Kataragama is the Hindu god of war and therefore would be an especially inappropriate object of worship for passive and non-violent Buddhists.

The answer to these two points are as follows: the reality of Sinhala worship of Hindu deities is widely studied and understood. Sinhala Buddhists view Hindu deities as subject to Buddhism and protectors of Buddhism. They simply integrate Hindu worship into their wider Buddhist religious milieu. There is therefore no fundamental contradiction. Second, the popularity of Kataragama, as argued by Gombrich and Obeyesekere, is a relatively recent development. Kataragama has essentially displaced the more passive Saman

36 *The lion and the cow*

and other deities of traditional importance.[122] The reason for this displacement is complicated, but the very fact that Kataragama is violent may be a key reason: Kataragama can get things done.

In keeping with this violent tendency, Kataragama desires flesh just as violent deities and demons do. Gombrich and Obeyeskere write that he is, 'ritually offered venison, and at one time, it is said [he] was even given iguana meat.'[123] This is inconsistent with the notion that 'good' deities should be offered vegetarian food. But Kataragama is not 'good' but is rather considered moody and potentially malevolent.

This is not to say that Kataragama is not subject to reform and it seems that Sinhala Buddhists are trying to cure him of his violent impulses. Every time I have visited the Katargama temple (over 10 years) it seems that vegetarian food is strictly offered. The offering is invariably a platter of fruits. Interestingly, after being blessed, the fruits are consumed by the worshippers and are often shared with nearby animals (especially cows though aggressive monkeys seem to monopolise most of the food available).

Despite Kataragama's thirst for blood, people aim to give him 'pure' foods. Naturally, this has the ironic effect of making the *pūjā* less effective. Perhaps those who want a particular good effect from their worship may supply meat as mentioned by Gombrich and Obeyeskere.

This desire to supply vegetarian foods to those who are considered pure extends also to royalty. This is suggested through a particular wedding practice. According to one up-country tradition, prospective grooms are supposed to dress in a distinctive wedding costume called a *nilamayi ænduma*. This attire, which was traditionally worn by the *nilamayi*, is associated with Kandyan royalty. Of course, today there are few limits on who can actually wear the costume and even those who are from the low country can wear it for their wedding. The only true obstruction is cost as *nilamayi ænduma* are expensive to buy and hire. But wearing one is considered very prestigious. Nonetheless, wearing this costume entails certain costs. For one, the groom must be vegetarian for the seven days before the wedding. The explanation given to me was that the *nilamayi* was also a representative of Buddhism and therefore should enact the virtues of the Buddha in the days leading up to the wedding.

Although the Kandyan royalty would not be considered gods, they are nonetheless elevated within the socio-metaphysical hierarchy and are considered to some extent morally pure. Therefore there is an apparent expectation that they eat vegetarian food. Since the royal family is now extinct this tradition has been passed on to those who embody them – namely those who wear the costume prior to the marriage ceremony.

Conclusion

The above materials demonstrate just how entrenched animal welfare discourses are in Sinhala Buddhist history, culture and society. This analysis has been a preliminary case that helps cement and contextualise what follows. Another feature of this discussion has been the fact that, in Sinhala Buddhist society, vegetarianism and animal ethics occupies a complicated position. On the one hand there is widespread acceptance within the relevant literature that non-violence and animal protectionism is important. There is even acceptance that, ideally, good Buddhists should adopt a vegetarian diet.

But this acceptance runs up against a violent impulse to kill animals and to eat animal flesh. This tension between the religious ideal and its practical reality will be a major theme of the rest of this book. What follows is an examination of this tension and a study of how that tension is resolved either through a total acceptance of Buddhist passivity or, alternatively, through a giving into the violent impulse and the associated bloodshed that this entails.

Notes

1. Another term sometimes used for the Sinhalese is the word *hĕḷa*, which means 'pure' or 'pristine.'
2. Obeyesekere, 2003: 199.
3. Pieris, 28.
4. Bartholomeusz, 37, 39, 54.
5. Ibid.
6. Tambiah, 1986: 122.
7. He is mentioned in some of the Sinhala vegetarian and animal welfare literature discussed in Chapter 2.
8. Fuller, 235.
9. Ibid., 93.
10. The food of very low castes, including the meat that they might come into contact with, is regarded as contaminated. Therefore, if a higher caste, such as the Brahmins, comes into contact with these materials then the transfer of this contamination can occur (Orenstein, 10). This requires complex and onerous decontamination rituals.
11. Douglas, 1966: 43.
12. Ibid.
13. Orenstein, 10.
14. Fuller, 94.
15. Khare, 229. For further details on this also see Fuller (93).
16. Ibid., 234.
17. Fuller, 93.
18. Khare, 234.
19. See: David Gray, 53. Of course, Gray observes that even though some Buddhist texts recommend the eating of human hearts, this does not stop other Buddhists from repudiating supernatural beings known as *ḍākinīs* for their perceived excesses in ritual meat consumption practices (50). In my mind this illustrates the native tension between vegetarianism and meat eating within some Buddhist communities – it is recognized that meat eating is not good, but it is also irresistible for a range of reasons.
20. Khare, 235.
21. Fuller, 102.
22. I.B. Horner, Early Buddhism and the Taking of Life, 1967: 3. D.N. Jha (2002) and Ludwig Alsdorf (1962) have also commented on the fact that Aśoka laid down a policy that protected animals from slaughter. A.L. Bashan has connected this explicitly to a desire for vegetarianism (2005: 56).

23 The likely inflation of these figures is noted by Bashan who also observes that the number of animals cited by Aśoka as being saved because of his policies is also almost certainly inflated (2005: 57).
24 A *cakravartin* is a Buddhist political concept that means 'a wheel turner', i.e. a monarch who rules righteously under Buddhist principles and in so doing advances the cause of Buddhism.
25 Basham, 59.
26 Ibid.
27 Ludwig Alsdorf, ix.
28 Ibid., 54.
29 K.M. Norman, 1.
30 Alsdorf, 55.
31 Gombrich, 2008, 186.
32 The relation between decadence and violence and the fall of Buddhism is completely consistent with the Pāli canonical texts. The *Cakkavatti-Sīhanāda Sutta* (DN 26, 385) tells a similar apocalyptic myth: as violence and warfare become more common, so too does Buddhism decline. After all, it is the non-violent character of Buddhism that keeps the zeitgeist for war in check.
33 Again, this notion that people live shorter and shorter lives the less moral they are is found in the *Cakkavatti-Sīhanāda Sutta*. This is a general pan-Indian concept however – longevity is related to moral excellence.
34 Gombrich, 1991: 336.
35 Guṇasēkara, 12.
36 Ibid., 13.
37 Obeyesekere, 2003: 199.
38 Guṇasēkara, 15–16.
39 Ibid., 18.
40 Ibid., 23.
41 Ibid.
42 Although the *Atthasālanī* is a Pāli commentary, and itself a para-canonical text, Buddhaghosa himself lived and worked in Sri Lanka the fifth century. Much of his inspiration is thought to have come directly from the Mahavihara tradition – itself a Sinhala Thēravādin lineage.
43 Animal flesh is routinely prescribed as a traditional medicine and this practice continues to this day as I discuss in chapter five.
44 *Atthasālanī*, 1.6, 137.
45 Ibid.
46 Ibid.
47 Ryan, 12.
48 Ibid., 5; also see, K.M. de Silva, 121.
49 *The Janavaṃsa*, 88. In mentioning this it is also interesting to consider the role that cannibalism plays in early Buddhist and Sinhalese writings. It is commonly brought up in discussions of meat eating as a potential pit fall in such dietary practices. Cannibalism is, of course, strictly outlawed in the *Vinaya Piṭaka*.
50 Ibid.
51 Ibid., 89.
52 Ibid., 88.
53 Young, 1995: 61.
54 Ibid.
55 Ibid., 90.
56 Ibid., 54; also see Blaze, 126.
57 The text is found in the *Rajāvāliya* and therefore cannot be reliably dated any earlier than the eighteenth century. As L.E. Blaze notes, however, the astonishment

illustrated here is at least evident of the surprise many Sinhalese would have had at the time for the actions and behaviours of the colonists (126).
58 Ibid., 54.
59 Ibid.
60 He is writing in the 1920s so we should disregard his Orientalist language which was common at the time.
61 Pieris, 150.
62 Ibid., 155.
63 Ibid., 150–151.
64 Locke, 327–328.
65 Knox, 43.
66 Ibid., 45–46.
67 Ibid., 46.
68 Ibid., 50.
69 Ibid., 42.
70 Ibid.
71 MV, 167.
72 Ibid., 41.
73 Ibid., 135.
74 Knox's rendition clearly relates to the term '*pav*' a term that means sinful or unmeritorious or productive of negative karma.
75 Ibid., 135–136.
76 Ibid., xvii.
77 Ibid.
78 Young, 1995: 51.
79 Ibid., 52.
80 Ibid.
81 Ibid.
82 Percival, 170.
83 Ibid., 212.
84 He writes, 'Fish, indeed, forms a considerable part of the food of the inhabitants...' (Ibid., 112).
85 Prothero, 281–302.
86 Ibid., 291. The full passage from *The Golden Rules of Buddhism* reads, 'One who buys butcher's meat or poultry violates the *gāthā*. For by paying the butchers for meat he has killed, the buyer shares his sins by 'sanctioning' his act' (Olcott, 2).
87 Ibid., 293.
88 Gombrich and Obeyesekere, 206.
89 Gombrich, 2006, 186.
90 Prothero, 1995: 297; Gombrich and Obeysekere, 1988: 214.
91 Anāgārika Dharmapāla, Return to Righteousness, 220.
92 Ibid., 224.
93 Ibid., 220.
94 Ibid., xxxiv.
95 Ibid., 160–161.
96 The term he uses *marakkalyā* has a derogatory sense.
97 *kristiyāni pāpatarayā dambadiva apavitra gudu chaṇḍāla saṇkhyāvaṭa gĕna tibĕnne harak mas, ūru mas kǣma nisayi. marakkalayā ūru mas kanne nǣta. ǣtǣm gōtravala brāmaṇayō kāli yakinniyaṭa pidū elu mas kati.* (Anagārika Dharmapāla, *Dǣnagata yutu karuṇu*, 2007: 38).
98 Ibid., 578.
99 He writes, 'vegetarianism I found universally admired, but rarely practiced' (1991: 305).
100 Gombrich and Obeyeskere, 28.

101 Ruegg, 234.
102 Obeyesekere, 1963: 145.
103 Gombrich, 1991: 298.
104 Ibid., 304.
105 Bond, 1992: 118.
106 Abeyesekere, 39.
107 Gombrich and Obeyeskere, 1988: 140. The extent to which non-violent alternatives are used has been disputed by Feddema, 1995: 142.
108 Feddema also disputes whether the demon is being 'tricked' (140).
109 Gombrich, 2006: 144.
110 Gombrich and Obeyesekere, 134.
111 Obeyesekere, 1963: 144.
112 Kapferer, 1997: 200.
113 Obeyesekere, 1963: 144.
114 Hugh and Deraniyagala, 146.
115 Kapferer, 1991: 194.
116 Ibid., 195.
117 Ibid. Again, this is disputed by Feddema (see note 104).
118 Bruce Kapferer, 1997: 119
119 Kapferer, 1991: 190–192. Kapferer observes that the offering also includes intoxicants such as betel nuts. Hungry ghosts crave luxuries of the human world, foods and other consumables that are considered polluting.
120 Ibid., 307.
121 Ibid., 243.
122 For details on the loss of these prominent deities amongst the Sinhalese see, for example, Obeyesekere and Gombrich (1988: 105, 190).
123 Gombrich and Obeyesekere, 175.

2 Eating, drinking, killing
Vegetarianism and animal welfare in Sinhala literature

One of the most telling Buddhist sutras in the Pāli canon is the story of a monk called Puṇṇa, who is asked by the Buddha what he would do if he visited a notoriously violent area called Sunāparanta where the people were known to be hostile to religious missionaries. When asked what he would do if he were attacked with the villagers' fists, Puṇṇa simply responds that he would be glad not to have been attacked with a club. When asked what he would do if he were attacked with a club, Puṇṇa replies that he would be glad not to have been attacked with a knife. When asked what he would do if he were killed with a knife Puṇṇa replies that he would be glad that he had finally found someone for whom he could exercise the Buddhist ideal of self-sacrifice through nonviolence.[1]

The point of the story is that Puṇṇa represents the pinnacle of the religious ideal of non-violence. Such examples of self sacrifice are even applied to the case of animals. Take, for example, Buddhaghosa's story of the Elder Piṅgalabuddharakkhita who, after being caught by a snake, refuses to kill the animal. He says, 'I will sacrifice my life but not the precepts.' Having had this good thought the snake releases him and departs.[2]

In these Buddhist texts, there is never a good reason to respond to violence with violence even in cases of self-preservation. This, of course, runs counter to many of our ordinary intuitions about violence. Many people, while accepting that unprovoked violence is never justified, vehemently argue that violence is acceptable in instances where we are acting in self-defence. The Buddhist sūtras, however, go against this notion arguing for total pacifism. The story of Piṅgalabuddharakkhita, unlike the story of Puṇṇa, extends this pacifism to animal kind. Even killing a snake in self-defence is considered inappropriate.

This pacifism is born from two causes. The first motive is the Buddhist virtue of compassion. A central tenet of the Buddha's dharma is the idea that we should act compassionately towards all living creatures and that we should pervade 'the four quarters' of the world with thoughts of loving kindness.[3] While many prioritise human beings in such an equation it is quite obvious from the *Sūtra Piṭaka* (though perhaps not the *Vinaya Piṭaka*, as we shall see) that the Buddha viewed non-human animals equally in this assessment.

The second motive for this extreme pacifism is more self-interested, however, and is derived from a strange kind of self-preservation. How is sacrificing yourself, as the monk described above was willing to do, an example of self-preservation? It is self-preservation only if you accept the metaphysical reality of karma and reincarnation.

If the monk were to act in self-defence and kill his attacker then he might survive, but he would also accrue negative karma from violating the first precept that forbids the destruction of another sentient life. Therefore, any act of killing whatsoever – even in cases of self-defence – is actually an act of self-destruction. Such an act does not give due consideration to the afterlife. The monk was not only compassionate towards his attacker for letting him live, he was being prudent about his future rebirth.

This extreme avoidance of killing has led some to think that other acts of resistance are necessarily required. The boycott of animal slaughterhouses is one such activity. A dietary preference for vegetarianism is another. What we find throughout the Pāli literature, peculiarly, is a fragile arrangement where the former boycott is promoted while the latter diet is not. It seems to me that this is an odd state of affairs, and this vacillation about what activities should be promoted in supporting animal welfare has led to much debate within – and outside of – Buddhist communities.

In setting up this vibrant debate about the limit of kindness towards animals I will begin by looking at modern Sinhalese literature on this topic. A great deal of Sinhala Buddhist literature has been written in support of greater animal welfare and greater support for vegetarianism.

Some material has been written opposing vegetarianism (there is no literature that I know of opposing the better treatment of animals incidentally). This pattern will be repeated in every chapter, in each case dealing with a slightly different group of Sinhalese. Here, we deal with the literary activists who try to persuade Sinhalese to give up meat eating through the written word. It is crucial, however, to consider the antecedent religious writings that influence these writers – in this case, the Buddhist canon.

Animal killing in the canon

In the previous chapter we looked at a wide range of Sinhala texts that highlight the role that animal welfare and vegetarianism play in Sinhala Buddhist society and Sri Lankan history. But perhaps one of the most influential bodies of literature that influenced Sinhala Buddhist opinion is the Thēravāda Buddhist canonical literature itself – the Pāli canon.[4]

The connection between the canonical texts and the practical matter of adopting vegetarianism has been discussed at length in the secondary literature. As we shall see, these issues have also received quite a lot of attention in modern Sinhala literature too. But it is important to here cover the facts about what the canonical texts actually say as a background for all the remaining ethnographical discussion.

Regarding the killing of animals, the *Sūtra Piṭaka* literature is quite clear that animal killing is absolutely prohibited.[5] This is born from the first, and arguably most importance, precept of the five precepts (*panca sila*). The five precepts lie at the heart of Buddhist ethics and act as the basic propositions under which a good Buddhist is supposed to live. These famous precepts are as follows: (1) abstinence from killing; (2) abstinence from stealing; (3) abstinence from sexual misconduct; (4) abstinence from lying; and (5) abstinence from taking intoxicants. In Sri Lanka, pious Buddhists will recite the five precepts as an oath whenever they attend the temple and most ordinary Buddhists will recite it on important religious occasions such as *poya*.[6]

The first precept is a vow to abstain from the taking of life. What the several Pāli terms for 'life' actually entail are vigorously debated, but it is generally understood that these various terms are limited to sentient life, i.e. life that has some consciousness and intentionality.[7] Lambert Schmithausen has maintained that plant life is a grey area in the Pāli canon and that it is possible that plants are also considered sentient, though sentient in a significantly diminished capacity.[8] Regardless of this, no Sinhala Buddhist seriously considers the possibility that plants are morally significant. However, it is incontrovertible that insects are considered to be sentient in the *Sūtra Piṭaka* and it is a virtual certainty that most Sinhala Buddhists accept that this is the case.

Regardless, except for especially scrupulous Buddhists, the Sinhalese routinely kill insects.[9] Mosquitoes and cockroaches are probably the most frequently massacred animals in Sri Lanka. Although this question is unstudied I suspect that allowances are made for insects for two reasons: (1) the negative karma produced from the killing of small insects is considered negligible. As I will reiterate again in a future chapter, in Sinhala Buddhist Sri Lanka there is a sliding scale of sinfulness in animal killing depending on the animal. The larger the animal, the more negative karma is produced; conversely, the smaller the animal, the smaller the karmic effect.

Also, (2) Because the negative karma produced is so negligible it is easy to negate those karmic effects through virtuous acts such as giving *dāna* (giving gifts) or saying *piriṭ* (reciting religious texts). Without needing to go into great detail, this latter view is probably not doctrinally sound: there is no real scriptural evidence that demerit can be cancelled out through good acts. This 'bank balance' view of karma, however, is ubiquitous in Sri Lanka and accruing a net positive balance of karma is a basic objective of most Buddhists. The basic goal is to realise a better future life, or even a better present life as the assumption is that karma can have an effect even in our current existence (even though, again, this is doctrinally questionable).

The view that is found in the *Sūtra Piṭaka* therefore, is that animal killing is wrong. For example, the *Sāleyyaka Sūtta* insists that violence towards living beings is, 'not in accordance with the Dhamma' and states that, 'here someone kills living beings, he is murderous, bloody-handed, given to blows and violence, merciless to living beings.'[10] The *Sutta Nipāta* meanwhile states that the good Buddhist lays aside, 'violence in respect of all beings, not harming

44 *Eating, drinking, killing*

even one of them.'[11] Such statements are common in the *Sūtra Piṭaka* and similar, or even identical, claims appear again and again throughout the canon.[12]

In fact, the punishment for killing animals in these texts is quite harsh. The *Sūtra Piṭaka* sometimes maintains that animal slaughter will result in rebirth in the hell realms. The most frequent point of discussion in relation to such a rebirth is the *Sūtra Piṭaka's* account of what will happen to professional animal slaughterers after they die. The punishment, as always, fits the crime precisely. A former sheep butcher is flayed alive in his afterlife; a hog slaughterer is sliced to pieces by swords; a deer hunter is killed by a shower of arrows.[13] The justice doled out by the forces of karma is always poetic and analytically precise.

We shall see momentarily that the operation of karma provides fertile ground for Sinhala Buddhist animal welfare enthusiasts who pen some very imaginative stories extolling the evils of animal slaughter and the punishment that such slaughterers receive.

Hunting animals in the *Jātaka Tales*

The para-canonical tales of the *Jātaka* contain numerous stories that illustrate the evils associated with animal slaughter. The *Jātaka Tales* – sometimes known as the Buddha's birth stories – contain many stories that, in particular, focus on the perils of hunting. Although the *Jātaka* is considered to be paracanonical within the scholastic community, traditional Sinhala Buddhists view it as *buddhavacana* – the Buddha's own words. Under the traditional view it is classified as being part of the *Sūtra Piṭaka*. From this view, the *Jātaka* stories play a crucial role in communicating critical Buddhist values.

The *Kuranga Jātaka* is a fine example of the anti-hunting agenda present in the *Jātaka Tales*. In this story the Buddha – when he was a bodhisattva – is born as a virtuous deer. Because of his wit, he avoids being trapped and killed by a hunter. The hunter, enraged, says, 'Begone! I've missed you this time.'[14] The Bodhisattva replies with the following prophetic words: 'You may have missed me, my good man; but depend upon it, you have not missed the reward of your conduct, namely the eight large and sixteen lesser hells and all the five forms of bonds and torture.'[15] Merely having the intention to kill a creature is warrant for a poor rebirth – though it should also be recognised that the fact that the hunter was attempting to kill a bodhisattva may also play a role in his fate.

This explicit repudiation of hunting is made also in the *Nigrodhamiga Jātaka*. The story tells of King Brahmadatta, the ruler of Benares, who is described as being 'passionately fond of hunting, and always had meat at every meal.'[16] Every day he mustered his followers to go hunting – even when this was detrimental to their business. His favourite sport was to hunt deer. The deer, 'at first sight of the bow...would dash off trembling for their lives' but would nevertheless be killed by volleys of arrows. The Bodhisattva was the king of these deer and eventually the deer came to complain about their mistreatment.

The Bodhisattva deer approached King Brahmadatta to negotiate an agreement. They agreed that instead of killing the deer *ad hoc* only one deer per month would be sacrificed. In time, however, a pregnant doe is selected to be killed and the Bodhisattva elects to go in her place. In awe of this demonstration of compassion King Brahmadatta vows never to slay deer again. But the Bodhisattva is not satisfied with this. He says, 'Sire, deer will thus be safe; but what will the rest of the four-footed creatures do?'[17] The King thereafter agrees to spare all these creatures too.

This *Jātaka* therefore illustrates that, (1) animal slaughter is wrong; and (2) that hatred, greed and violence can be overcome through acts of compassion and self-sacrifice.

The *Jātaka Tales* preach weariness of hunters in other ways. For example, the *Lakkhaṇa Jātaka* describes a story where the bodhisattva is reborn as a king of the deer. The Bodhisattva instructs his fellow deer to avoid hunters during the harvest season. He warns, 'Anxious to kill the creatures that devour their crops, peasants dig pitfalls, fix stakes, set stone-traps, and plant snares...so that many deer are slain.'[18] The Bodhisattva goes on: 'My children, [it] is now the time when crops stand thick in the field and many deer meet their death at this season. We who are old will make shift to stay in one spot; but you will retire each with your herd to the mountainous tracts in the forest and come back when the crops have been carried.'[19]

Unfortunately one rogue deer refuses to listen to this advice and strays close to humankind and is thus killed. We learn that this deer is none other than the Buddha's arch-nemesis Devadatta in a previous life. The story is a metaphor for the life of the renunicate: those who follow the Buddha's advice (the bodhisattva deer) will be able to avoid a poor rebirth (being killed by the human hunters); those who ignore his advice will meet a poor fate. Devadatta is an example of what will happen when you fail to follow the Buddha.

The *Jātaka Tales* are full of examples of non-violence towards animals. As is clear already, much of it is specifically against hunting. This resonates already with the Sinhala *Mahāvaṃsa* where King Devānaṃpiyatissa gives up his hunting expedition due to the power of Buddhism. The *Jātaka Tales* are quite explicit that killing animals is wrong and that, amongst other things, a poor rebirth will result from such actions.

The Vinaya and moral hierarchies

The *Sūtra Piṭaka* and the *Jātaka Tales* have strong opinions on the killing of animals. The *Vinaya Piṭaka* – the monastic rulebook that reports the Buddha's instructions to his own disciples – contrasts considerably with the *Sūtra Piṭaka*, however. While the *Vinaya* agrees that animal slaughter is completely unacceptable and disallowed, the relative seriousness of the offence is questionable.

The circumstances under which the Buddha bans animal killing for monks can be found in the *Pāṭimokkha* of the *Vinaya*. The story concerns a rogue monk called Udāyin. The discourse states that Udāyin, 'having shot crows, having cut off their heads, put them in a row on a stake.'[20] The Buddha is alerted to these events and states that, 'whatever monk should intentionally deprive a living thing of life, there is an offence of expiation.'[21]

Note, here, that the offence is one of expiation (*pācittiya*). Expiation is a punishment that involves the monk admitting to his wrongdoing publically and undertaking a vow never to repeat the action. Sometimes a demotion is entailed. One unpleasant aspect of this punishment is the embarrassment of being put on trial in front of one's peers. This act of expiation is to be distinguished from an offence that entails expulsion (*parājika*). Killing humans, stealing, sexual impropriety and boasting about one's spiritual attainments result in this punishment. Expiation is a lesser offence. It is obvious, then, that from a jurisprudential perspective there is a difference between killing an animal and killing a human being.

Indeed, killing an animal – according to the *Vinaya* – is no worse than walking alone with a woman.[22] Certainly, killing an animal is absolutely not justified by the *Vinaya*, but the seriousness of the punishment is quite at odds with the harshness of the *Sūtra* literature.

As we shall see, this curious indifference to animal killing in the *Vinaya* seems to have influenced the wider monastic community. Many of the monks studied in my interviews were quite unenthusiastic about animal welfarism and this might be owed to the fact that animals occupy a lesser moral significance in the *Vinaya*. On the other hand, the *Sūtra Piṭaka* – including the *Jātaka* stories – take a more serious view of animal killing. These same texts, especially the *Jātaka*, are popular with laity as they provide an accessible – and sometimes entertaining – insight into the Buddha's teachings. This may help explain the apparent divide between monastic and lay opinion when it comes to the seriousness of animal slaughter.

These subtleties do not interfere with the fact that animal slaughter is fundamentally considered morally wrong in the *Vinaya*. Like the *Sūtra* literature, the *Vinaya* bans the killing of animals completely. The disagreement is only over how serious the offence is.

Despite the *Sūtra Piṭaka's* warning that killing animals will result in rebirth in hell, there is evidence that even lay people do not always take animal killing all that seriously. The *Vinaya* incorporate a hierarchical structure where killing humans is much worse than killing animals. Sinhala Buddhists, in their day-to-day lives, also seem to apply a ranking system of moral offence depending upon the relative size of the animal being killed.

Scholars have commented on the fact that the animal slaughter profession is not popular amongst the Sinhala Buddhist community in Sri Lanka and that such activities are generally left to non-Buddhist minorities. Cattle slaughter is almost exclusively conducted by Muslims.[23] Fishing is generally carried out by Sinhalese Christians who live on the coast. As we saw, indigenous texts such as the *Janavaṃsa* are quite critical of those Buddhists who support fisher-folk. As we shall see in Chapters 5 and 7, Sinhala Buddhists are very critical of cattle slaughter. But they are much more permissive when it comes to the killing of fish. Indeed, fish eating is entirely ubiquitous within the Sinhala Buddhist community.

As with the case of insects discussed earlier, this may partly because fish are small and therefore considered less morally significant. As a result, killing and eating fish will only result in a trivial amount of negative karma being created. Cows, on the other hand, are very large and therefore only a very morally incompetent person would think about killing them.

Buddhaghosa lends support to the notion that small animals matter less. He writes: 'Among small animals devoid of virtues, it is a slight misdeed to kill in the case of a small creature and a great misdeed in that of a large one.'[24] Buddhaghosa explains that the difference in wrong doing is owed to the difference in effort required to kill the animal in accord with its size.[25] Harvey confirms this idea by pointing out that, 'it is preferable to eat the meat of an animal which is less intelligent, and/or smaller, than the opposite.'[26] Killing animals is bad, but killing big animals is worse.

In tension with this hierarchical approach within the lived Buddhist community is the claim in the *Sūtra Piṭaka* that killing animals will lead one to be reborn in hell. Meanwhile, the *Vinaya* takes a more relaxed attitude towards animal killing and maintains that a monk can simply apologise if he happens to kill an animal. So there are a range of different moral hierarchies that illustrate the relative seriousness of killing animals and humans, big and small.

It is also clear that, despite the *Sūtra Piṭaka's* threat that animal killing will result in a poor rebirth it is apparent that at least some Sinhala Buddhists do not pay this much attention. But regardless of these complications, the textual sources are at least clear that animal killing is completely wrong. The only disagreement is over *how* wrong it is and what the relative punishment is for violating the strict rules against animal killing.

Vegetarianism in the canon

Despite these subtleties, the canonical texts practically call for a boycott of slaughterhouses. What we do not find, however, is the next logical step in the escalation of animal welfare actions namely, a call to boycott the consumption of meat. The foundation for vegetarianism in Thēravāda Buddhism, while philosophically in keeping with the Buddha's attitude of non-violence towards animals, is very doctrinally weak indeed.

The critical point of contention over meat consumption centres around the issue of whether the meat is *trikoṭi parisuddha* or 'pure in three ways.'[27] This discussion appears in both the *Sūtra* and *Vinaya* literature.[28] In both instances the Buddha insists that meat eating is acceptable but only if that meat satisfies three conditions: that it is not seen, heard or suspected that the animal was killed *for* the monks who were to receive it.

In short, the animal was killed for some other purpose, not for the monks, and they just happened to have been given the meat. The notion here is that the monks should not be directly associated with the animal's death. The Buddha clearly wanted to exonerate the *sangha* of any potential allegations of responsibility for an animal's death. Of course, it's also not out of the question that an animal might be killed *for* the *sangha* but that the monks were satisfied that this wasn't the case anyway. In short, it seems to be the case that the monks simply *should not know that the animal was killed for them*, which is not quite the same as the animal actually being killed for them.

In the *Jīvaka Sūtra* the Buddha is accused by a Jain ascetic of eating meat and that the meat was killed on his behalf.[29] The Buddha responds sternly that he allows for meat eating provided it meets the above criteria. Again, this nicely skirts the issue of whether *in fact* the animal was killed for him – just that he sincerely should be able to say that *he did not know*. In any case, it is quite obvious that the Buddha did eat meat. The *Aṅguttara Nikāya* records a case where the Buddha was given a meal that included meat.[30] There is also the notorious final meal of the Buddha which, purportedly, was either mushrooms or pork – depending on how one translates the relevant term in the *Dīgha Nikāya*. Most scholars believe the mushrooms translation is fanciful, though it is a moot point given the above-mentioned *Aṅguttara Nikāya* sutra.

Another significant matter is the case of Devadatta. Devadatta is the Buddha's rival and nemesis who sought to reform the *sangha* to accommodate his own ideas. The canonical texts depict him as a divisive figure who would have destroyed the *sangha* had the Buddha not intervened at the right time. Devadatta also supposedly attempted to assassinate the Buddha on several occasions. He is therefore the de facto villain of the Buddhist tradition and, interestingly, is a threat that originates *from within* the Buddhist *sangha* itself. In other words, the greatest threat to the viability of Buddhism is not an external force, but rather internal division. This is an important point to remember when considering the Buddha's decision to disallow the introduction of mandatory vegetarianism.

Devadatta approached the Buddha with the suggestion that, amongst other reforms, the Buddha make vegetarianism compulsory. The texts do not provide any justification for this request except that Devadatta was motivated from bad intentions as he supposedly knew that this would split the *sangha* apart. In the interests of unity, and in an attempt to avoid the collapse of Buddhism as an institution, the Buddha refused his request. There is therefore considerable ambiguity about the Buddha's decision to disallow mandatory vegetarianism. After all, it seems that he disallowed it because it was imprudent not necessarily because it was not morally right.

The awkwardness of this situation perhaps also explains the awkwardness of the *trikoṭi parisuddha* rule mentioned above. The rule allows meat eating, but brackets it off and puts conditions on it thus directly suggesting that meat eating is morally hazardous. On the other hand, Devadatta's association with vegetarianism also suggests that vegetarianism is morally tarnished too.

Western scholars and Sinhala commentators alike tend to oversimplify the question of vegetarianism in Buddhism. The consensus tends to be that the Buddha did not make it mandatory and therefore meat eating is not intrinsically immoral. These views overlook the aforementioned ambiguities about the Buddha's decision about vegetarianism. They also overlook the complicated political and social context of the Buddha's decision about vegetarianism.

The role of Jainism in shaping this internal debate is also unavoidable. Mahavira, the founder of Jainism, was a contemporary of the Buddha. Jainism was a movement that was known to advocate mandatory vegetarianism even during the Buddha's time. Recall that in the *Jīvaka Sūtra* it was a Jain called Jīvaka that confronted the Buddha about his meat eating habits.

From a Jain point of view, the fact that the Buddha allowed meat eating is a moral embarrassment given that he so fiercely opposed the killing of animals. Jīvaka was bringing attention to this embarrassment. Whether the Buddha sufficiently redirected this unwanted attention by citing the *trikoṭi parisuddha* rule remains a matter of debate, but it seems to me that it only amplified these dietary difficulties. In any case, it is plausible – though impossible to know for sure – that the Buddha's reluctance to introduce mandatory vegetarianism was because it would constitute a concession to Mahavira and the Jains. Such a concession would have been politically destabilising as it would have suggested that the Jains and Buddhists essentially agreed morally and, worse, that the Buddha arrived at that conclusion only after Mahavira did.[31]

The solution to this political conundrum is to allow meat eating with some restrictions, and, at the same time, suggest that *mandatory* vegetarianism in Jainism is an example of Jain extremism not in keeping with the core Buddhist principle of following a middle path between two extremes.

Regardless, Buddhists have since been frequently criticised for not biting the bullet and making vegetarianism mandatory. Just as the Buddha regards the Jains as extremists, the Jains accuse the Buddhists of decadence. One key Jain text, the *Sūtrakritāṅga*, describes Buddhist lay people as inveterate animal killers subservient to the clergy: 'They kill a fattened sheep, and prepare food for the sake of a particular person; they season the meat with salt and oil, and dress it with pepper.' The monks are even worse, however, 'You are irreligious, unworthy men, devoted to foolish pleasures, who say that partaking hertily of this meat you are not soiled by sin.'[32]

The case for vegetarianism is therefore problematic from a strictly doctrinal perspective and many who oppose Buddhist vegetarianism know this. The response from pro-vegetarian Buddhists is diverse. The first option is to simply ignore the above facts and continue to argue that vegetarianism is an ideal diet by way of implication rather than as a direct statement made by the Buddha. This is the most feasible approach.

The second option is to deny many of the above observations. Some scholars have attempted torturous intellectual contortions in an attempt to make this second option work. Roshi Philip Kapleau, for example, has insisted that the Buddha was a vegetarian himself and advocated vegetarianism.[33] A few of our lay informants also took the view that the Buddha was a vegetarian. We know from the above discussion that such a view is doctrinally mistaken.

The first option is by far the better option in defending ethical vegetarianism in Buddhism. It relies on the fact that the Buddha was in favour of animal welfare and was against the killing of animals. It observes that the Buddha promoted the encouragement of non-violence towards animals and that this entailed a boycott of slaughterhouses.

It also observes that the Buddha merely made vegetarianism optional – it is neither mandatory nor outlawed. Given the optional nature of vegetarianism, the view amongst some will be that the best Buddhists will voluntarily be vegetarians. It is, in short, a moral test. Of course, this awkwardly implies that the Buddha was morally defective. This, needless to say, is completely untenable. The intractable problem of vegetarianism is therefore clear.

Buddhist revenge literature

The above textual sources illustrate that the case for vegetarianism in Buddhism is complicated. But what is not complicated is the fact that the source materials condemn animal killing. This condemnation of animal killing has clearly filtered through to modern Sinhala literature.

One source of regular entertainment that exploits such ideas is the Sri Lankan newspaper *Lankadīpa* and its insert *Taksalāva*. In that newspaper is a series of letters concerning the subject of karma and revenge. It is implied that the letters are based on real events and come from one basic theme: the karmic punishment of villains for crimes they have committed in their own life. Although not all these letters are concerned with crimes committed against animals a large number of them are, and this already illustrates just how important animal welfare is for many Sinhala Buddhists. These letters also reflect themes already clear in the Pāli literature: a concern over the lives of animals and a fascination with the tortures that meet those who harm living creatures.

In a Chapter 5 I will discuss the letters specifically concerned with cow-related crimes and their commensurate punishments. Again, of all the letters concerning animal violence, around half the letters were concerned specifically with cows – so not only is animal welfare important, cow welfare is particularly important.

The stories in these letters are not only thematically similar they also follow stereotypical plot points. The structure of the stories are as follows: a morally unscrupulous individual harms part of an animal's body; almost immediately the individual develops an illness on an identical part of their own body; they seek either Western or traditional medical treatment which usually fails; but in cases where the treatment reduces the illness, even in a temporary fashion, the individual still cannot resist continuing with their pastime of harming animals; finally, the illness then continues on – or returns – and as a result the individual dies in agony. It is remarkable how predictable the stories are in following these particular steps. This tells us something about the operation of karma: it is very predictable and mechanistic in its meting out of punishment.

Take for example one story titled *'The man who killed and consumed goats who lived in the temple'*.[34] The story describes how a particular man would sacrifice goats as part of his religious observances. Note that the implication here is that the man was Hindu since some Sinhalese believe that Hindu believers routinely sacrifice goats as part of their temple activities (this is only rarely true, of course, and we saw in the last chapter animal sacrifice is going out of vogue in mainland India).[35]

The story makes a point of describing the anguish of the goats: 'When the goats are brought to the *pūjāva* they cry out because they know they are going to be slaughtered.'[36] Providing a detailed account of the animal's misery is a basic trope of this type of literature. But the mere fact that this man sacrificed goats is not the only immoral aspect of the man's character – he is also depicted as extraordinarily cruel. The story says, 'Once a female goat tried to save itself by jumping from his grasp. The man ran and with some difficulty caught it. "You (derogatory) can't escape from me *that* easily! I will teach you a lesson," he said and stabbed her in the eye with a knife. Because of the sharpness of the blade it cut deep into the eyes and [they] bled. He gleefully looked at the animal, grabbed it, and then, in a precise manner, cut its throat.'[37]

The injustice of such cruel acts does not escape the metaphysical law of karma. The story goes on to say that after this especially inhuman act he suddenly developed an eye disease. Despite attempts to treat the illness with medicine the eye disease got worse and worse. The author of the story writes, 'Because both his eyes were worsening the doctor said they must be removed'.[38] But as is the case with immoral people they cannot reform their ways so easily. As a result, the man continued to do *pūjā* that involved the routine sacrificial slaughter of goats. After stabbing a goat in the throat with a knife the story has it that, 'When he walking around in the yard blinded he stepped on a spike'.[39] Gradually, the wound got bigger.

Finally he had to have the leg removed as well. At last the man died after developing a throat disease because he persisted in cutting the throats of goats. Because he had no eyes or leg his attendants assisted him in this task, though this does cause one to wonder whether his attendants are also culpable in these activities. Regardless, it is compelling just how proportionate, according to these accounts, karma is the man stabs out a goat's eye, so he loses his eyes; he stabs a goat's throat, so he is stabbed; he cuts their throats, so harm befalls his throat, and so on.

The accuracy of karma here is reflective of several things: (1) the expectation amongst many Sinhala Buddhists that metaphysical justice will be done even if an individual escapes human justice; and (2), the poetical nature of this justice whereby the individual suffers the exact same fate that he himself applied to others. Finally, (3) this literature, it seems to me, is a kind of revenge literature. That is, it is not *only* about distributing sober justice, it is also about exciting feelings of satisfaction in the reader when the perpetrator is finally punished. Indeed, the more violent and bloody the punishment is, the better.

Take for example the story titled, *'The man who killed pigs'* (*ūran mærǣ minihā*). The story begins by describing an individual who was Sinhala and a Buddhist. This is not incidental. In the previous story concerning the goat killer there was a strong implication that the man was a Hindu. This story, however, stresses the fact that karma is unbiased in its application and is concerned only with deed, not one's religion. The story maintains that this man raised pigs with the intent of slaughtering them later. As mentioned in the discussion of the *Sūtra Piṭaka*, such an occupation is considered to be un-Buddhist and this is reflected in this story where the man is described as a pig slaughterer *in spite* of the fact that he is a Buddhist.

It reads: 'Having needed to kill a pig it was put in a sack and tied up. The pig that he put into the sack was beaten with a pole. The pig would die in the sack. If, after pounding the pig, it was still alive the custom was to stab it with a knife. People knew about [what he did] and called him 'the pig killer.' Even the monks knew about him.'[40] Not only did the monks know about him, they were happy to accept the pig flesh that he produced as an offering. It seems to me that this point is a veiled criticism of the monastic practice of receiving flesh as an offering. There is also an implicit implication that the villagers tacitly supported his activities. The point is, perhaps, that evil deeds are more easily carried out with the support of a community.

One day, the man got in a quarrel with the villagers. 'The fight went on for some time. People bought big sticks and hit him with them. At the end, with broken limbs, he fell to the ground.'[41] Despite attempts to heal him with traditional medicine the man would not get better and eventually died. The story describes his death in lurid detail, 'With great suffering the man died tragically in his own urine and feces.'[42]

Another example of the extreme violence in these stories comes from a *Taksalāva* letter titled, *'The man who cut off the dog's penis'*.[43] The protagonist of the story is an alcoholic who stumbled upon two dogs copulating in a marketplace while trying to find a place to urinate. The story continues: 'The man said, 'Stay there, I'm going to teach you a lesson for your (derogatory) vulgarness,' and pulled out a sharp knife and cut the penis off the dog who was still connected to the bitch. The dog bled profusely, howled and ran away [presumably to die]. The bitch painfully whimpered and moved away.'[44] This incredibly violent and gory scene subsequently leads to a similarly violent scene of retribution. 'Exactly one week after that, the man went for a walk in the evening around the [village] area using bad language [because he was a drunk]. After watching a film and having lit a torch-branch a group of young men who were walking by got to look at the man whose sarong was lifted up [i.e. he exposed himself to the group of young men]. They loudly swore at him, grabbed the torch-branch and put it on his groin. With his groin burning in pain the man ran away. The youths laughed loudly.'[45]

As with the previous story concerning the priest who was forced to get his attendants to slaughter the goats on his behalf one wonders whether these youths were also subject to karmic retribution for their own violent actions. On the other hand, perhaps the view is that agents of karma, i.e. those who are simply cosmic instruments, do not suffer punishment. This is not clear from the story, nor is it especially clear in the wider Buddhist metaphysical picture. In any case, the story ends saying, 'Because of the burn and the wound that was created he suffered a great deal and passed away'.[46]

The elaborate and detailed violence in these stories seems to highlight the importance of the punishment rather than justice. It is the equivalent of letting a murder victim's family watch the execution of the murderer. In other words, there is an element of satisfaction in witnessing someone get their come-uppance. On top of this, the fact that the perpetrator is invariably described as dying in extreme agony and suffering further reinforces this as a key motive in the development of these stories.

There are many other stories that fit this same format and I will briefly describe a few here. One story called *'The Priest Who Tortured a Cat'*[47] describes the case of a priest who tied a cat to a tree, 'pulled out both its eyes' (*æs děkama gælavuyěya*) and then later lashed it to death 'because of his hate' (*krōdhaya nisā*). Later, the priest developed cancer in both eyes. They attempted to cure it by putting 'boiled greens on his eyes' (an ayurvedic treatment). Prayer would do nothing either. In the end the eyes had to be removed. But even after the surgery bumps began to appear all over his body: 'Doctors told him that the cancer from his eyes had ran throughout his body. He died in great suffering at the monastery.'[48]

Examples like this multiple in the newspaper literature. *'The youth who impaled monitor lizards'*[49] tells of a young man who hunted monitor lizards and impaled them on spikes. One day while chasing a monitor lizard up a tree, the boy fell out and was impaled on a sharp branch. Again, the offender dies in agony: 'From the pain of those wounds he screamed for many days before he finally passed away.'[50]

The basic points of this story is repeated in a similar tale about a man who hunted elephants (*The man who killed elephants fell into the pit that was made for the elephants*).[51] As with the monitor lizard story, the man is eventually killed in the same manner as the trap that he set for the animal. 'At a certain time in the night, while looking for elephants, the man fell into the pit trap [he had dug]. When he fell his legs were wounded by the spikes. ... Because he was wondered for several days he suffered and finally starved to death. ... His dead body was found in the jungle because of its stench.'[52]

The story about the elephant hunter also illustrates another factor in these stories: that of desire. The elephant hunter is motivated entirely out of greed – namely, he wanted to take the tusks of the elephants for profit. The role of avarice is in fact a key point in many of these stories. In each of the cases described above, the perpetrator *could not help* but engage in their illicit behaviours. Take for example the alcoholic who cut off the dog's penis: it was his desire for alcohol that led to his undoing. Likewise, the Hindu priest who engaged in goat slaughter was practically addicted to the act of sacrificing goats. The role of desire, and its unavoidable allure, will arise again as a factor in meat consumption in Chapter 3.

Of course, the basis for all evil deeds in Buddhism is ultimately desire. The purpose of the Buddhist path is to bring desire under control and, in so doing, eliminate evil deeds and their associated negative karma. But what these stories also tell us is that human evil is a tragic affair born from our intrinsic tendency to crave even when those cravings lead to pain and misery. These stories are therefore tragedies in the Greek sense of the term because, in many ways, it was inevitable that these individuals were to carry out these deeds and consequently reap their unhappy punishments. There is also a cathartic element to the stories. So although the lurid details in the story lead one to conjure up feelings of justice and retribution, there is also an element of pity here. The feeling of pity is critical, however, because it allows the reader to feel that they are being compassionate. The reader is distracted from the fact that they are also celebrating the villain's pain. After all, that would be un-Buddhist.

One of the underlying purposes of these stories is that they be a tool to reassure the reader that there is real justice in the world. This is especially important when one considers that Sri Lanka is a nation that has serious problems with corruption and where the course of public justice can be easily perverted.[53] In such circumstances it is perhaps comforting to know that metaphysical justice can be realised and these stories further confirm the reality of this phenomenon. Despite the stereotypical nature of these stories it seems that they exist outside the literary world and also find a place in the oral tradition too. I have heard more than one story from informants that roughly fits the same format at these stories that appear in *Taksalāva*.

These stories are also derivative of Pāli canonical and commentarial sources and are no doubt partly inspired by them. We have already encountered examples of this in Chapter 1, namely the case of the monk in the *Rajāvaliya* who was boiled alive for killing an ant in a previous life. Another excellent example of this is a story told by Buddhaghosa in his *Atthasālanī*. He describes a monk who in a previous life was a cowherd who tormented a reptile by trapping it in a hole without food and water for seven days. Because of this past misdeed the monk was reborn in a circumstance where he too was trapped in a cave without food or water. Buddhaghosa writes that he was trapped there and then after seven days (as with his original crime) he died after 'all his days had expired.'[54]

The notion of karma as a precise instrument of revenge is similarly highlighted in the *Sūtra Piṭaka* described earlier where animal slaughterers are reborn in conditions where they are tortured in ways that echo the crimes they committed to animals in a previous life.

The revenge literature in *Taksalāva* takes these mechanistic stories of karma and transforms them into salacious stories that prey upon the readers desire to see punishment inflicted upon wrong doers. The stories offer cathartic experiences for the readers but they also confirm the role of karma in day-to-day affairs. Moreover, they confirm the immorality of animal killing.

Pro-vegetarian Buddhist authors

It is perhaps unsurprising that most of the Sinhala authors who have chosen to write on the subject of animal welfare are in favour of the better treatment of animals through the boycotting of meat and the adoption of vegetarianism. There is a reasonable range of pro-vegetarian literature available in Sri Lanka, but it should not be assumed that this automatically implies that a majority of Sinhala Buddhists would automatically agree with vegetarianism.

One author that does argue in favour of vegetarianism is J.D. Sudasinha. His key work here is *Let's all adopt a vegetarian diet (nirmānsha āhārayakaṭa purudu vemu)*. His starting point for the importance of vegetarianism comes from a sympathetic attitude to the suffering of animals. His initial premise is a refrain heard frequently amongst those who support better treatment of animals: animals suffer just like us. He writes, 'Every creature in this world does not want to die'[55] and 'Just like us humans, all animals go through pain and suffering at the time of death. No animal can die from their own consent.'[56] This argument appeals to the notion that humans and animals are not different from each other. Such arguments are a hallmark of many Sinhala Buddhist ethicists. It draws upon the basic Buddhist principle of compassion and, more importantly, unselfishness or sympathetic joy *(mūdita)*. Animals and humans are not so dissimilar, according to this view, and Sudasinha appeals to our own experiences in order to motivate us to respect and care for other animals.

Sudasinha is generally critical of other religions for their lack of commitment to animal welfare. For example, Hinduism – which we already know from the previous chapter to sometimes advocates vegetarianism – is subject to some criticism. Sudasinha writes that, 'Some denominations of the Hindu religion reject meat food. Despite that, the Hindu religion frequently utilises milk and milk products. They consider the cow as a god and in India Hindu believers have completely banned the slaughter of cows in certain areas. In their society the consumption of cows flesh has been conquered. Anyone who consumes beef is cornered in that society. *Despite that, some Hindu denominations take goats and chickens and other animals for use in various blood sacrifices*' (my italics).[57] Although he does celebrate the fact that Seventh Day Adventists are vegetarians, he notes that, 'Amongst those who believe in [Christianity] it seems that there is no apparent instruction for them to reject flesh food.'[58] As for Judaism and Islam he observes that those religions allow for the slaughter of animals provided they are killed in a ritually pure way.

It seems to me that the point of these comparisons is to contrast Buddhism with these other religions. Given our earlier analysis of the Buddhist canonical texts this seems like an odd strategic decision given the fact that, unlike religions such as Jainism, Buddhism does not explicitly encourage vegetarianism at all.

Nonetheless, this does not stop Sudasinha from providing a vigorous defence of Buddhist vegetarianism.

He writes, 'In Buddhism, is flesh food allowed?' His answer is, first of all, that Buddhism is very diverse. Nonetheless, regardless of denomination, Sudasinha believes that 'for Buddhists taking flesh food is not appropriate.' Though it is not appropriate Sudasinha does accept that variation in culture and climate can lead to the consumption of meat as a necessity. 'In modern times, the Buddhist religion is in force in the countries of Thailand and Tibet and when [monks] go on alms rounds they receive a lot of meat in their begging bowl. Similarly, because of the various geography, climate, and cultures in difference countries there are various different food types.'[59]

Sudasinha's main Buddhalogical objection to flesh food consumption is that, in cases where meat eating is optional (which is certainly the case in Sri Lanka, he would maintain), it can only be the case that monks eat that flesh out of desire. This feeling of extreme desire is, however, contrary to Buddhist doctrine. But these obligations extend to the laity as well. 'If it is possible to live life with healthy food without taking meat food then it is appropriate for the Buddhist laity and the monks to avoid follow a diet without meat.'[60]

The responsibility that the laity have in supplying meat is a matter that will be again considered in Chapter 4.

For Sudasinha, what follows from this is a set of directives that he believes emerge from the first precept not to take life. 'If a person follows the Buddha's teachings which are the five precepts and the three points then that person should not kill animals for food or any other cause. That person should also not advise other people to do so. If there is an animal who is due to be killed that person should set that animal free. He should teach others about showing compassion towards animals. Going to the market and buying meat also makes us participate in the act of animal slaughter.'[61]

These religious observations form a part of his argument for vegetarianism. But a large part of Sudasinha's book is concerned with a secular analysis of why vegetarianism is ideal. He laments the ubiquitous nature of animal slaughter in Sri Lanka. He regards this as being a consequence of widespread meat consumption. In his chapter titled *The consumption of flesh food in Sri Lanka* (*srī lankāvē mānsha paribhōjanaya*) he states that, 'The number of animals that are killed is statistically even more than [the official incomplete governmental data].' He adds that, 'Out of devotion, a lot of individuals give relief for cows and oppose cow slaughter for merit.' He describes how these animals are collected in isolated locations, lifted by mechanical arms onto trucks and then taken to be slaughtered.

In his previous chapter, titled 'The Method of Suffering that Accompanies Animals that Are Slaughtered for Food'[62] Sudasinha provides ghastly detail as to the various techniques used for slaughtering a range of different animals.[63] Of course, alerting readers to the macabre nature of the abattoir is a basic part of animal welfare literature both in Sri Lanka and elsewhere in the world.

Apart from these concerns about the animal's suffering, Sudasinha also points out that there would be a number of human benefits from switching to vegetarianism. He says, 'If people did not do this and practiced a vegetarian diet then hunger and death amongst the world's population would not occur.'[64] Instead of raising animals, land can be used to grow crops and grain: 'ten million acres of forest lands are used annually for meat production. It would be beneficial to use this land for agricultural purposes. From this, the entire world population can be provided with healthy food.'[65]

This endorsement of vegetarianism continues with other writers. Take, for example, Shrīya Ratnakāra. His book *Give us space to live (apaṭa jīvat vĕnna iḍa dĕnna)* covers some of the same topics as Sudasinha and is based fundamentally around the same issue of advocating for the better treatment of animals and the adoption of a vegetarian diet. Like Sudasinha, Ratnakāra deploys the argument from sympathetic understanding, namely that animals and humans are not so different – we both love our lives. He says, 'You and I also like to live' (*obat mamat jīvat vīmaṭa kæmættō vĕmu*).[66]

Also like Sudasinha, Ratnakāra believes that the first precept against the taking of life implies that we should not eat flesh. He writes, 'Buddhists eating meat contravenes the first four learner verses.'[67] This is a rather bold claim given the earlier analysis of the canonical texts and also speaks of Ratnakāra's confident approach to this subject.

Ratnakāra's view is that all four of the precepts ultimately arrive back at refusing to eat meat. Take, for example, the verse not to steal. He writes, 'I will not steal what belongs to another person. Likewise, when you consume flesh isn't it stealing another person's life?'[68] Supporting the killing of animals through eating meat is itself a kind of stealing – the theft of a living being's life. Ratnakāra maintains that this is also the case with the verse not to lie. He writes, 'I will not tell a lie. I did not kill that animal.' Isn't saying such statements deceptive? Isn't it because of our love of meat that the animal was killed?'[69]

This, of course, contravenes the assumption behind the *trikoṭi parisuddha* rule. For Ratnakāra, however, the logic of this rule appears to be a incorrect. Ratnakāra also applies this logic to the precept against taking intoxicants: 'Essentially, the mind of people who eat meat with their food are, to a certain degree, confused? Is it possible to avoid the impulse to do wrong?'[70] Ratnakāra's aim here is to associate the confusing effect of intoxicants with our dizzying craving for flesh.

Apart from these imaginative alternative readings of the precepts, Ratnakāra also appeals to more conventional moral arguments. For example, he cites the *Mettā Sūtra (The Loving Kindness Sutra)* as general evidence that the Buddha dharma advocates non-violence towards animals and therefore vegetarianism. But he notes the hypocrisy in how this song is used in ordinary Buddhist affairs. He writes, 'Individuals who go to the temple and receive the five precepts and sing the Mettā Sūtta come home afterwards and take chicken out of the freezer and cut it into pieces in order to consume it.'[71]

He concludes the passage by observing that, 'Loving kindness should apply to every animal alike' regardless of how small they happen to be.[72] His point here is that people don't pay attention to animal life when the satisfaction of one's stomach is in question. This is manifestly unjust, he would argue. His comments also overturn the common assumption that small animals matter less than big ones. This concludes his chapter titled 'Let all animals be without suffering' (siyalu sattvayō niduk vĕtvā).

Ratnakāra's text is highly polemical and relies to a great extent on emotive imagery and the widespread deployment of rhetorical questions. This use of rhetorical questions, a device explicitly intended to draw the reader into question their ordinary assumptions about what constitutes a 'good Buddhist', is already apparent from his idiosyncratic discussion of the five precepts. Here is another example of this method of questioning: 'Have you ever thought how many lives can be liberated by just one person who does not consume meat?'[73]

This rhetorical flair extends in other directions. For example, he sometimes anthropomorphises animals and has them speak directly to the reader, 'Nevertheless, from us they pleaded for mercy, from the beast's questioning voice, [it says] quietly 'Oh! Don't kill us.''[74] Having animals appeal to the reader from their own perspective is a trope in Sinhala Buddhist animal welfarism. This appeal to emotion is also exemplified by his description of the unpleasant process by which cattle are selected and transported for slaughter: 'Going from place to place and selecting cows, goats, pigs, and chickens, purchasing them and packing them into lorries and taking them to cattle sheds, they are imprisoned without food in cages, and they go on a journey of many miles knowing that at the end they will be executed.'[75] He goes on, 'Fear, pain and anger is sunken into every piece of meat and doesn't this make the meat poisonous?'[76]

All these remarks clearly illustrate Ratnakāra's commitment to uncovering the evils of the animal slaughter industry. His arguments for vegetarianism are based around a combination of Buddhist metaphysics, Buddhist ethics and an appeal to our bare emotions.

Consider his argument for vegetarianism in the chapter: 'Are we eating the flesh of bodhisattvas?' In this chapter he asks, 'How many [times] were we previously born as animals [in order] to receive a human soul?' In discussing the fact that the Buddha, in his previous existence as a bodhisattva, was reincarnated as a range of animals, Ratnakāra says, 'We have heard that the Lord Buddha has been born as a horse, cow, tiger bird and many more species. Therefore, there is a possibility that someone like the Lord Buddha is born amongst those species today. If so, there is a possibility of us consuming bodhisattva flesh.'[77]

This argument has some strong implications because in Theravāda Buddhism, unlike Māhayāna Buddhism, there is only one bodhisattva in existence – the bodhisattva Maitreya. He is prophesied to be the next Buddha and it is Maitreya that will begin the next epoch of Buddhism after the current era of Gautama Buddha finally ends.[78] As we know from the *Jātaka* tales bodhisattvas quite often exist in the animal realm before they are reborn as a human Buddha. They exist in this realm for the purpose of doing good deeds and working towards the goal of buddha-hood.

Effectively Ratnakāra is arguing that there is a possibility that when we eat meat we might actually be eating the dead body of the bodhisattva Maitreya. It is a doctrinal fact, of course, that the killing of an enlightened being is a capital crime and rebirth in hell is an inevitable result of such conduct. Presumably eating a bodhisattva carries with it a similarly harsh penalty. This possibility, Ratnakāra believes, should be enough to dissuade any remotely devout Buddhist from eating meat.

As a side note, such an argument should be much stronger in the Mahāyāna case for the simple fact that there are *many more* (perhaps even *infinite*) numbers of bodhisattvas in the world. Hence the chance of killing and eating a bodhisattva is dramatically increased in Mahāyāna Buddhism and Ratnakāra's argument applied in such cases is even stronger.

In another chapter titled 'Only man acts against nature'[79] Ratnakāra argues that human vegetarianism is the more natural dietary path. He writes, 'Wild animals are divided into two types: meat eaters and vegetarian eaters. From those some animals are extremely small. Some more of them are extremely big. Yet from the formation of bodies of the meat eating animals and vegetarian animals there is enormous variation. Their legs, teeth, tongues, mouths, and their way of drinking are all different.'[80] These points directly contradict the assumption that small animals matter less, a point discussed earlier.

He then spends some time looking at the physiological and behavioural differences between carnivorous and herbivorous animals and then concludes the chapter by saying, 'From this [analysis] observe that human beings' bodies are very similar to animals that take vegetarian food, they are analogous. An animal that takes vegetarian food, however hungry he is, is different to animals that do not eat the flesh of the dead. You have heard the saying, "How many hungry lions refuse to eat grass." It is not in an animal's nature to eat other food. Human [actions] contravene nature.'[81]

Ratnakāra's argument here seems to be that (1) human beings are similar to vegetarian animals and can eat vegetarian food; (2) unlike animals like lions, human beings can choose to only eat vegetarian food. They are not forced to eat one type of food (recall in Chapter 1 that Sinhalese are frequently associated with lions). So Ratnakāra thinks that our tendency to choose to eat meat contravenes our essentially omnivorous nature. Nonetheless, it seems to me that his same argument can be used against his own pro-vegetarian position – it would be unnatural for humans to only eat vegetarian food since human beings are *also* not forced to only eat vegetables – they *can* eat meat. Such arguments that appeal to naturalness are often deeply problematic. Nonetheless, Rathnakāra's arguments offer an important perspective of vegetarianism.

60 *Eating, drinking, killing*

The Vegetarian Society of Sri Lanka

The Vegetarian Society of Sri Lanka (*srī lankā nirmānsāhāra samtiya*) has produced a considerable amount of pro-vegetarian literature. One of the interesting aspects of this society is that it deploys a range of different arguments in favour of vegetarianism and does not limit itself to only Buddhist arguments. Take for example the following flier. This flier naturally applies arguments that appeal to the reader's moral sentiment, but also utilises arguments of a more prudential nature.

> Today throughout the world hundreds and thousands of people abstain from eating animal and have a vegetarian lifestyle.
> Why is that?
>
> - Everyone accepts that animals have a right to live.
> - Animals are bred for food and killed in cruel and heartless ways.
> - Only being a vegetarian can prevent harm to animals and horrible things happening to them.
> - Recent research has shown that there are several substances that cause meat food to be bad for your health.
> - Vegetables, fruits, grains and ancient herbs are healthy and beneficial in every way, and are completely nutritious because of this lets be vegetarian and follow a path of non-violence and lets not take away the cow's right to live.
>
> You should be a vegetarian and enter the path of non-violence.
> They have a right to live [several images of different animals are inserted here: pig, hen, calf, goat, dolphin and another pig]. Let's not take away their lives.
> Sri Lankan Vegetarian Society.
> [Address and telephone number][82]

This document uses conventional moral arguments, namely that eating animals presupposes that they suffer and are killed, but it also depends upon arguments of prudence, i.e. eating animal flesh is unhealthy. In this piece the author obliquely refers to 'substances' (*duvaya*) and as we shall see in Chapter 6, this refers to chemicals that are consumed by slaughter animals. The moral arguments do draw upon Buddhist principles – such as referring to the notion of non-violence – but these ideas are not restricted to Buddhism only. For example in Chapter 1 we saw that these ideas are also present in Hinduism.

Even though this pamphlet is not overtly religious in its pro-vegetarian arguments, other types of literature produced by the Society do have a religious message. Take for example a pamphlet titled, 'Let all beings be happy!' (*siyalu sattvayō suvapat větva*) which is a common Buddhist exclamation especially uttered by monks. The background of the cover of the pamphlet shows an elephant watering the Buddha. The text reads as follows:

'Compassion does not belong to any religion or race. Compassion does not have an owner and it doesn't depend on any relationship. If an individual respects humans, animals and trees alike, we can call him a compassionate person.'[83]

This passage is an excellent example of an inclusivist ethos that goes against the ethnic and religious politics often present in the animal welfare movement. Still, despite the plea that compassion is a universal good, it is still a quality fundamental to the basic ethical framework of Buddhism. As we have already seen in the discussion of Pāli Buddhist literature, compassion is a basic Buddhist virtue and the principle of non-harm is considered an extension of this critical moral sentiment.

But the Vegetarian Society of Sri Lanka does take a pan-religious view of vegetarianism. In the above pamphlet there is mention of the following figures with accompanying quotes that support vegetarianism: Buddha, Jesus, Krishnamurti, Gandhi, Einstein and E.W. Adikāramitumā. There is therefore a mix of religious persuasions here – Buddhist, Christian and Hindu. E.W. Adikāramitumā was a Sinhalese educator of some note. His quote reads, 'I do not eat meat and fish because that can be a reason for an animal's death'.[84] Einstein also appears routinely as an exemplar case of vegetarianism and is mentioned by other pro-vegetarian authors such as Sudasinha. The point of including these figures is simply to add credibility to the vegetarian cause by suggesting that there is authority behind vegetarianism. After all, intelligent and famous people are in its favour. This appeal to authority is considered persuasive by these authors.

But the Society continues to press the point with the following discussion from the same document: 'Why should you be a vegetarian? 1. It results in animal cruelty and death; 2. For the health of the body; 3. For the safety of society and the environment; 4. For economic benefits; 5. For mental well being.'[85] As will be clear in Chapter 5, item (3) mainly depends upon the assumption that the slaughter industry pollutes the environment and therefore subsequently causes deleterious health effects in humans. Therefore, apart from the conventional moral and religious arguments, and also their rhetorical arguments based upon authority, many of the Society's points in favour of vegetarianism are prudential. These prudential health arguments will be investigated more fully in Chapter 5.

An anti-vegetarian author

Sudasinha and Ratnakāra both adopt the view that vegetarianism follows necessarily from the basic moral premises of Buddhism. They regard the first precept (and in the case of Ratnakāra the other four precepts as well) as being the basis for a vegetarian diet. Both authors attempt to find ways to avoid the problem of the Buddha eating meat. In general, their overall position seems to be that vegetarianism is in keeping with the core of Buddhist principles regardless of any other factors.

Not all authors are so forgiving of these considerations however. Gñanananda Thēra is the author of the book *The Problem of Vegetarianism (nirmānsha prashnaya)* and his view is that vegetarianism has no relation to the fundamentals of the Buddhist teaching. He opposes any attempt to read the Buddha, implicitly or otherwise, as a proponent of vegetarianism. Gñanananda Thēra exploits the awkwardness of promoting vegetarianism when the Buddha himself explicitly refused to make it mandatory. Gñanananda Thēra's overall attitude is representative of many of the monks that I interviewed in my research. Individuals that shared the same outlook as Sudasinha and Ratnakāra were absolutely in the minority amongst the clergy. In general, the clergy are much more concerned with avoiding doctrinal inconsistencies than radical laymen such as Sudasinha and Ratnakāra.

Gñanananda Thēra's book is structured as an interview between himself and an interlocutor who seems to favour vegetarianism. The purpose of the book is to dissuade this interlocutor of this erroneous and un-Buddhist view. In many respects, the interlocutor can be exchanged for Sudasinha and Ratnakāra who Gñanananda Thēra would view as adversaries spreading a doctrinally unsound view of Buddhism.

Indeed, Gñanananda Thēra doubts the sincerity and moral character of ethical vegetarians. He knows this because he was himself a vegetarian for a time and consequently was able to see its limitations as a moral pursuit. The interlocutor asks if it is true that he was a vegetarian, and Gñanananda Thēra replies, 'It is true. Not only was I a vegetarian then, but I also spoke about vegetarianism a great deal. I also managed to convince people to be vegetarians. I could not stand the sight of people who consumed meats and flesh. I often sae these people as a part of society that is backward and undeveloped. Because of this, regarding my vegetarianism, I remained arrogant.'[86] The implication in this discourse is that vegetarians are defective because they are overcome by feelings of haughty superiority. Such feelings would be an obstruction to the Buddhist path since Buddhism recommends the cultivation of equanimity and recognition of our intrinsic equality. Arrogance is therefore contrary to those sentiments. In this manner, Gñanananda Thēra's objection is a soteriological issue as much as it is a muted insult to the vegetarian movement.

Unlike pro-vegetarian authors like Sudasinha and Ratnakāra, Gñanananda Thēra does not think the first precept that prohibits the taking of life has anything to do with the first precept. To begin with, he points out that the five precepts are not to be considered on their own, but are to be considered in context to the Buddha's other teachings which include wisdom and meditation. He observes that the Buddha was against animal slaughter, and that he also rejected the consumption of various types of meat.

However, he is quick to point out that the banning of those meats was a response to monks who had engaged in illicit acts that were rooted in unnatural desires. He writes, 'One day a monk (possessed by a demon) went to a place where pigs are slaughtered. He ate raw pig flesh and drank raw blood. Afterwards it is said that the demon was satisfied and left the monk. And the monk recovered afterwards.'[87]

Subsequently, the Buddha banned the consumption of raw flesh. It seems that there is a presumption that the presence of raw flesh leads to the promotion of unnatural vices and is indicative of the presence of evil forces. This resonates with a point mentioned in the last chapter where raw flesh is associated with violence. In other words, the Buddha's response was driven by a concern for the moral credibility of the monks, and a need to ensure that they participate in the Buddhist path correctly, not necessarily out of a concern for the animal.

Another key point for Gñanananda Thēra is that vegetarianism is aligned with the Jain tradition and represents an extreme diet not consistent with the Buddha's middle way path. 'Friend, the philosophy of Lord Buddha consisted not only in benevolence (compassion). It consisted also in great wisdom.'[88] He adds that some people erroneously try and compare the Buddha's compassion to the Jain view when in fact the Buddha's compassion is incomparable. To illustrate the impropriety of the Jains, Gñanananda Thēra writes, 'The Jain Nathaputha was an extreme vegetarian. He was a person who did not brush his teeth because he didn't want to harm anything living in his mouth. Neither did he wash himself for the reason that he did not want to harm anything living on his body. At present, male Jains cleanse the bodies of Jain monks using damp pieces of cloth. Jains usually carry peacock feathers wherever they go'[89] Again, Gñanananda Thēra continues with his original thought that vegetarianism is an extremist diet that leads to the cultivation of vices, namely arrogance. The Jains are engaging in extremist ascetic behaviour inconsistent with the basic premises of Buddhism.

Later in his book he comes back to the first precept. His move here is to separate the relation between eating and killing animals. As one would expect, the issue is to do with intention. He writes, 'Friend, people who eat meat are directly associated with animal slaughter. Namely a person that hunts. Such a person hunts animals. He then comes and eats the meat. That individual is most directly connected to the verse for life. It's because he had the intention and idea to harm and slaughter the animal. After having this intention to harm, the result is that the animal is killed.'[90]

The hunter violates the first precept, not because he ate the animal, but because he killed the animal. Gñanananda Thēra makes a point in defence of meat eating that we will return to again later in the book, namely that merely eating meat is not a sin. It is the killing of the animal that is a sin. Gñanananda Thēra does not accept that there is a causal relation between buying and killing. For him, properly following the *trikoṭi parisuddha* rule mentioned earlier is enough to inoculate the meat eater from any possibility of moral hazard. As long as the animal wasn't killed *for you* then there is no sin.

Ultimately, Gñanananda Thēra does not object to people being vegetarians – though he does regard it as a potentially dangerous activity as it might lead to the development of un-Buddhist feelings of arrogance and pridefulness.

64 *Eating, drinking, killing*

Rather, Buddhists can be vegetarians as long as they do not maintain that it is a doctrinal decision. Gñanananda Thēra puts it like this, 'Friend, I cannot talk about the tastes of all the monks who live in this country or their preaching. Nevertheless there is a thing I should say. Namely, if certain monks have a private opinion about vegetarian food then there is no problem. But if confusion stems from this discussion about the Vinaya and Dharma and such a discussion is contemptuous of a certain compulsory part of the middle path then they should doubt that one-sided view of the Dharma that they have.'[91] He adds, 'If a monk has learned the wisdom of the Vinaya and Dharma correctly, and if they have an appropriately enlightened mind, and if they have the right intention and are completely aware of the contents of the Dharma, and that monk speaks the truth and preaches Buddhism instead of trying to solely promote vegetarianism.'[92] For Gñanananda Thēra, being a good Buddhist has nothing to do with vegetarianism. Indeed, being a vegetarian may well obstruct one in developing the correct Buddhist attitudes. His point here is that one can be an excellent Buddhist monk and still not be a vegetarian.

The problem of the Buddha's eating habits

One of the most persuasive pieces of evidence on Gñanananda Thēra's side is the fact that the Buddha himself appears to be a meat eater. Much of the pro-vegetarian's argument hinges on the Buddha's opinion on meat eating. How do pro-vegetarians try and answer this problem? Sudasinha, for his part, does attempt to address this issue.

He writes, 'Statements that Lord Buddha's final offering (*dānaya*) was composed of pig flesh distort the Buddha's character and is mere balderdash.'[93] He adds that, 'It can be thought that this generalisation of flesh eating as a quality of the Buddha is simply a debased contrivance.' Why is it a contrivance? Because, amongst other things, the Buddha never ate meat as his last meal. Sudasinha is a proponent of the theory that the Buddha's last meal actually consisted of mushroom truffles. There has been a long running controversy concerning the Buddha's last meal because the Pāli term that is used, *sukkara maddava*, is sufficiently ambiguous such that no one is quite sure what the meaning is, but it is routinely translated as 'pig's delight' which is taken to mean that it is some kind of delicate pork dish. On the other hand, proponents of the vegetarian argument suggest that the implication is not that it is pork, but rather that it is a food that pig's delight in, namely truffles that have been dug out of the ground.

For Sudasinha, the arguments in favour of the Buddha's purported meat eating stems from the view that his last meal was meat. Sudasinha believes that his last meal was, in fact, mushrooms. He explains this in the following way: 'There is an idea that blossoming in the ground is a certain type of mushroom named 'pig's mushroom' (truffles).'[94] He goes on, 'Because lots of types of mushroom dishes, after getting soft and delicate, start to look like meat and between these two things there is an abundance of protein so it [the mushroom] provides a meat-like taste.'[95] In other words, it is entirely unsurprising that the Buddha has historically thought to have eaten meat for his last meal. After all, truffles and meat are of a similar texture and appearance when cooked. For Sudasinha the confusion is understandable.

He continues, 'It is not possible to consume every variety of mushrooms that grows in the ground due to the poisonous nature that some of them have. Poisonous mushrooms can cause problems ranging from minor abdominal pain to death. An amateur could not understand that this particular type of mushroom is not suitable as food due to the fact that they look and smell the same as the ones which are edible.'[96] An amateur, such as Chunda – the man who prepared the Buddha's last meal – might accidentally prepare a dish made from mushrooms that are poisonous, a mushroom that might in fact cause illness and death. Because the canon is clear that the Buddha died whilst suffering from some type of gastrological ailment Sudasinha concludes that he was poisoned by mushrooms.

Sudasinha's two pieces of evidence that the Buddha's last meal was mushrooms are as follows: (1) the similarity between cooked mushrooms and meat; and (2) the fact that mushrooms can cause abdominal illness and even death. The Buddha died from some cause or complication of an unknown abdominal illness. Sudasinha's inference is therefore that the Buddha certainly did not eat meat for his last meal. But Sudasinha is not the first person to speculate that the Buddha's last meal was a type of toxic mushroom. In 1982 R. Gordon Wasson and Wendy Doniger O'Flaherty released an article that argued that the Buddha's last meal may well have been a type of psilocybin mushroom.[97] Wasson and O'Flaherty's argument is based on a combination of historical analysis and contemporary anthropology. Needless to say, the idea that the Buddha may have died from overdosing on hallucinogenic mushrooms is not well received by many scholars. Interestingly, Sudasinha also speculates about the various different types of mushrooms that may have led to the Buddha's illness – one of which is, in fact, psilocybin.[98]

Predictably, Gñanananda Thēra will not entertain any such notion that the Buddha's last meal was vegetarian. In answering his interlocutor's question as to whether the Buddha's last meal was meat, Gñanananda Thēra replies in reference to the *Jīvaka Sūtra*: 'One thing is made clear about this problem from the *Jīvaka Sūtra*. Namely, that the Buddha was a person who ate meat.'[99] The *Jīvaka Sūtra* concerns an accusation from a Jain that the Buddha ate meat that was not *trikoṭi parisuddha* (pure in three ways). The Buddha only denies that he ate impure meat, not that he did not eat meat. In fact, in this Sutra, the Buddha makes it clear that meat eating is not banned for Buddhist disciples. From this Gñanananda concludes – not unreasonably – that the Buddha ate meat and that therefore any question about the Buddha's last meal is moot. Whether he ate meat or not for his last meal, the Buddha was not a vegetarian.

Whether the Buddha is a vegetarian or not is important because one way or another it leads to a horned dilemma for the pro-vegetarian. If the Buddha was a meat eater, then according to the pro-vegetarian the Buddha was morally defective. This is, of course, unacceptable. On the other hand, if the Buddha was a vegetarian then this contradicts the canonical texts thus implying the canonical texts are defective. This too is unacceptable. There is no simple answer to this problem for the pro-vegetarian except to argue that the Buddha was privately in favour of vegetarianism but for complicated social and political reasons was unable to enforce it. But although the vegetarian position is awkward, so is the position of the Buddhist meat eater because it implies that the Buddhist doctrine – when taken to its logical conclusions – is itself imperfect because it does not adequately recognise the connection between buying a product and supporting the continued production of that protect. When it comes to meat eating, it seems that this contradicts the first precept to do no violence to animals. Whatever the case may be, the issue of vegetarianism remains a problematic issue.

Conclusion

The preceding discussion begins to reveal some of the dynamics of the animal welfare and vegetarian movement in Sri Lanka. To begin with, we can see that there are a number of different motives for why one might adopt a vegetarian diet from a Buddhist perspective. The first motive is a fear of punishment in the afterlife. We can see from the gruesome stories sent to *Taksālava* that there is a genuine belief that cruel deeds towards animals will result in punishment not only in a future life, but also in the present one. These stories also have an entertainment value, but at the same time they reinforce an expectation that karma is real and that we should consequently be wary of acting improperly.

Pro-vegetarian authors take this concern for animal welfare one step further by arguing that we have a responsibility to treat animals well immediately and not merely chide others for their moral failures. Like the *Taksālava* stories, animal welfare authors like Sudasinha and Ratnakāra rely upon violent descriptions of animal slaughterhouses and processing facilities to appeal to the reader's emotional vulnerabilities. In this case, the purpose is less driven by a desire to entertain and primarily concerned with delivering the facts to the reader in as stark a way as possible. The important move that these authors make is to personalise these accounts and bring the reader's responsibilities into the assessment. Now the reader is not just assessing the moral worth of others – as with the *Taksālava* articles – he is assessing his own moral worth. These pro-vegetarian authors appeal less to the reader's fear of other-worldly punishment but instead draw upon the Buddhist necessity of compassion and loving kindness.

Notice that these two motives – self interest versus other orientated compassion – are already explicitly present in the Pāli Buddhist literature. These stories and pro-vegetarian tracts develop these ideas and apply them to contemporary Sri Lanka. But this dependency on the canonical texts also causes these pro-vegetarian authors to have to deal with the awkwardness of their own arguments in context to the indifferent attitude the canonical texts have to vegetarianism. Authors such as Gñanananda Thēra capitalise on this by pointing out that the canonical literature is not in the least bit sympathetic to any argument that makes vegetarianism mandatory.

This tension between the pro-vegetarian philosophical implications of the Buddha's teaching, versus his explicit denial of the necessity of vegetarianism, will return again and again throughout this book.

Notes

1 SN, 35.88(5), 1168.
2 Atth, 137.
3 Ibid., 41.7, 1325.
4 The Pāli canon is traditionally broken up into three basic components (hence why it is known as the *Tripiṭaka*, or 'three baskets'): the *Sūtra Piṭaka*, or the recorded sayings of the Buddha; the *Vinaya Piṭaka*, or the monastic regulations; and the *Abhidhamma Piṭaka*, or the 'higher teachings' of the Buddha. For our purposes, the *Sūtra Piṭaka* and the *Vinaya Piṭaka* are the most important teachings in understanding the moral rules that govern animals and diet. The *Abhidhamma Piṭaka* is more of a scientific study that deals with the metaphysical structure of reality and has little concern for morality.
5 Take for example the following passage from the *Dīgha Nikāya*, 'abandoning the taking of life, the ascetic Gotama (i.e. the Buddha) dwells refraining from taking life, without stick or sword, scrupulous, compassionate, trembling for the welfare of all living beings' (DN 1.1.8, 68). A number of scholars have pointed out that the first precept extends to animals (Keown, 2005: 41; Phelps, 2004: 49; Harvey, 2000: 156; Chapple, 1993: 22; Bodhipaksa, 2009).
6 Poya days are full moon days and, in Sri Lanka, they are special religious holidays intended to celebrate the enlightenment of the Buddha (purportedly, the Buddha gained enlightenment on a full moon day). On poya days, devotees will attend temple, participate in minor austerities, engage in religious ceremonies such as doing *pirit* (recitation of Pāli texts), and sometimes meditate.
7 For a discussion of the various terms used for 'life' in the Pāli texts, see Waldau's *The Spectre of Speciesism* (2002: 146).
8 Schmithausen, 1997: 13. Elison Findly's study is another example of how plants may have some moral significance in Buddhism (2002).
9 Gombrich actually mentions this tendency in his own work: 'Monks will also slap at insects in a way scandalous to pious Hindus. Not that they would ever deny this to be a sin – they just don't care that much' (1991: 306).
10 MN, 41.8, 380.
11 SN, 1.1.3, 4.
12 For example, AN, 10.3.21, 23; Iti, 3.7, 131; MN, 51.14, 449; DN, 1.1.8, 68.
13 SN 19.2, 702–703.
14 Jat, 21, 58.
15 Ibid.
16 Jat, 12, 39.
17 Jat, 12, 40.
18 Jat, 11, 35.
19 Ibid.
20 Vin-Pat, 3, 132.

21 Ibid.
22 Vin-Pat, 61: 1, 62: 3.
23 Gombrich writes that, 'To be a butcher is considered wrong for a Buddhist, and most butchers in Ceylon are indeed Muslims' (1991: 304).
24 Att., 129.
25 Ibid.
26 Harvey, 161.
27 Ulrich has argued that this permission to eat meat is a peculiar artefact of the conflict between Buddhism and Jainism (239).
28 'Monks, one should not knowingly make use of meat killed on purpose. Whoever should make use of it, there is an offence of wrong-doing. I allow you, monks, fish and meat that are quite pure in three respects: if they are not seen, heard, suspected (to have been killed for the monk)' (MV v1 325; also see CV vii 277). These remarks are repeated again in the *Jīvaka Sūtra* (MN 55.5, 474).
29 MN 55.5, 474.
30 AN 5.44, 41. This is also pointed out by Harvey (160), Waley (347) and Gñananda Thēra (see below).
31 For further discussion of this possibility see my article 'The Question of Vegetarianism and Diet in Early Buddhism' (2010).
32 Jacobi, 416.
33 Kapleau argues that it is impossible that the Buddha would argue against vegetarianism given the first precept. The fact that the texts indicate that he did argue against it only shows, for Kapleau, that the texts have been corrupted. I think this argument is obviously flawed (54). The textual evidence only shows that there are awkward inconsistencies in the canon, as I have already argued.
34 *dĕvālayaka eluvan kæpū minihā.*
35 The article simply states that he belonged to a 'certain religion' (*eya ek āgamakaṭa ayitiya*).
36 *pūjāvaṭa eluvan gēna vita un maha haṇḍa nagā ennē maraṇayaṭa taman gaman karana bava dannā sēya* (Lankadīpa Taksalāva, September, 8, 2013).
37 *varak elu dĕnaka ohugē grahaṇayĕn bērī ivataṭa pænnāya. minihā duvavit amāruvĕn ū allā gattēya. tŏṭa magĕn bērĕnna echchara lēsiyĕn bæ. hiṭapiya tŏṭa hŏṇḍa pāḍamak uganvanna kiyamin hĕtĕma pihiyĕn ægē æs dĕkaṭa ænnēya. pihi talaya vædīma nisā æs dĕkama yaṭaṭa kæpīlē vægirĕnnaṭa viya. prītiyĕn ū dēsa balā piṭi hĕtĕma ū allāgēna gŏs niyamita tænadī bĕlla kæpīya* (ibid.).
38 *æs dĕkama narak vī æti nisā ēvā galavā dæmīmaṭa vēvadyavaru kīha* (ibid.).
39 *ohu æs nætiva vattē ævidina viṭa kaṭuvak kakulaka æṇiṇa* (ibid.).
40 *ūraku maranṭa vuvamanā vū viṭa ohu karannē ū gōniyaka damā bænda gænīmayi. esē gōniyaka dæmū ūrāṭa ohu pŏllakin gasayi. gōniya ætuḷē ūrā marahaṇḍa dĕyi. hŏṇḍaṭama talā ū eliyaṭa gēna tavat paṇa tibē nam pihiyĕn æṇīma siritaya. mē gæna dannā kavurut gamē ohuṭa kiyannē 'ūru maruvā' kiyāya. pansalē hāmuduruvŏt ohu gæna daniti* (ibid.).
41 *raṇḍuva digaṭama giyēya. minissu diga pŏlu gĕnavit ohuṭa pahara danha. avasānayēdī aṇḍupaṇḍu kæḍī ohu bima væṭiṇi* (ibid.).
42 *vindimin siṭa mala mutra mædama kĕdajanaka lēsa miya giyēya* (ibid.).
43 *ballāgē lingaya kæpū minihā.*
44 '*ohŏmma hiṭapiyav tŏpē valatta kamaṭa hŏnda pāḍamak uganvanna*' *kiyamin hĕtĕma hiṇĕn ul pihiyak æda bælliya hā bæduṇu ballāgē lingaya amu amuvē kapā dæmmēya. ballā lē vaguravamin kæ gaha gaha divēvēya. bælliya vēdanāvĕn kĕndirigāmin ætaṭa giyāya* (Lankadīpa Taksalāva, October 27 2013).
45 *īṭa hariyaṭama stiyakaṭa pamaṇa pasu ē minihā kuṇharupa kiyā ræ kālayē gaman gattē anduru pĕdĕsakini. ræ chitrapaṭi balā hulu attak pattu karagēna ena karuṇa pirisakaṭa sarama lassāgēna yana minihā dakinnaṭa læbiṇa. hayiyĕn kuṇu harupa kiyana ohuṭa hŏnda pāḍamak uganvannaṭa. situ taruṇayan kaḷē pattu kaḷa hulu*

attak ohugē lingika pradēshayaṭa ælīmaya. tamangē lingika prdēshaya piḷissīmĕn mahat vēdanāvaṭa pat minihā duvannaṭa viya. taruṇayō maha haṇḍin sinaha vūha (ibid.).
46 *minihā piḷissīma nisā haṭagat tuvālavalin balavat dukvīnda miya giyē* (ibid.).
47 *bæḷaliyaṭa vada dun pūjakayā* (ibid.).
48 *æsē piḷikāva ænga purāma duva æti bava vēdyavaru kīha. Hĕtĕma ārāmayaṭa vit balavat duk maraṇayaṭa patviya* (Lankadīpa Taksalāva, October 20, 2013).
49 *talagŏyi ula tæbū taruṇayā.*
50 *ē tuvālavala vēdanāvĕn dīna gaṇanak kǣ gasmin siṭi ohu antimaṭ miya giyēya* (Lankadīpa Taksalāva, November 3, 2013).
51 *alinṭa kæpū baḷaṭa væṭī mæræṇu ali vǣrǣ miniha* (Lankadīpa Taksalāva, October 13 2013).
52 *ek vatāvaka rātriyē ætun sŏyā yana gamanē ohuma mē bŏruvaḷaka væṭiṇa. eya ætuḷē ulvala ohugē kakul vædī balavat lēsa tuvāla viya. ohu kētaram væsam kaḷat bŏru vaḷĕn eḷiyaṭaēmaṭa nŏhæki viya. dina gaṇanakma tuvāla nisā duk vinda hĕtĕma sāginnĕma maḷēya. gajamutu sĕvīya natara vūyē mē andamaṭaya. ohugē maḷasirura pasuva kæḷē dī hambavuṇē kuṇu ganda gasana viṭaya* (ibid.).
53 In 2012 Sri Lanka was placed 79th on the Global Corruption Perception Index with North Korea last at 174. So according to that index Sri Lanka is quite corrupt. The website for this data can be viewed at www.transparency.org/news/pressrelease/20121205_sri_lanka_placed_79th_in_global_corruption_perception_index.
54 Atth, 361.
55 *mĕlŏma ipida jīvat vana sǣma satvayĕkuma maraṇayaṭa akamætiya*. In *Let's all adopt a vegetarian diet (nirmānsha āhārayakaṭa purudu vĕmu)*, J. D. Sudusinha, Vishrā Vidhyā aḍyāpana niladhārī.
56 *apaṭa mĕn ma sǣma sathvayĕkuṭa ma maraṇayē vēdanāva eka sē pŏduya. kisidu sathvayĕku sva kæmætten maraṇayaṭa pat nŏveti* (1).
57 *hindu āgamē samahara nikāyayan mānsha āhāra pratikśēpa karati. enamut hindu āhgamikayan kiri saha kiri niṣhpādana bahulava āhāraya piṇisa ganiti. ovun gavayā dēvatvayē lā salakana atara, indiyāvē hindu bhaktiyan bahulava vasana pradēshavala gava ghātanaya sapurā tahanam vē. gava mas kannan ovungē samājayen kŏnkara damati. enamut samahara hindu āgamika nikāyayan, vividha bili pūjā sandahā eluvan kukuḷan væni sathun yŏdā ganu læbē* (9).
58 *mĕma āgama adahana aya atara mānsha āhāra pratikśēpa kirīma pilibanda etaram prakaṭav pĕnĕna nīti rīti dakvā nŏmæti* (ibid.).
59 *vartamānayē vuvada budu dahama prabalava pavatina tāyilantaya, ṭibĕṭaya væni raṭavala bhikśūnvahansēlāgē pātri tuḷaṭa piṇḍusigā yēmē dī mānshamaya āhāta læbē. esēma bhǣgōlīya vividhatva, dēshaguṇika vividhatvaya, sanskrutika vividhatvaya væni hētu nisā raṭin raṭa āhārayē vividhatvaya da vĕnas vē* (13).
60 *mānsha āhāra nŏgĕna vĕnath pōṣhyadhāyī āhāra magin jīvithaya pavatvāgĕna yāmaṭa hækiyāva tibē nam bauddha gihiyĕku men ma bhikśūn vahansē kĕnĕkuṭa da uchita vannē evæni mānsha āhāravalin væḷækī siṭimaṭa ya* (13).
61 *kĕnĕku pancha sīlaya trikŏṭikava rakinnē nam ohu anivāryĕnma sathun nikarunē hō mas piṇisa ghātanaya nŏkaḷa yutuya. esē kirīmaṭa anubala nŏdiya yutuya. ghātanayaṭa niyama vū satĕku vĕt nam un nidahas karagata yutuya. satva hinsāvēādinava an ayaṭa kiyā diya yutuya. vĕḷĕdapŏḷaṭa gŏs mānsha āhāra mila dī gænīmĕnda karanusē aniyam ayurakin apa īṭa sahabhāgī vīmaya. mē sandahā apa dāyaka vannē adāḷa ghātanaya sandahā aniyamva mudal yĕdavīmĕni* (14).
62 *mānsha piṇisa sathun ghātanaya karanu labana vēdanā sahagata krama.*
63 Ibid., 47–57.
64 *mĕya nŏkara nirmānsha āhāra vĕlvalaṭa minisun huru purudu vannē nam atu vishāla lōka janagahanayakaṭa baḍaginnē miya yāmaṭa sidu nŏŏvanu æta* (ibid., 92).

70   Eating, drinking, killing

65   *lōkayē vanāntaravalin vārśikava akkara miliyan 10k pamaṇa pramāṇyan mas piṇisa satun æti kirīma sandahā væya vē. mēma iḍam mānava kruśikarmāntaya sandahā āhāra niṣpādanayaṭa yōdā gænīma ya* (ibid., 93).
66   Shrīya Ratnakāra, 7.
67   *mas mānsa kana bauddayā paḷamu shikśhā pada satarak ma ullanganaya karannē ya* (ibid., 5).
68   *mama an satu dēyak sŏrā nŏganimi. esē nam mas mānsa kæmē dī sŏrā gannē thavat kēnakugē jīvitayak nŏvannē da?* (ibid., 5–6).
69   *mama bŏruvak nŏkiyami. oya satā mæruvē mā nŏvēyi. esē pævasīma musāvak nŏvannē da? apa kana nisā nē da satā maruṭa bili vūyē?* (ibid., 6).
70   *mas mānsa sahita āhāra minisāgē manasa vyākula tattvayakaṭa sihi kalpanāvak tibē da? varadaṭa pēḷambīma vælækviya hæki da?* (ibid.).
71   *pansil gēna karaṇīya mētta sūtriya gāyanā kara kussiyaṭa yana æya pihiya ataṭa gēna kuṭṭivalaṭa kapannē shītakaṇayĕn eḷiyaṭa gannā kukuḷā ya* (ibid., 4).
72   *siyalu ma sattvayanṭa mētrīya dakvannē elēsaṭa ya* (ibid.).
73   *mas mānsa anubhavayĕn tŏra jīvitayak gata karana eka pudgalayakuṭa pamaṇak kĕtaram sattva jīvita maraṇayĕn galavā gannaṭa puluvan vē dæyi oba sitā balā ædda?* (ibid., 7).
74   *ehĕth apagĕn abhayadānaya illamin 'anē api maranna epā' yæyi nihaṇḍa va haṇḍa tirisan sattvayāgē haṇḍa apaṭa næsē* (ibid., 8).
75   *thænin thænaṭa gos gavayan. eluvan, urran, kukuḷan thŏrā berā gena, milaṭa gena, lorivala gāl karagena, kuḍuvala hirakaragena nirāhāra va sæthæpum gaṇṇāvak yana gamana keḷavara porakaya bava ovuhu danithi* (ibid., 14).
76   *biya, duka vēraya kindā tibĕna ē sæma mas kællaka ma ættē viśa nŏvannē da?* (ibid., 14).
77   *as, gava, kŏṭi, sā, pakśi yana apamaṇa ātmavala upaṭa læbū bava api asā ættēmu. sathyā eya esē budu bava paṭana kēnaku ada sattvayan atara ipida siṭinnaṭa puluvan. pakśīn atara siṭinnaṭa da puluvana. mas mānsa kana apa bōdhisat mānsa kannan vannaṭa da idha tibē. apa rasa kara kara kannē mēvan bōdhisattva mas vannaṭa da bæri næta* (ibid., 25).
78   The previous chapter provides one Sinhala account of how the end of Buddhism will arrive. As I point out, the circumstances of the end of Buddhism are concerned with a failure to treat animals with non-violence.
79   *dharmatāvaṭa paṭahæniva kriyā karannē minisā pamaṇi*.
80   *tirisan sattva vargayā dĕkŏṭasakaṭa bĕdē mānsa budinnō hā nirmānsa budinnō. mĕyin samahara sattva visheśa itā kuḍā ya. tavat samaharĕk itā vishāla ya. esē vūva da mānsa budina sattvayan hā nirmānsa sattvayangē dĕha vilāsayĕhi vishāla vĕnaskam pihiṭa tibē. ovungē dĕpā, dat, diva, kana, bŏna krama vĕnas ya* (ibid., 27).
81   *mē anuva balana kala minis sirura da bŏhō sĕyin nirmānsa āhāra gannā satunṭa samāna bava pĕnī yayi. nirmānsa āhāra gannā satĕk kŏpamaṇa hāmaṭē siṭiya da vĕnat sataku maragĕna mas nŏkayi. kĕtaram baḍagini vūva da sinhayā taṇa nŏkayi yana kiyamana oba asā æta. sattu ovunŏvungē dharmatāva anuva āhāra anubhavayĕhi yĕdĕti. mē dharmatāva ullanganaya karannē minisā pamaṇi* (ibid., 30).
82   *ada lōva purā lakśa gaṇan janayā sathun anubhava kirīmĕn vælakī nirmānsāhārika divi pĕvĕtaṭa pivisĕti. ē æyi? 1. satunṭat jīvat vimaṭa ayitiyak æti bava ada kavurut piḷiganiti; 2. āhāraya sandahā satun æti karannēt marannēt itā krūra, dayāvirahita lēsaṭa ya; 3. satunṭa erĕhi va karana daruṇu aparādavalin væḷkiya hækkĕ nirmānsāhārika vimĕn pamaṇaki; 4. mānsāhāra saukyaṭa ahitakara nŏyĕk duvayavalin piri æti bava nūtana paryēṣaṇavalin hĕḷi va æta; 5. eḷavalu, palaturu, dhānaya, ādi shākāhāra saukyavalin hæma atin ma hitakara ya, pōṣaṇaguṇayĕn sampūrṇa ya. bavat nirmānsāhārika va aginsā māvataṭa pivisĕnva. mŏvungē jīvatvīmē ayitiya. api udurā nŏganimu* (Vegetarian Society of Sri Lanka, Flier 1).
83   *karuṇāva kisima jātiyakaṭa āgamakaṭa ayiti dēyak nŏvē. eyaṭa himikaruvaku da nŏmæta. eya paudgalika hitamiturukam mata da nŏpihiṭayi. yamĕk manuśaya*

Eating, drinking, killing 71

vargayāṭa měn ma, satā sivipāvāṭa da æḷaṭa dōḷaṭa gahaṭa kŏḷaṭa eka sē mituru bava paḷa karannē nam ohu karuṇāvantayěk vē (Vegetarian Society of Sri Lanka, Pamphlet 1).

84 *mama mas mālu nŏkannē eya satungē maraṇayaṭa hētu vana bævini* (Vegetarian Society of Sri Lanka, Pamphlet 1).

85 *oba nirmānsika viya yuttē æyi? 1. sattva hinsanaya hā eya sathungē maraṇayaṭa hetu vana nisā; 2. shārīrika suvatāva sandahā; 3. sāmājiya hā pārisarika surakśitatāva sandahā; 4. ārṭika pratilābaya sandahā; 5. mānasika suvatāva sandahā* (Vegetarian Society of Sri Lanka, Pamphlet 1).

86 *esē ya. eya sathyayaki. ekala mā nirmānshīva shudda shākāhārīva siṭiyā pamaṇak nŏvē, ē gæna mahat garvayakin yutuva puna punā varṇanā kaḷa kěněkmi. emen ma an ayava da nirmānsha āhāra bhakśaṇaya piṇisa pŏrŏndu karavā gat kěněkmi. eměn ma mas mālu anubhava karana aya duṭuviṭa eya mama nŏ rissū kěněkmi. eya balavat lēsa piḷikulaṭa lak kaḷemi. mas mānsha anubhava karana aya mā duṭuvē mahā nŏ diyuṇu pirisak hæṭiyaṭa ya. enisā ma mama nirmānshī āhāra anubhavaya kirīma piḷibanda mahat sē udam anamin siṭiyěmi* (ibid., 13).

87 *dinak ē bhikśuva (amunuśaya āvēshayěn) ūran maraṇa tænakaṭa giyē ya. gŏs amu ūru mas kævē ya. amu lē da bīvē ya. eviṭa ē amunuśaya dōśaya duru viya. ē bikśuva suvapat viya* (ibid., 30).

88 *pinvath, apa gē shāsthru vū budurajāṇan vahansē samanvita vūyē mahā karuṇāvěn pamaṇak nŏvē. mahā prañāven da samanvita vana sēka. enisā unvahansē gē karuṇāva nihganṭha nātaputta gē 'parama avihinsāva' yæyi kiyā gannā lada prāyōgikava galapā gata nŏ hæki huděk vāda vivāda karagannā druśṭhiyak sē nŏ vūyē ya.*

89 *nātaputra nigaṇṭha těmē parama nirmānshī kěněki. hē bukayē jīvat vana satun haṭa hinsāvak věti yi kiyā dat nŏ mædděya. ænga pata nŏ sěduvē ya. ada pavā nigaṇṭha shrāvakayan gē niruvat sharīraya pirimi bætimatun visin tēta mātu karana lada rědi kæbali valin pirisidu karana ayuru mavisin dæka tibē. nigaṇṭhayō yana yana tæna mŏṇara pil kalambak rugěna yati* (ibid., 31).

90 *pinvata, mas māna anubhava karana udaviya prāṇaghātayaṭa kělin ma havul vana avasṭhā tibē. enam, kěněk aḍayamē yayi. hē satěku daḍayam karayi. hē pæmiṇa ē masa pisa anubhava karayi. ē tænættā srujuva ma prāṇaghātayaṭa sambanda vū kěněki. sæbævin ma ohu prāṇaghātayaṭa huval vūyē mas anubhāva kirīma nisā nŏvē. chētanātmaka va vadhaka adahasin ema satāva ghātanaya kirīma nisā ya. ohu thuḷa vaḍaka chētanāva haṭa satāva maraṇayaṭa pat karanu læbūyē* (ibid., 42).

91 *pinvata, mē raṭehi vædasiṭina siyalu svāmīn vahansēlā gē ruchi aruchikam gæna hō baṇa kīm gæna hō mama vaga nŏ kiyam. ehět eka děyak kiva yutuya. enam, yam svāmīn vahansē namak paudgalika ruchikatvaya mata nirmānsa āhāra vaḷandat nam ehi kisidu gæṭaluvak næta. namut eya ḍarma vinaya vashayěn paṭalavāgěna eya shī laya bavaṭa huvā dakvamin anyayanṭa garahamin eya ma ārya mārgayěhi anivārya vashayěn huvā dakvat nam unvahansēlā gē ḍarmāvabōdaya piḷibandava ekāntayěn ma sæka kala yutu ya* (ibid., 69–70).

92 *yam svāmīn vahansē namak tathāgata dharma vinaya nuvaṇin yuktava hadārā tibē nam, yōnisōmanasikārayěhi yědī tibē nam, chētanāvak kriyātmaka vannē kěsē dæyi dharmaya tuḷin nirākula lēsa avabōda kara gěna tibē nam, e svāmīn vahansēlā pavasannē chaturārya satyayaṭa adāla dharmayak misa nirmānsha āhāra gæna nŏvē* (ibid., 70).

93 *budurajāṇan vahansēṭa avasan dānaya sandahā ūru mas aḍanga vī tibiṇi yæyi prakāsha kirīma budda charitaya vikruti kirīmē tavat pralāpayaki* (Sudasinha, ibid., 27).

94 *eya pŏḷŏvē pipěna ūru hatu namæti hatu vishēśayak bavat ek matayaki* (ibid., 28).

95 *bŏhō hatu varga vayānjana lēsa sækasu viṭa mŏlŏk vū mas měn pěněnana atara ehi aḍangu adhika prōṭīn pramāṇaya nisā mānshamaya rasayak da īṭa læbē* (ibid., 28).

96 *pŏḷŏva mata vardanaya vana sæma bimmal vishēyakma āhāraya piṇisa gata nŏhæki ya. bimmal varga atarin samahara varga viśa sahitaya. Ema viśa varga magin sulu*

parimāṇayaṭa sǣdĕna udara vĕdanāvĕ siṭa maraṇaya atkirīma dakvā vana viviḍa viśa varga rusak evǣni bimmal tuḷa aḍanguya ... esĕma matupiṭn bǣlūbǣlmaṭa kisiyam bimmal vargayak kǣmaṭa sudusuda nǣdda yanna āḍunikayĕkuṭa tĕrum gata nŏhǣki ya. Īṭa hĕtu vannĕ kǣmaṭa gannā bimmalvala hǣḍaya, suvanda, pǣhǣya ǣti ĕ hā samāna viśa bimmal varga da tibīmaya (ibid., 28).
97 Wasson and O'Flaherty, 591–603.
98 Sudasinha, ibid., 30.
99 *jīvaka visin asala lada mĕma prashnayĕn eka dĕyak pǣhǣdiliva pĕnĕ. enam unvahansĕ mas mānsha vaḷandana kĕnĕk bava yi* (Gñanananda, ibid., 53).

3 Food of compassion

Vegetarianism in modern Sinhala Buddhist lay communities

One of the most important Sinhala Buddhist rituals is the *buddhapūjā*. In this ceremony, worshipers place a *pūjāvaṭṭiya* – an 'offering tray' – before an image of the Buddha. The tray has various foods and drinks arranged on it. This activity is performed both at home (*gĕdara*) and at the temple (*pansal*), though the temple is a space where the ceremony has the greatest efficacy since it is a place of greater spiritual significance. The purpose of the exercise is to celebrate the excellence of the Buddha and, in so doing, create merit (*pin*) for the worshipper. Through the accumulation of this merit the devotee hopes that they will be fortunate in their future endeavours. Food, therefore, is a critical part of the economics of Sinhala Buddhist ethics.

The composition of this tray of food is of the utmost importance. At a temple, the *buddhapūjā* is always done in context to a *dāna*, the ceremonial act of feeding temple monks. At the Kaha temple in Colombo, devotees prepare the offering tray by carefully selecting the best pieces of food from the *dāna* preparations.[1] Often elaborate and unusual foods are used in these preparations. Devotees try and second-guess the preferences of the monks. It is not enough to give simple dhal, for example, the lentils must be prepared with aromatic spices and tossed through with vegetables such as spinach. Speciality and time-consuming dishes such as eggplant brinjal or mango curry are prepared. In general, food served to monks must always be of the highest quality. The goal is to impress the monks and satisfy their stomachs. There is also plenty of meat available. Although Sinhalese in their normal affairs tend to restrict themselves to the consumption of fish, and sometimes other seafood, many types of meat are prepared for monks. Chicken, for example, seems to be a favourite. It is essential that monks be lavished with the finest and most expensive foods.

The preparation of these foods for monks indirectly leads to the arranging of the offering tray for the *buddhapūjā* ceremony. The various types of food prepared for the large *dāna* are picked over and only the very best are placed into small brass, ceramic or steel bowls (*pātriya*). There is already a hierarchy of moral significance here. First, the best dishes are prepared for the

74 Food of compassion

assembled monks, and from that the best portions are selected for the offering tray meant for the Buddha image. Once selected, these bowls are put on the offering tray and they are then assembled around a central ritual vessel containing rice. Fruit and sweets are also placed on the tray. Over this, a special cloth is positioned so that the food does not become contaminated. Although flies and other insects may land on the food prepared for the lay people and even the monks, every measure is taken to avoid the same fate for the Buddha's meal.

What foods find their way onto the offering tray is of critical significance. At the Kaha temple, the devotees quite explicitly refrain from including any of the meats in the offering tray. Meat, it would appear, is a suitable – perhaps even necessary – meal for the Buddhist clergy, but for the Buddha it is considered inappropriate. The Buddha will take only vegetarian food. This, in part, relates again to the issue of contamination. The Buddha's food must be pure not only from contaminating forces such as insects and other pests, but also from potentially morally impure substances such as meats, a food that may be regarded as morally suspect.[2]

Not all devotees insist upon this vegetarian principle, yet it would seem that, increasingly, more Sinhala Buddhists are beginning to shun the use of meat in *buddhapūjā* ceremonies. We will see that providing vegetarian food at *buddhapūjā* ceremonies is now mandatory in at least some Buddhist temples. This vegetarian impulse is sometimes taken even further than the Buddhist image house, however. Some laity are beginning to think that meat is not suitable for human consumption either and many devout Buddhists are now turning to a strict vegetarian diet. Such people believe that vegetarianism is a diet that best represents the first, arguably most important, principle of the five Buddhist precepts: the precept of nonviolence. To eat meat is to condone violence towards animals and animal violence is explicitly condemned by the Buddha himself.

From this, many infer that the Buddha would – or perhaps *should* – condemn vegetarianism. If the Buddha should not eat meat, the argument goes, then a good Buddhist should not either. But as we saw in the previous chapter, the Buddha did eat meat and was not a vegetarian. Nonetheless, as we will see repeatedly in this chapter, many Buddhists think a good Buddhist should be a vegetarian regardless of this fact.

The first precept

At the heart of the issue of vegetarianism and Buddhism is the first precept of non-violence. On *pōya* – full-moon days – Buddhists will assemble at temples to participate in religious activities. Elderly lay people and devout practitioners will conduct lengthy meditation sessions in special meditation halls (*bhāvanā shālāva*). But devout or not, all Buddhists solemnly recite the five precepts in the presence of the clergy. As we saw in Chapter 1, the first precept is a fundamental part of Buddhist ethics. In Chapter 2 we also noted that the first precept motivates some Sinhala Buddhist writers to advocate vegetarianism. Vegetarian Buddhists the world over cite the first precept as a pretext for abstaining from meat.

Yet in their book *Buddhism Transformed* (1988), Gombrich and Obeyeskere state that, for Sinhala Buddhists at least, the first precept of non-violence has, 'not generally been so interpreted as to impose' vegetarianism.[3] This claim stems in part from their observation that Buddhists are often indifferent to vegetarianism. Gombrich states elsewhere that, 'vegetarianism I found universally admired, but rarely practiced'.[4] Obeyesekere gives the most vivid description of all in the following comment: 'Sri Lankan Buddhists have become huge consumers of meat; vegetarianism is touted but it is the rare exception to the rule.'[5]

Seyfort-Ruegg supports these claims when he writes, 'Although the idea of ahimsa, "non-harming" is generally proclaimed and respected in Buddhist thought and practice, what might seem to be its logical corollary, namely abstention from eating flesh of animals killed for their meat is far from practiced in most parts of the Buddhist world.'[6] Robert Knox, writing, concluded that vegetarianism was well respected and considered a pious dietary choice, though it was nonetheless not widely adopted.

It is clear that Buddhists accept the first precept of nonviolence, and they are aware that harming or killing animals is a sin of the Buddhist religion. Yet according to these authors Buddhists do not link this principle with vegetarianism, a practice that would ostensibly combat animal violence.

But it would appear that things are slowly changing and the first precept appears to now be considered an important factor amongst some Sinhala Buddhists who choose to be vegetarians. This is not to say that the disconnection between the first precept and vegetarianism does not exist. In Chapter 2 we observed that Gñanananda Thēra explicitly made the point that the first precept did not imply vegetarianism. It should be noted that for many Buddhists who favour meat eating this point is obvious.[7]

Nonetheless, many of the Sinhala Buddhist informants I interviewed for this research were quite supportive of vegetarianism and typically regarded the first precept as an excellent justification for a vegetarian diet. For these Buddhists, vegetarianism typically centres around both the first precept of non-violence and the *buddhapūjā* ceremony. The interconnectedness of diet, conduct and the treatment of the Buddha image is summed by one informant named Chamika.[8]

Chamika is a devout Buddhist and strict vegetarian. At the time of the interview she was in her final year of school. She had two other siblings and her father was a rickshaw driver. When asked about meat and the *buddhapūjā* ceremony Chamika answers, 'I don't give meat because this meat is another life. To take another life so that you can satisfy your stomach is not deserving. Therefore we do not offer it to the *buddhapūjā* and we don't take it for sustenance.' This idea of 'not deserving' relates to what constitutes right and proper conduct when relating to a Buddha image. For Chamika, as in the case of the Kaha temple above, it is not right to give meat to a Buddha image because giving meat involves the slaughter of animals and this is forbidden by the first precept.

Although Chamika alludes to the first precept indirectly, other informants are much more explicit in their discussion of the first precept and vegetarianism. Charuni, another lay vegetarian, argues that eating meat is an offence to the first precept. She says, 'One of our precepts is to refrain from killing animals. The Buddha, having told us this…means that it's not good for us to offer it to the Buddha image. To say that we should refrain from killing animals is to say that we should reconcile with that non-killing every single day. The harming of animals has been completely forbidden.' Again, Nawanga, perhaps the most devout lay Buddhist that was interviewed, states that, 'As Buddhists the first precept of the five precepts is, "do not take life" and this means "don't take life from what has life".' For Nawanga this means that Buddhism demands vegetarianism, 'So in protecting that directive, if everybody stopped eating flesh in that village, or in that province, butcheries and the killing of animals would disappear.'

Buddhist vegetarians support the idea that the first precept for non-violence implies that a good Buddhist should abstain from meat eating. This seems to run counter to the observations made by earlier ethnographers. Of course, it may be quite unsurprising that Buddhist vegetarians see the first precept in this way. Maybe they are the sorts of people that would naturally interpret the Buddha's teaching to promote vegetarianism. What is perhaps more surprising then, and more telling, is the fact that many non-vegetarian Buddhists tend to interpret the first precept to imply vegetarianism too.

Take for example Roshani Nonā, a lawyer who lives in a large house in our research area. She is not a vegetarian. Yet she nonetheless says, 'It's hard to say whether a Buddhist should be a vegetarian, but it's good to be like that. When we take the precepts, if we say the verse for life, then we should live like that. That is the right way. Even I eat salted fish, but I don't eat meat. But it's best not to even eat that.'

Another meat eater, Rohini, who is a lecturer at a polytechnical college, tends to agree. She states that you should not give meat at a *buddhapūjā* ceremony because, 'It is bad to harm animals. There are the five precepts after all. There is a bad character in harming animals.' Again, although she herself was not a vegetarian, Charuni's elder sister Sanduni Akka believes that the first precept implies some degree of vegetarianism, 'I think that Buddhists say that the Buddha preached the view of non-violence. Therefore it's not good to condone the eating of meat and fish.' Yamitha, an Abhidhamma teacher at a local Sunday school similarly insists that the first precept is important in judging what food should be consumed. He says, 'I have an idea to stop eating meat and fish. I have this idea because we're eating the animal's flesh, right? We bring back meat after we kill an animal. At this point we get entwined in the verse for life. The first precept is not to take the life of another creature. We try to refrain from breaking the precept but in a roundabout way we get caught in it by eating meat.'

A number of informants, vegetarian and non-vegetarian, therefore reject meat eating in large part because it is viewed as an *indirect* violation of the first precept. The fact that some of these informants nonetheless persisted in eating meat in spite of the fact that they believed to be improper is puzzling. Sanduni Akka addresses this issue in one of her answers: 'From a young age we are used to eating meat and fish and therefore we like it. Otherwise meat and fish is something you receive when you have destroyed the life of another being. Other people kill it because we eat it. Therefore, we are used to it, right? Because we're used to it, we crave it.'

Sanduni Akka uses the word *tanhā* (craving) here and this word has important Buddhist implications. *Tanhā* is a strong desire that binds beings to the cycle of rebirth. As such, it is considered the root of suffering and human misery. But desires of this sort can also lead to temporary satisfaction and hence they are difficult to give up. An archetypal example of this type of craving might be the craving of sensual pleasures. The satisfaction of these cravings only leads to further cravings. When the cravings cannot be easily met, however, there is great suffering. To avoid suffering altogether, the cravings themselves must be eliminated. This is one of the central psychological tenets of Buddhism. Meat eating, for Sanduni Akka is another example of *tanhā:* it is hard to give up because it is associated with temporary pleasures, but in the long run immoral and likely to lead to future suffering.

In light of this idea, Buddhists like Sanduni Akka may be aware of the problems associated with meat eating, but due to a weak will they find it hard to give it up. In Sri Lanka, this difficulty is emphasised by the fact that the consumption of fish is especially prevalent.

Sri Lanka is an island nation and therefore a fishing nation, so fish eating is pervasive, especially along the coast. Giving up meat is one thing, but giving up fish is another matter. Informants who spoke of vegetarian relatives especially praised those who had given up the eating of fish and *umbalakaḍa* (Maldive fish flakes). But for all them, the first precept is indirectly violated through the consumption of meat because eating meat fuels and supports the killing of animals. As we shall see, this mental connection between meat eating and the first precept is remarkably absent amongst the monks interviewed.

Supporters of vegetarianism

As already indicated, in this study many informants regarded vegetarianism as an ideal Buddhist diet, even if they themselves did not follow it. This intriguing situation reveals the extent to which Buddhist identity has been tied to diet. To be a good Buddhist is not just about attending temple on specified days, nor is it just a matter of reciting *pirit* or mechanistically giving alms to monks, it is a matter of monitoring one's behaviour and ensuring that the ethical standards of Buddhism are evenly applied in all dimensions of one's life. Living an ethical life also involves the devotee eating and drinking the right things too.

In Buddhism, moral conduct is described in terms of purity. The Pāli word for 'pure' is *sudda* and it is this same word that is applied in the case of the Sinhalese language. In this way, the religious sentiment of the source materials finds its way into the everyday language of the Sinhala people. Aiming for a pure and unblemished life is the goal of Buddhism and the more areas of ones life that are pure in thought and deed, the better.

Vegetarianism is one way to accomplish purity in terms of one's diet. Some Buddhists believe that vegetarianism is a sign of moral virtue. In Sri Lanka, people especially celebrate Buddhism on *pōya*. A *pōya* day is a day when the moon is full – the Buddha is said to have gained enlightenment on such a day. On *pōya* Buddhists attend the temple, pay homage to Buddha imagery, and participate in other temple activities. Many Buddhists also adopt a vegetarian diet on such a day. Buddhist food shops (known as hotels) will sometimes only serve vegetarian food on such days. At one notable shop that I frequented in Kalubowila there was a sign hanging that states clearly: 'Every pōya day only vegetarian food is served'.[9] The shop proprietors are so committed to their Buddhist values that they actively restrict what customers can buy on particular days. This is likely construed as an act of piety on the part of the owners: a financial sacrifice made for good merit.

One informant who takes vegetarianism very seriously is Nawanga. He is a middle-aged man, married, with three children. At the time of the research only one of his children still lives at home. Nawanga is an accountant but works itinerantly throughout Sri Lanka. Nawanga is an important case because he illustrates a general point about vegetarianism: the more pious a devotee is, the more it seems that they are likely to endorse a vegetarian diet.

Every night he recites *pirit* – the reading of Pāli passages – over an image of his family. Through reciting these sacred texts he hopes that his family will be blessed with fortune and good karma. He has also expressed a desire to join the *sangha* once all his children leave home. Nawanga can often be found at the temple hall meditating. Increasingly, he has taken to wearing white: the clothing that indicates that one is an *upāsaka*, a person completely dedicated to the Buddhist religion. Nawanga is a paradigm case of a good Buddhist.

He is also a vegetarian. As mentioned, Nawanga's vegetarian views are rooted in the first precept. But it is not simply a matter of seeking to avoid violating the first precept, there is also a positive dimension to his vegetarian diet. Nawanga believes that abstaining from meat is a compassionate action that helps protect animals from suffering.

He is critical of those who arbitrary care for some animals but not others. As will be clear in Chapter 5, the cow, for example, is treated with special respect and care. Nonetheless, 'is it only the cow that has a life? If you look at small animals, every animal has a life. Every animal like its life. The desire is the same: like a caterpillar, like an ant. If you try to touch them they get scared because they're frightened of death.' Animals and humans are similar insofar that they want to continue their life. To prematurely end that life does harm to that animal. Nawanga believes that Buddhism demands that we treat all animals in a kind and compassionate manner: 'In the sūtras of the Buddhist religion it teaches that all animals, not just four legged ones, love their life.'

He concludes the interview poetically by again restating the similarity between humans and animals: 'Even if I am lying on my death bed, even if I know I am about to die, when I have completed my age, and I know that my time for death is right, it's possible that I want to live even for another second longer, every animal is like that.' This argument based upon sympathetic understanding is a staple of the animal welfare movement and we have already encountered it in the previous chapter with the pro-vegetarian authors.

This deep compassion towards animals is what leads Nawanga to adopt a vegetarian diet. He does not want to support activities that involve the unnecessary killing of animals. Nawanga's idea that we should not privilege a human life over an animal life is echoed in the activist Sinhala blog *Tahanam Vachana (Censored Words)*. On a web article dedicated to the animal activist monk Bowatte Indaratane Himi – a contemporary monk who will be again discussed in Chapter 7 – a *Tahanam Vachana* correspondent writes that, 'There is no division between "yours" and "theirs".'[10] Quoting the *Saṭṭipatana Sutra*, the author concludes that, 'Thus my life and their life should not be regarded as two among different things.' This attitude sums up an important dimension of Sinhala Buddhist vegetarianism: the idea that human beings are not exceptional and that they are connected to animal lives in inextricable ways.

This notion depends upon the concept of rebirth and the Buddhist idea of *paticcasamuppāda* or dependent origination. Rebirth is the principle that when we die we will inevitably be born in a new form dependent on our karma. Dependent origination is the mechanism that underlies this transformation. According to this doctrine, all causes must have an effect and all effects must produce a further cause. Human existence depends upon antecedent causes and our future lives depend upon the actions we perform now. This mechanism has already been intimated in the previous chapter in the form of the Pāli canon and then with the Buddhist revenge literature. In both instances the injury and killing of animals led directly to a poor rebirth.

Because of this metaphysical doctrine, direct compassion towards animals may therefore lead to inadvertent kindness towards human beings. Conversely, Ratnakāra argued that killing animals may result in us accidently killing a bodhisattva. But harming animals can also mean we indirectly harm former human beings we knew previously too.

Jayawardane Nonā, a mother in her 40s, describes the matter in these terms: 'Sometimes the thing that we eat is the flesh of an animal, but if we go back to our past life when we travel between one life and the next the person that was an animal is one of our people, that we turn into meat that we eat. It is possible to think this.' Jayawardane Nonā observes that, according to Buddhist doctrine, we should be aware that the food that we consume could very well be a past relative who has been reborn in a different form.

80 Food of compassion

This unpalatable idea is, she thinks, enough to make one think twice about consuming meat.

Sanduni Akka also considers the morality of animal welfare and its relationship to rebirth. She recalls a story of a man who was a lorry driver. One day he was driving his lorry and, due to inattention and carelessness, ran over a large python that was sunning itself on the road. Later, the man had a son. When his son was born, he was horrified to learn that the child had a devastating birthmark running across his abdomen. It was, Sanduni Akka tells us, in the shape of a tire mark.

This story, of course, is somewhat at odds with a strict understanding of karma as the harm should have been inflicted on the father, not the innocent son. After all, it was the father who did the wrong, not his child. The point Sanduni Akka makes is nonetheless instructive: if you do a harm to an animal, then that harm may very well be visited upon you.

These stories, whether they are told by lay people like Sanduni Akka or in classic works of literature that we have already examined, or in the form of letters to *Lankadīpa*, indicate the way Sinhala Buddhists take seriously the importance of animal welfare. Showing compassion towards animals is important not only because it is mandated by the first precept, and not only because it is a virtue to be compassionate, but it is important because it is a simple matter of prudence. Killing animals, and supporting the killing of animals, can lead to harm falling upon the aggressor. For some, vegetarianism is a way to combat this animal cruelty and the troubles associated with it.

Detractors of vegetarianism

So far, this discussion of vegetarianism might lead one to conclude that there is unanimity amongst the informants as to the virtues of vegetarianism. In fact, some of the informants were less enthusiastic about its importance. Renuka, a 90-year-old matriarch of a large family, believes that harming animals is not justified by the Buddhist religion. But like previous ethnographers have emphasised, she does not connect this to the practice of vegetarianism.

She says, 'Buddha has said that harming animals is not good. You don't need a single thing if your heart is pure. It's okay to even eat water and rice. Your heart is what needs to be good.' Renuka thinks that intentions are more important than actions. A good-hearted meat eater is better than a maliciously minded vegetarian. Suspicion over the motives governing vegetarians is a concern raised also by Gñanananda Thēra in Chapter 2. For Renuka, examining what one eats is an unreliable method of assessing moral worth. She adds that this is supported by the fact that meat eaters typically do not kill the meat they eat: 'I don't encourage vegetarianism. We don't go and kill animals. We bought a thing that was for sale. Is that sinful?' On the other hand, purposefully seeking out the death of an animal really is a sin. She says,

'If we said, "Somehow bring two fish from the sea," we would have done wrong because it was killed for us.' Intention, for Renuka, is critical. Simply buying meat from a shop is not evil because the buyer was not directly responsible for the animal's death. This point is especially important for monks, as we shall soon see.

Another informant echoes Renuka's sentiment. Kanthi Aunty, an informant from the Kegalle participants, argues that vegetarianism is unnecessary from a Buddhist perspective. 'There is no rule that says to only eat vegetables. It's okay to eat whatever you want, even if you are a Buddhist.' Her explanation is that eating meat does not imply any responsibility for the killing of the animal. 'We do not say to kill it. People do lots of different jobs to stay alive. Some people breed animals and kill animals. We don't say to kill. If you go to the market you can give money and get it. There is no rule to say to only eat vegetables.' This view can be contrasted with informants, such as Nawanga, who believe that market forces combine to encourage the slaughter of animals. Individuals are responsible for an animal's death insofar that they support the industry that is responsible for their killing. Renuka and Kanthi Aunty reject any such connection.

Kanthi Aunty and Renuka both believe that vegetarianism is unnecessary because, so long as they themselves are not killing the animal, there is no blame associated with buying and consuming meat. Some other person has committed a sinful act, not them. Such arguments are rooted in the *trikoṭi parisuddha* ruling made by the Buddha in the Pāli canon. These views have evidently influenced even lay Buddhists.

Ānanda, a rickshaw driver, is similarly indifferent towards the importance of vegetarianism though his objections to vegetarianism are entirely prudential rather than moral. For Ānanda, vegetarianism is simply bad for your health: 'The blood in your body doesn't work properly when you only eat vegetables.' Nonetheless, he is somewhat uncertain as to the reliability of this fact. He says, 'The doctors tell you to eat meat too, right?'

The point is actually instructive. Some informants were quite unclear about the simple facts around vegetarianism, medicine or even basic biology. A surprising number of informants did not understand chicken reproduction and had no grasp of the concept of fertilisation. This will be discussed later.

We can see from these cases that there are many ways that people approach the issue of vegetarianism. Some people support vegetarianism while others reject it. What is clear, however, is that a number of informants supported vegetarianism and only a few were actively critical of it. This is not a trivial matter given how common meat consumption is in Sri Lanka, especially the consumption of fish. It is clear that some Buddhists have misgivings about meat eating, and most link these misgivings to their Buddhist convictions.

However, this affection towards vegetarianism is illustrated by other Buddhist activities. For many, vegetarianism is demonstrated not only through one's own diet, but also the way other people eat, hence the importance of the *dāna* ceremony.

The alms giving ceremony

The sharing of food is a critical part of Sinhalese culture. Preparing food for others is a way to create and cement social bonds. The feeding of others is a way of nurturing others and sustaining their life. In this way, food offering is, in many ways, the most important act of charity one can participate in. Food offering is therefore a fundamental part of day-to-day Sri Lankan social customs. Food preparation and offering is generally matriarchal and so female kin come to be especially associated with acts of generosity that lead to the nurturing and sustaining of life.

As we shall see in Chapter 5, rice is just one of two foods that are considered critical in Sinhala culture. The other important food is milk, and this too is given during moments of ceremonial significance.

This act of giving life through food is exemplified through a traditional ritual whereby family members are fed food by hand. The first meal of a child is often *kiri bat* (milk rice), a porridge made of rice and coconut milk, which is typically fed by hand from the mother to the child. As we shall see in Chapters 5 and 6, the role of milk is critical in such actions since milk is viewed as a unique source of nutrition. Similarly, on special days such as birthdays, weddings or on *pōya*, family members will feed each other *kiri bat*. This action of sharing *kiri bat* is a symbolic act to encourage the flourishing of the family. Indeed, rice itself is regarded as a food of special, almost sacred, significance because it is a staple of the Sri Lankan diet and symbolises prosperity. More specific comments about food consumption will be discussed in Chapter 6.

The act of giving food can take on a more explicit religious significance however, and this religious impulse is exemplified through the act of alms giving. Generally, alms giving is restricted to the clergy. Sometimes, usually on important religious days such as *pōya*, Buddhist devotees will hand out food parcels to the poor. Even giving food to stray animals is considered an act of kindness and expressive of moral purity. Nonetheless, giving alms to the clergy is considered the most auspicious and meritorious act of generosity.

The clergy represent a special space of merit cultivation, sometimes called a 'field of merit', because they are official representatives of the Buddhist religion. To feed and nurture the clergy is, therefore, to feed and nurture Buddhism as a whole. Such actions trump lesser forms of giving, such as giving to the poor or stray animals, because the personal benefit associated with giving to the clergy is so much greater.

This is the case even though the clergy are less in need of alms. Many temples are well resourced and complicated rosters for alms giving ceremonies need to be created because there are more families wishing to give than there are meal times. This can sometimes lead to conflict when families begin to compete with each other to see who is responsible for giving alms at the more prestigious temple.

For temples, alms giving involves the offering of various items, not just food. Soup, razors, toothbrushes, begging bowls, new robes and incense are all considered suitable items to give to a monk. Traditionally, there are eight items considered appropriate for giving and this is known as an *aṭa pirikara* (eight requisites). As a general rule, the list of what is considered appropriate to give is quite short, as it would be considered unmonkly for clergy to accept lavish or expensive items. Clergy are supposed to be individuals who have renounced the world and therefore it is expected that they will only take what is necessary for them to live in a minimally comfortable and hygienic manner. This minimalistic living is intended to be harmonious with the Buddhist notion of desirelessness. According to the Buddhist religion, the root of all suffering is desire and the goal of monastic living is to gain control of desire. Consequently, monks live austerely and with few modern comforts.

This does not stop the laity from hosting opulent banquets for monks, however. Of all the alms one can give the clergy, food offering is the most important. The giving of food alms is known as a *dāna* ceremony. *Dāna* simply means 'giving' in Pāli. It is a fundamental act of generosity that leads to merit production. Because food giving is such an important way of cementing social bonds, giving food to monks is especially important because monks are very much at the heart of lay religious life.

Many lay people will have a favourite monk who they regard as especially pious, well versed in the religious canon, or who has special powers that illustrate his monkish credentials. A good example of this is Magalkande Sudātta Himi Thēra, a monk of some note who even has an online social media presence.[11] He is best known for his ability to encourage cows to bend before him in worship. This ability has brought great favour upon him. These favoured monks will often be singled out for special attention during the alms giving. The laity will prepare the best food for monks with an eye for what they believe will be a favourite dish amongst the clergy. It is thought that the more a monk enjoys the meal, the more merit will be produced.

The idea of giving monks a lavish meal to satisfy their stomachs is not considered appropriate by everyone, however. Some informants believe that monks should be offered only vegetarian food because vegetarian meals are more morally appropriate. Chamika, for example, says that, 'In our house we give meat, but I say it's not right to give it. That is to say, the monks eat it because we give it. When we give a *dāna* we ought to know not to give it. That's what I say.'

Chamika would like to give vegetarian food at *dāna* but her family insists that meat should be supplied. Nawanga throws light on why this is, 'The way things are a lot of the time, the way society is, that is the way that we should work. A lot of the time if I go about my own decision society looks at me differently. That is to say, they might think that I am stingy – "Maybe that's why he doesn't give meat" they would say, "he doesn't give flesh because he's stingy".' Of course, not all lay people are determined to produce lavish banquets for monks and another school of thought is that monks should only be given plain food that is perceived of as healthy. For example, it was reported to me that some lay people believe monks should only be given simple foods such as red rice and banana flour (*kehel mal*) – foods that are thought to be healthy.

But although there is a school of thought that monks should be given plain food predominately people try and give them the very best food available. This is confirmed by Obeyesekere. He writes that, 'In a famous temple in Kandy one of the monks in charge of coordinating almsgiving for monks, insists that the lay devotee supply chicken. The laity in turn can no longer supply vegetarian food to monks (fish maybe if meat is considered not kosher by lay-folk).' Although it seems to me that this desire to pleasing the clergy's palate is the norm, the situation Obeyesekere describes is probably not widespread and my experience has been that monks do not explicitly dictate what foods should be supplied – except in very exceptional situations such as at the Māligāva.

Despite the fact that Nawanga and Chamika wish for their *dāna* ceremonies to be vegetarian enormous social pressure prevents them from being able to realise this goal. Part of the goal of a *dāna* is to impress the monks, but there is also an element of impressing others who gather at the *dāna* ceremony. Saving face in front of friends and family is often a more pressing matter than the cultivation and encouragement of religious piety.

Giving alms is largely governed, therefore, by social expectations. It matters little what the individual thinks about what is 'right' or 'proper'. Instead, the social convention is the chief determining factor. Social conventions dictate that meat should be provided because meat is expensive and therefore an impressive item to serve for a meal. One of the young monks at the Kegalle *piriveṇa* explains, for example, that the majority of *dāna* ceremonies performed at his temple are vegetarian. That is only because, however the givers (*dāyaka*) are largely impoverished and could not afford meat. If they could, he explained, they almost certainly would give it.

Impressing monks and lay people is important, but the monk's individual palate is also relevant. Since monks are not allowed to express a desire for food, lay people will generally try and second-guess what a monk might like to eat. They watch closely during a *dāna* to see what a monk will take and what he will leave behind. Some dishes are less popular than others and it is unlikely that those dishes will be prepared again in the future. The goal is to create a perfect feast for the clergy. What they ought to eat, therefore, is somewhat irrelevant in these considerations.

This is made clear by comments from informants such as Charuni. Charuni, of course, is herself a vegetarian, yet she gives meat and fish to monks at *dāna*. She says, 'If there is a person who eats meat then we have to offer it. We give it for our merit. If someone gives me something I say "Thank you" and take it but if I don't want it I give it to someone else.' This way of dealing with a *dāna* through prudence, rather than through ideology, is echoed by others such as Ānanda the three-wheel driver. He says, 'We give meat to the monks. I give chicken and fish, but not beef. Monks don't eat beef, right?'

Again, what governs the composition of the menu is the desires of the monks, not the desires of the laity. Even Nawanga, the arch-vegetarian, will give meat to the monks. 'If we're going to a big *dāna* we generally find out if giving meat is a problem. That is to say, it's okay for us to offer what the monks are going to eat otherwise it's a waste.' For some, the most important thing about giving alms is intention, not what is actually given. This is clear from Charuni comments. She says, 'There is also this thing: imagine that I am a hunter. If the Buddha came and all I had was meat because I am a hunter, I would devoutly offer it.'

The word Charuni uses here for 'devout' is *saddāva*, which can also mean 'faithfully'. Because the thought is pure what is actually given is not very important. This relates back to Renuka's claim that you can consume only water and bread, and so long as you have a pure thought (*hŏnda adahasa*) then the action is morally sanctionable.

Many of these comments run up against prevailing views by other ethnographers and Buddhist Studies scholars. Peter Harvey says that, 'If [monks] are given flesh food, and it was pure as described above, to refuse it would deprive the donor of the karmic fruitfulness engendered by giving alms food. It would encourage the monks to pick and choose what food they would eat.'[12] The same idea is echoed by Ruegg, '[Monks are] morally bound to accept any alms offered in good faith by a pious donor.'[13] According to this view, monks must accept whatever they are given. This is a common reading of the directions of the Pāli canon, though this interpretation can be disputed. Such an interpretation originates from direct instructions from the Buddha himself, but also from indirect instructions, as we saw in Chapter 2, that monks should not eat excessively. Clearly this lay enthusiasm to meet the clergy's wildest culinary desires is completely contrary to this ethos of moderation.

Despite this, we can see from informants like Charuni and Ānanda, monks display preferences for food all the time. This is underscored by the fact that laity recognise and attempt to satisfy the unique desires of monks. It was perceived by some informants, for example, that monks do not like green beans due to their commonness, nor did they like overly oily food. In fact, at numerous *dāna* ceremonies I attended there were routine complaints between the laity that monks would not eat certain dishes. In addition to this, some monks are vegetarians – as we shall see in the next chapter – and for them maintaining a vegetarian diet was trivial; they would simply refuse any meat offered to them. A monk's aspiration to conquer desire can therefore be made more difficult by the laity's desire to impress their peers.

There are efforts to control these temptations, however, and this is clear from other ethnographic studies based in Sri Lanka. Take, for example, Michael Carrithers report of a particularly idiosyncratic monk: 'At the end of the sermon [the laity] offered him kerosene and honey, which he accepted; and a large bowl of fruit which he rejected. He told them, "It is not proper to offer monks fruit after twelve noon. They may accept things which keep, such as kerosene and honey, but they may not accept food".'[14]

This shows two things: (1) that there are efforts to institute limits on what is given to monks thus protecting the ideal of moderation; and (2) contrary to claims made by other scholars, that refusing food items is sometimes necessary to maintain this ideal. If we think of a case where a monk is offered alcohol they would have no choice but to refuse it. The idea that monks may never refuse food is therefore not a practical rule and is, moreover, not in keeping with the ethos of the Buddha's intentions.

The having of preferences, and the refusal of certain types of food, is therefore not considered an obstacle to being a good monk. Lay people are similarly largely indifferent to what food is given to monks. Some would prefer it if monks were vegetarian and they praise those who are. Yet from a lay perspective, doing *dāna* is more about meeting social expectations than it is about improving or cultivating monastic decorum. The case of alms giving, however, can be contrasted with the *buddhapūjā* ceremony which is, for peculiar reasons, largely an exclusively vegetarian affair.

Feeding the Buddha

As is clear from our analysis in Chapter 2, a sober reading of the Pāli texts indicates that the Buddha was not a vegetarian. To recap: the Pāli canon uncontroversially reports that the Buddha consumed meat on at least one occasion.[15] Furthermore, the Buddha stipulates in both the *Vinaya* and the *Jīvaka Sūtra* that monks may eat flesh provided that they did not hear, see or suspect that the animal was killed for them. This is the basis of the *trikoṭi parisuddha* ruling. There are also other restrictions, for example monks may not eat certain types of meat such as elephant flesh, lion flesh, hyena flesh, and so on. But within these constraints monks, and therefore the Buddha himself, are free to eat meat.

As already established in Chapter 2, there is great controversy over the composition of the Buddha's last meal. The possibility that the Buddha's last meal was vegetarian has encouraged some to conclude, contrary to the facts, that the Buddha was a vegetarian more generally. Despite the fact this inference is faulty, it has nonetheless had some influence over the attitudes and beliefs some Sri Lankans have had about the Buddha's diet. More importantly, this has influenced the views they have about whether a Buddha image can be offered meat, or whether it is more appropriate to only offer vegetarian food.

The issue, therefore, concerns the composition of the *pūjāvattiya*, the offering tray upon which the food items are arranged. The tray, once prepared with suitable food items, is then ritually placed in front of a Buddha image. This Buddha image is usually a *buddha piḷimaya* (Buddha statue) located at a shrine at home, though sometimes the *buddha piḷimaya* will be replaced with a framed picture of the Buddha. This offering ceremony is known as a *buddhapūjā* and, as in the case of the *dāna* ceremony described above, the main purpose of this ritual is to produce merit in order to cultivate a more fortuitous future.

In principle, the spiritual goal of the gathering of this merit is to ensure a better rebirth that will allow future conditions whereby the devotee can be reborn in a future era under a new Buddha. It is only at this time that nirvana can be achieved. In reality, most lay people believe that the *buddhapūjā* and *dāna* ceremonies provide the conditions for a better and more prosperous future in *this* life. An associate of one informant repeatedly did *buddhapūja* and other religious activities such as the doing of *bāra* (a vow),[16] in order to help cure terminally ill relatives. For some, especially the clergy, this latter view is regarded as a corruption of the true essence of Buddhism.

As with the *dāna* ceremony, the laity wish to provide the Buddha image with the best foods. Again, because the *buddhapūjā* is a ritual in which food is offered there is an important social dimension here. The ritual symbolises the nurturing of the Buddha's body directly which indirectly nurtures the mind and therefore strengthens the Dharma, the intellectual core of Buddhism.

It may even be argued that the feeding of the Buddha image is more spiritually important than the feeding of monks during a *dāna* because it is the Buddha that is being fed here. This is especially evident in cases such as the Srī Daḷadā Māḷigāva where the image of the Buddha has become deified through historical contact with Hinduism. In other instances, however, it is recognised that the Buddha is not actually present. Instead, it is the mere intention to feed the Buddha that is most important.

The Buddha, therefore, can only have the best food. But what 'best' means in such instances varies from case to case. Again, as with the *dāna* ceremony, expectation is a key variable in this analysis. Devotees want to provide the Buddha with what they believe he should eat which can mean both what he *did* eat, but also what is *fitting* for the Buddha to eat. These two accounts of what is 'best' intersect in complicated ways and also relates to the question of what his last meal was.

Some of the laity were completely unaware of the facts around the Buddha's diet. Srilal, a young family man and entrepreneur, states that, 'There is this thing where he unknowingly ate a piece of meat and he rejected it. Therefore we don't offer it.' Srilal, however, reports that he happily fed monks meat because monks were fond of it. It is clear in these cases that the composition of religious food offerings is dictated very much by what the assumed preferences of the recipient is. Srilal thinks the Buddha doesn't like meat so he doesn't give it; monks, however, typically do like meat, so they are provided with a veritable feast of meats. Srilal has no time for the intrinsic merits of giving or not giving meat.

Like Srilal, Jayawardene Nonā believes that the Buddha was a strict vegetarian. 'There is nothing written to say that the Buddha ate meat. It isn't stated anywhere that meat was eaten by him, rather mushrooms were brought to him. There's a place in the Buddha's teaching that says that mushrooms were received by him that looked like meat.'

In this explanation, the Buddha was a vegetarian who never touched meat, but the controversy arose because the mushrooms that he ate in his final meal supposedly looked like flesh. Yasitha comes closest to the more accurate account of what the source materials claim. This is, perhaps, unsurprising as he is an Abhidharma teacher and therefore is conversant with the Pāli canon.

He says, 'There's something like this: there's no accurate recording of the Buddha eating meat that I've seen. One thing is a thing called the *sūkara maddava*. It has been said that the Buddha had a stomach upset after it was consumed. That's the only instance where we think he could have consumed meat and fish.' Of course, as discussed in the previous chapter there are instances elsewhere in the Pāli literature where the Buddha ate meat.

Perhaps the idea that the Buddha was a vegetarian goes some way to explaining the belief that it was inappropriate to offer meat at the *buddhapūjā*. For example, Buddhika, a young carpenter who lived in Kegalle, states that he did not give meat and fish at a *buddhapūjā* because, 'the Buddha did not eat meat and fish, therefore we don't give it.' Similarly, Srilal also made the same claim. He said, 'The Buddha doesn't eat meat or fish and because it is not eaten by him we don't offer it [to the Buddha image].'

The composition of the offering tray was not entirely determined by the perceived diet of the Buddha, however. Overwhelmingly, informants refused to give meat at a *buddhapūjā* and this was so for a variety of reasons. Usually it was because they believed the giving of meat to be an indirect violation of the first precept as discussed above. Six of the lay informants stated that they did not give meat and fish at a *buddhapūjā* because it violated the first precept. But there were other reasons too. Nawanga and Priyanka stated that, because they themselves were vegetarians, they did not offer meat to the Buddha image. Nawanga: 'As the head of the household, because I don't eat meat or fish, I think it is good to give the things I eat and drink to the *buddhapūjā*.'

Ānanda had an unusual but interesting reason for why he would not give flesh at a *buddhapūjā*. 'You don't offer it to the Buddha. There are germs (*pili*). You don't offer it because of germs.' As mentioned earlier, the *pūjāvattiya* is to be covered with a special cloth to prevent it from becoming contaminated. Flesh is at special risk of contamination because, according to Sinhala lore, meat attracts *pili* or germs. For example, after you attend a funeral it is customary to wash yourself so at to eliminate germs. A thorough wash is also customary before one attends a temple. This prevents any *pili* one is carrying from contaminating the temple grounds. Bruce Kapferer's study of Sinhalese exorcism rituals also illustrates the contaminating nature of meat. Kapferer's study discusses how meat is used as a bait to lure demonic forces from their host's body.[17] Demons are uniquely attracted to meat because flesh is associated with death and violence which is the domain of these evil spirits. Ethnographers have also observed that vegetarian food is provided for more morally pure supernatural beings such as *deviyo* or gods.[18] Meat is therefore not only associated with physical contamination, as we learn from Ānanda, but also is connected to moral contamination. In the transcendent realm of gods, devils and buddhas, meat is fit for the impure, while vegetarian food is meant for the pure. These matters were discussed at length in Chapter 1.

Vegetarian food is, therefore, customarily given to the Buddha image because it is considered an appropriately pure offering. The extent to which vegetarian *buddhapūjā* is practised is also revealed indirectly by informants such as Niromi. Niromi was a very poor low-caste washer woman. She states that you should not give meat and flesh at the *buddhapūjā* but she simply did not know why. Clearly, there is a level of social expectation surrounding the necessity of a vegetarian *buddhapūjā* and some are not aware of what the governing reasons are for this custom.

Although giving vegetarian food at the *buddhapūjā* was very popular, not everyone agreed that it was necessary. Isuru, for example, gives meat and fish at a *buddhapūjā* because, 'the Buddha has not said not to eat meat or fish. He's only given a limit.' Sanduni Akka, on the other hand, gave meat and fish at the *buddhapūjā* and was indifferent as to whether others should give it too: 'That's their want. Different people have different ways. In our house we cook meat and fish, therefore the thing I cook, the first portion of what I cook I give to the Buddha. Some people may not like it, but that's each person's idea.' Here Sanduni Akka refers back to the importance of giving the choicest food to the Buddha image. In this case it just so happens to be meat.

As previously described, giving food is a solemn social activity and honoured guests are served first and given the best pieces of food. The Buddha, the most revered guest of all, is therefore given the very best of the best. Nonetheless, these cases of individuals giving flesh at the *buddhapūjā* are outliers and the vast majority of informants supplied only vegetarian food. This is exemplified by the case of the Pinwatte Temple described at the start of the chapter.

The difference between a *buddhapūjā* and a *dāna* is therefore striking. In the *buddhapūjā* vegetarians and non-vegetarians alike only put vegetarian food on the offering tray. By contrast, in the case of the *dāna* ceremony, even vegetarians gave meat to monks. In both cases the social conventions are different. With the *dāna* there is great pressure to give meat because there is a desire to impress both monks and lay onlookers. The *buddhapūjā* is much more private, however, and therefore less governed by public accountability. Furthermore, the social dynamics of the *buddhapūjā* is different because the Buddha is regarded as exceptionally pure and therefore he requires special food items. It is already clear that vegetarian food is intended for the highest gods so it would be incoherent to not also offer vegetarian food to the Buddha himself.

There are, however, other pressures in play here. In particular, there are special religious spaces that model the proper conduct of *buddhapūjā* ceremonies at home and at temples. These special religious spaces uniquely demand that only vegetarian food and as such lay people begin to repeat these demands in their private rituals.

Critical religious spaces

The Kataragama dēvālaya premises in Kataragama is a popular pilgrimage site for Sri Lankans regardless of religious affiliation or ethnic identity. The Kataragama site is sacred not only for Hindus, but also to Buddhists and Muslims. Kataragama is most well known as for its Kataragama temple.

Kataragama, otherwise known as Skanda, is the son of Śiva. He is regarded as a potent deity who protects the southern lands of Sri Lanka.

His violent and wrathful nature make him especially sought after as an object of worship because it is thought that he is more potent in answering prayers. The composition of his offering tray is complicated. He is nominally given vegetarian food in accord with the idea that gods should receive 'pure' vegetarian dishes. However, his violent nature invites participants to supply flesh – the food that he really craves. In other words Kataragama occupies an odd space between that of a god and demon. He is a god with faults. But this disparity between what the particular gods want, and what he actually received, reveals the expectations devotees have about the moral nature of their deities.

At the rear of the Kataragama temple is a venerated Buddhist stūpa called the Kiri Vĕhĕra.[19] It is called the Kiri Vĕhĕra because it is a milky white colour. Buddhists flock to Kataragama not only to honour Kataragama himself – who is worshipped by Buddhists and Hindus alike – but also to worship at the Kiri Vĕhĕra. It is customary for Buddhists to circumambulate the Kiri Vĕhĕra stūpa before they participate in subsequent Kataragama rituals at the Kataragama temple. The idea is that the Buddha should always take priority even over important gods such as Kataragama. Sometimes, devotees will also visit the *buddhage* or the Buddhist image house. At the *buddhage* devotees will participate in a *buddhapūjā*. What is remarkable about this *buddhage* is the instructions concerning the *buddhapūjā* and what sort of food may be provided.

There are clear instructions written on the side of the *buddhage* that the food be vegetarian only: 'In this Buddha offering house please deposit inside all vegetarian offerings. This place is entirely devoid of meat, fish, salted fish, eggs, Maldive fish. You ought to kindly consider this – the Temple Authorities.'[20] This stipulation is remarkable because it is quite unlike the requirements of other *buddhage* from other areas in the country. Ordinarily, lay people are allowed to place whatever food they want in front of the Buddha image. At the temple in Kataragama, however, the opposite is the case. Only vegetarian food is permitted there.

The *buddhage* itself is quite unusual and is very modern in its design. It is made of glass and steel. Observers can look through the glass walls directly at the Buddha image housed within it. This is not the convention with other *buddhage*, which are of a more traditional design and are enclosed within a stone or cement structure and hidden from view from the outside. Not only is this *buddhage* non-traditional in terms of its dietary stipulations, it is also of a non-traditional and modern design.

The head monk (*nāyaka*) of the temple insisted that his temple enforces mandatory vegetarian offerings at the *buddhage* because the Buddha encourages you not to kill. This attitude is extremely uncommon amongst the monks interviewed. As a rule, monks insisted that the first precept had little to do with any decision to become a vegetarian. Like some of the lay people, the head monk was also aware that there is dispute over whether the Buddha was himself a vegetarian. It is clear, then, that the head monk of Kiri Vĕhĕra has adopted some interesting and non-traditional views about how Buddhist practices about food should be conducted at his temple.

The case of Kiri Vĕhĕra at Kataragama can be compared with the case of the Srī Daḷadā Māḷigāva in Kandy (hereafter Māḷigāva). The Māḷigāva is undoubtedly the most important Buddhist pilgrimage site in Sri Lanka. Devotees come here to worship the Daḷadā, the sacred tooth relic of the Buddha. The Daḷadā is an extremely sacred Buddhist site because it contains a relic of the Buddha, the equivalent of the Church of the Holy Sepulchre in Jerusalem. In Sri Lanka it is rivalled only by the Ruwanvăelisaya Stūpa in Anuradhapura, a *stūpa* which purportedly contains the Buddha's forehead bone. Worshippers flock from all over Sri Lanka to the Māḷigāva. It is said that simply gazing upon the Daḷadā for even a moment is enough to secure a good future rebirth in the era of Maitreya Buddha.

Some devotees, and only those who have special affiliations with the Māḷigāva authorities, are able to provide special *buddhapūjā*, known as the *daḷadā pūjāva* or *murutæn pūjāva*, directly to the tooth relic. Participating in this immensely meritorious ritual is highly regarded and there is enormous competition to secure a place as a participant in this sacred ritual activity. Most Māḷigāva attendees are only able to briefly shuffle past the inner sanctum and glimpse the Daḷadā through a small window. Offering food, on the other hand, is a great and rare honour. Only a select number of families a year can participate.

The items to be placed on the special offering tray must be vegetarian. Devotees who participate in the *daḷadā pūjāva* are supplied with a detailed list of ingredients that must be given to the Māḷigāva authorities prior to the day of the *daḷadā pūjāva*. The ingredients are all vegetarian. In addition, the lay people may not prepare the offering themselves and instead the food is made by special cooks on the Māḷigāva premises.[21] These cooks are required to wear masks so as not to contaminate the food with germs (*pili*), and also to prevent them from inadvertently smelling the food – it is considered an offense to consume food meant for the Buddha and this includes even smelling his flowers, incense or food.

As with the *buddhage* at the Kiri Vĕhĕra, this mandatory vegetarian offering at the Māḷigāva is quite unusual. Why do the authorities of these important Buddhist pilgrimage sites demand only vegetarian food be given? The head monk at the Kiri Vĕhĕra claims that it is because it is a potential violation of the first precept. There are, however, other important socio-cultural considerations that can be brought to bear on this question.

In both the case of the Kiri Vĕhĕra and the Māḷigāva there is an element of hinduisation involved. This is clear especially in the case of the Māḷigāva. The Daḷadā relic has increasingly come to take on a deity-like character, which is quite unusual from a conventional Buddhist perspective. Though the Buddha is dead his relics are nonetheless viewed as retaining living power and hold the capacity to be able to answer wishes (*prāthanā*) directly. The Daḷadā has taken on a godlike quality that is otherwise unheard of in

Thēravada Buddhism.[22] This special treatment of the Daḷadā is likely to stem, in part, from the influence of Hinduism on Buddhist practices. It stems originally from interaction with Indian Hindus and indigenous Hindu Tamils. One example of this is the case of Kandyan royalty marrying Indian royalty.[23] Not only did these individuals transport themselves to Kandy, they also transported their entire Indian retinue. These Indians continued their religious practices and this lead local Buddhists to adopt foreign Hindu religious customs. Of course, the antiquity of Hindu–Buddhist relations predates this late case, but this is a concrete example of how Indian and Sinhalese were cross-pollinated with different religious ideas.[24] It is plausible that these Hindu influences have partly resulted in the increased deification of the Daḷadā relic.

Hindu influences certainly seem to be a relevant factor in the vegetarian character of the *daḷadā pūjāva*. A monk from Kandy who was directly involved in *daḷadā pūjā* activities acknowledged this: 'By the time meat and fish came to Nuwara (Kandy) there was a Hindu influence.' Originally, meat and fish were hard to get in Kandy, and by the time it was common vegetarianism was already made popular because of Hinduism. Furthermore, the monk explains that the vegetarian nature of the *daḷadā pūjā* was originally also a way to help resolve the karmic debt of King Kīrti Sri Rajasiṃha. He says, 'Even though, as a Buddhist, the King helped in the deeds of the Buddha dharma, he was a debtor. Through this, there is a lot of refusing meat and fish, not just in the Māḷigāva, even today in a lot of places, in temples, during *buddhapūjā*, meat and fish are removed.' It is clear that Buddhism and Hinduism dovetail together in these cases.[25]

Hinduisation is also a factor in the case of the Kiri Vēhēra. Because the Kiri Vēhēra *buddhage* is located in such close proximity to the Kataragama temple it is likely that practices at the temple influence practices at the *buddhage*.[26] If Kataragama is to be given vegetarian food because of reasons of moral purity then it would not stand for the Buddha to also not be offered similarly pure food. It is plausible that this sort of competition between Hindu practices and Buddhist practices is what led to the use of vegetarianism in the *buddhapūjā* originally.

As the monk at the Māḷigāva already explained, these vegetarian practices at critical religious sites such as the Māḷigāva and the Kiri Vēhēra influence wider *buddhapūjā* practices throughout the country. It is plausible that these cases help explain why lay people were eager to supply vegetarian food at their local *buddhage* and at their private shrines at home.

Lay Buddhists pay close attention to the details of the religious practices mandated by authorities at these locations and model these rituals accordingly in the context of their private affairs. The popularity of vegetarianism as a Buddhist diet may itself stem indirectly from these practices. If the Buddha should be given a vegetarian *pūjā* then it implies that a vegetarian diet itself is holy and perhaps something a good Buddhist should himself adopt. If it is good for the Buddha then, in principle it is good for one and all.

Egg eating

One final matter in considering vegetarianism in Sri Lanka is the role of egg eating. Vegetarianism in Sri Lanka generally entails abstinence from egg consumption even though it quite often involves the eating of Maldive fish. This common definition of vegetarianism is quite at odds with the definition known in the West, where the contrary is assumed: vegetarians eat eggs but not fish while vegans do not eat either. Sometimes vegetarians who do not eat eggs *or* fish are referred to as 'pure vegetarians' in Sri Lanka.

In any case, the eating of eggs itself deserves special attention in part because of some of the unusual ideas underlying it. As a point of departure, consider what Gombrich has to say about egg eating in Sri Lanka: 'A true vegetarian Buddhist eats no eggs: even educated people think that all eggs are fertilised, and when I tried to tell people that a hen could lay without prior assistance from a cockerel, I was never believed, but probably considered crazy.'[27]

Things seem to have changed little since Gombrich's research in the 70s. Many of the views surrounding eggs were confused. Chamika, for example, suggests that all eggs were automatically fertilised: 'Eggs mean there is a male or female chick [inside]. *There is some life in it, right?* There was a lot of sin (*pav*) because it was in the belly. That means that before the chick even comes into the world we've already satisfied our stomachs and that is a big sin (*loku pavak*)' (my italics).

Renuka, the elderly matriarch, echoes this idea: 'I think there is a baby inside it [the egg],' she said, referring to all eggs. Nonetheless, it appears that she was confused over whether all eggs contain chicks. She subsequently implied that not all eggs had chicks and therefore it was sometimes appropriate to consume eggs. Her explanation for how eggs become fertilised is as follows, 'The reason I think it is right [to eat eggs] is because with just an egg the chick doesn't come. You need a *current* [English word, as in electricity] as well or you need a female, and a hen needs to come there [and sit on the egg].'

Another unusual view about egg fertilisation came from Priyanka. She says: 'I eat eggs. The reason I eat eggs is that the chicken's flesh is entirely in the egg. So the hen gives birth to life, but only after she sits on it does it have life in it. If you remove the egg, or if you bought the egg to the market, that egg is never going to have life. If the egg is with the hen for 21 days then it has life in it.' Priyanka did not seem to be aware that more was required than just the egg being incubated – fertilisation was also required.

This view leads Priyanka to not eat eggs that have been sat on too long because it is 'bad', i.e. morally hazardous. In other words, the chick develops *only* if the hen sits on the egg for a sufficient period of time.

These views seem to confirm Gombrich's observations that some Sinhalese are not knowledgeable about the life cycle of the hen. Only a few of the lay people interviewed had a good understanding of egg fertilisation. Still, those who had a good knowledge of the hen's life cycle were often less troubled by the prospect of eating eggs. Kanthi Aunty says, 'Sometimes there are eggs that don't have chicks in them. There's no problem if you eat those.'

Nawanga has the most to say about egg eating. In accordance with his vegetarian diet he says that he did not eat eggs, 'I don't eat eggs because actually some people say that there is a life inside the egg. Some people say there is no life.' For Nawanga, it just isn't clear whether there is or isn't a chick in an egg. Given this, eating eggs is potentially morally hazardous and should be avoided. Being involved in the death of a chick is not worth the karmic consequences.

He also argues that any amount of egg eating, however small, will lead to an excess of egg consumption. For him, the danger of a slippery slope towards excess is in-itself bad and therefore he rejects egg consumption regardless of whether there is life in the egg or not. The reason for this is unclear, though it may be based upon the more traditional Buddhist view that excess eating is bad. Moreover, excess eating entails the presence of a craving which is un-Buddhist. Nawanga says, 'Other people [non-vegetarians] assume that they [vegetarians] don't get enough vitamins and therefore they are offered more eggs. When that happens you get used to eating eggs. So I decided I wasn't going to eat eggs or egg-products.' When asked what he would do if he knew that there was no life in an egg he replies, 'Then you should reduce the amount of eggs you eat. That means you should eat enough to supplement your lack of eating flesh, but there is no need to eat a heap of it.' In general, he was sceptical of egg eating and considered it a crutch that detracted from the religious intent of a vegetarian diet.

As for the other vegetarians none of them ate eggs. Jayawardane Nonā notes that her vegetarian husband does not eat eggs and Charuni says that she does not eat eggs though she has no special reason to support this decision: 'I just don't think about it very much.' Some meat eaters also refused to eat eggs though their reasons were often arbitrary. In particular, Niromi reports that although she likes to eat eggs she never does because her family refuses them. When asked why, she simply says that it is the custom. She could not elaborate further. But most meat eaters ate eggs as a matter of course.

The clergy were also asked about egg eating. Some of the monks, being better educated, were much more aware of the biological necessities of egg fertilisation. The head monk of one temple says that there is no 'rooster involvement' – a rather charming euphemism – and that this means, 'there is no life in it.' This being so, eating eggs is acceptable. His deputy maintains a similar view, 'Society now has divided eggs into fertilised and unfertilised [literally eggs with seeds and eggs without seeds].' A monk at the large monastic university (to be discussed in the next chapter) states that eating eggs without a seed (*biju*) is acceptable. When pressed most monks gave plausible biological explanations for the origin of hen eggs.

As is clear from above, this was not always the case with the laity. As is obvious with Nawanga, this led to uncertainty as to whether an egg had a chick in it or not. Gombrich reports that this has led to a market for so-called 'Buddhist eggs' or 'pre-cracked eggs'.[28] A Buddhist egg is an egg that is already broken, either on purpose or by accident, and is then sold at a discounted rate to pious Buddhists. In this way the Buddhist egg eating can be assured that there is no life in the egg (the food hygiene standards of this practice is, of course, quite questionable). Intrigued by this, I was sure to ask the informants about the existence of so-called 'Buddhist eggs'. Every informant, however, was totally unaware of what a Buddhist egg was and many thought that the idea was ridiculous.

Still, after further investigation it seemed that Gombrich's observations still hold today. When I visited the Colombo Egg Centre in Bambalapitiya, the staff were happy to show me two large trays of pre-cracked eggs that they sometimes sold to Buddhist customers. It turns out that these pre-cracked eggs are just eggs that have been damaged in transit. Rather than disposing of them they are sometimes able to sell them at a reduced rate. They did note, however, that pre-cracked eggs are not popular. It is plausible that the practice of buying and eating so-called Buddhist eggs has gone somewhat out of favour since Gombrich's research in the 70s.

In general, it is hard to say how popular egg eating is. Simoons claims that eggs are eaten in Sri Lanka only rarely.[29] I have doubts about this claim. For one thing, eggs are commonly eaten in Sinhala savoury pancakes called hoppers (*āppa*). So-called Sri Lankan omelettes – omelettes with pepper, chilli, tomato, onion and spices – are popular. Unless a Buddhist is already a vegetarian, people generally do not object to eating them. Furthermore, a 2003 medical study by Wickramasinghe *et al.* showed that a major source of protein for school age children were milk and eggs.[30]

Obeyesekere also observes that egg consumption has not always been unfashionable and states that: 'unmarried men, particularly students in the university dormitories, eat raw eggs in the morning to enhance strength and vitality.'[31] This research was also conducted in the 70s. This suggests that egg eating has always occupied a complicated place. In any case, Obeyesekere's explanation for eating eggs is that it will help with vitality and energy owing to the fact that the egg is a symbol of fertility.[32] Egg consumption can have an *āyurvedic* function and it is considered a good food for rebalancing the humors and restoring vitality.[33] I will discuss *āyurvedic* medicine more in Chapter 6.

I would add that this could also be connected to the fact that meat consumption is associated with an improvement in martial prowess and therefore an improvement in energy and aggressiveness (as discussed in Chapter 1). But this highlights that egg consumption is caught up in the same tensions meat eating is caught up with: it is a potentially morally hazardous activity but its use may entail significant benefits.

Conclusion

Vegetarianism remains a contested diet in Sinhala Buddhist communities. Nonetheless, there is evidence – contrary to previous research – that vegetarianism has some popularity within segments of the lay Buddhist community. Not only are very pious Buddhists in favour of vegetarians, sometimes meat eaters also regard it as a moral ideal. The vegetarian diet can extend to every aspect of Buddhist religious practice. Not only do Buddhists themselves adopt vegetarianism, they demand that their idols also adopt the diet too. Vegetarian food is routinely offered to Buddha images, it is also prepared for honoured deities.

Of course, despite the fact that vegetarianism is regarded as being a virtuous diet there are a range of factors that confound its widespread use. For one thing, vegetarian food is comparatively cheap and so its use during important social and religious occasions is problematic: religious virtuosity can easily be confused with miserliness. Meanwhile, the temptation of offering meat to deities is sometimes irresistible. Some deities, such as Kataragama, prefer meat and it is thought that giving them flesh will result in better rewards.

Vegetarianism may be a religious ideal. It may even be relatively popular in Sri Lanka. But this ideal is easily hamstrung by social expectation and the desire for having one's religious wish fulfilled. As Sanduni Akka correctly points out, vegetarianism is a hard path in the face of desire.

Notes

1 This temple is to be discussed again in detail in Chapter 2 where we will look at the views of the monks associated with the temple.
2 Douglas' observation about the role food can play as a contaminant is relative in this analysis.
3 Gombrich and Obeyesekera, 28.
4 Gombrich, 1991: 305.
5 Obeyesekere, 2003: 194,
6 Ruegg, 234.
7 A note on caste: the topic of caste (*kula*) identity is a very sensitive matter and it is impossible to ask what someone's caste is directly. Caste can only be established indirectly – either through the reports of others, through reference to surname or prename, or through inference from occupation. These methods are, of course, quite fallible. In any case, based on the meagre information available, it would seem that caste has no particular impact. Of the data available the caste breakdown was *goyigama* (13), *kārava* (1), *rodiya* (1), unknown (6). For a detailed analysis of caste in Sri Lanka see Ryan (1953).
8 In accordance with the ethics approval guidelines all names have been altered to pseudonyms.
9 *sǣma pōya dhinakama eḷavalu kǣma pamaṇayi.*
10 The site is accessible at http://thahanamwachana.blogspot.com.au/2013/05/thero-indarathana-and-us.html.
11 See his Facebook page at www.facebook.com/magalkande.sudaththahimi.5.
12 Harvey, 160.
13 Ruegg, 239.
14 Carithers, 262.
15 Harvey (59). Other authors that make the same point include: Thomas (129), King (282), Keown (48), Ruegg (234), D.N. Jha (64) and Horner (11). Indeed, the observation that the Buddha allowed meat eating is made over and over again in numerous scholarly works.

Food of compassion 97

16 The *bāra* is an interesting example of a religious wish (*prāthanā*). It is a wish is a sort of mercantile promise. For example, the devotee will wish that a particular event may happen (their relative will be cured of a sickness, they will get a promotion, they will find a good bride, etc.) and in return they will do, for example, ten *buddhapūjā* next month. Sometimes these promises are written on flags and hung near *bo* trees in temples.
17 Kapferfer, 1995: 195; also Gombrich and Obeyesekere, 140.
18 Obeyesekere, 1963: 144.
19 The Kiri Vĕhĕra temple is associated with Sinhala Rāvaya, a political movement that will be discussed in Chapter 7. Sinhala Rāvaya launched a petition against cattle slaughter from Kiri Vĕhĕra. Sinhala Rāvaya's involvement with Kiri Vĕhĕra illustrates just how vegetarianism and animal welfarism in Sri Lanka is tied up with ethno-political conflict.
20 *mĕma budda pūjā mandiraya tuḷa tænpat karaṇa siyalu pūjā davayayat nirmānsha (mas mālu karavala bittara umbalakaḍa valin nŏra) viya yutu bava – karuṇāvĕn salakanna. mĕyaṭa vihārādhipati.*
21 Seneviratne (125) describes the process for how people come to donate food offerings for the *daḷadā pūjāva*.
22 For more on the influence Hinduism has on the tooth relic cult see: Seneviratne (124), Trainor (160–161).
23 De Silva, 143, 160.
24 De Silva explains the antiquity of Hinduism in Sri Lanka, its popularity with Sinhalese and its later presence in Buddhist courts, 'Although the spread of Buddhism in the island was at the expense of Hinduism, the latter never became totally submerged, but survived and had an influence on Buddhism which became more marked with t he passage of time. Vedic deities, pre-Buddhistic in origin in Sri Lanka, held their sway among the people, and kings who patronized the official religion, Buddhism, supported Hindu temples and observed Brāmanical practices as well. Hinduism was sustained also by small groups of Brāhmans living among the people and at the court' (50).
25 Previously it was noted, for example, that Kataragama has become a major object of veneration by Sinhala Buddhists. Also see Holt for details on the worship of Viśnu by Sinhala Buddhists (2004).
26 The intersection between Buddhism and Hinduism is already very apparent at the Kataragama precinct. See Gombrich and Obeyesekere (1988: 45, 182–189, 411); Obeyesekere (1977); Pfaffenberger (1979).
27 Gombrich, 1991: 305.
28 Ibid.
29 Simoons, 151.
30 Wickramasinghe, 117.
31 Obeyesekere, 1976: 214.
32 Ibid.
33 Ibid.

4 The disciple's diet

Monastic views on vegetarianism and animal welfare

The Māligāva's alms-giving hall (*dāna shālāva*), though critical to the functioning of the temple, is nonetheless located in an unassuming position near the tooth relic reliquary room. It is in the *dāna shālāva* that monks from the Asgiriya and Malwatta monastic chapters come to receive food and other requisites of monkish life from white-clad pilgrims. The Māligāva itself is indicative of the complications associated with monastic attitudes towards vegetarianism. As mentioned, the Daḷadā relic only receives vegetarian offerings. Yet in the Māligāva alms giving hall meat is commonly supplied to the monks there. The alms giving hall, and the types of food supplied there, influence alms giving practices in Sinhala Buddhist temples throughout the entire country.

The arrangement of the *dāna shālāva* is simple. A series of trestle tables are located in the centre of the room. It is on these tables that vessels containing alms food are placed. Flanking these tables are long benches upon which monks receive their food. The chairs upon which the monks sit have short legs and plain white fitted sheets draped over them in accordance with regulations stipulated by the *Vinaya*.

These are requirements stipulated by the *Vinaya Piṭaka* that are intended to help convey the simplicity and modesty of the monkish life. A large white buddha image (*buddha piḷimaya*) is located prominently at the front of the hall. Around its head are a series of garish flashing bulbs that symbolise the dazzling spectacle of the Buddha's enlightenment. It is a modern flourish that draws attention in this otherwise stark and clinical environment. Along with the lay pilgrims, Māligāva support staff ferry the plates of food and alms and arrange them on the central table in preparation for the entrance of the monks.

The laity are required to sit on the floor near the alms tables. Special woven mats called *pǣdura* are laid on the ground for this purpose. Elderly people are allowed to sit off to one side on chairs. Although monks are supposed to project an air of modesty and equanimity they are nonetheless considered superior to the laity and this is symbolised by their physical elevation above the laity who sit on the ground. Their superiority is both moral and metaphysical in nature. Monks are not only ethically pure, unlike the blemished masses, they are also closer to a better rebirth – that is closer to enlightenment – and therefore are on a higher metaphysical plane than ordinary people.

This intrinsic respect for the clergy is further demonstrated by the complex rituals attached to lay–monk social interactions. Laity are always required to refer to monks in the formal tense. A lay person will always use the formal *ŏba vahanse* (your excellence) when talking to a monk rather than the informal *ŏyā* (you) that is used in common conversation. Monks must be acknowledged first by an act of worship a ritual in which the worshipper gets on one's knees and touches the feet of those they seek to respect. The clergy are also regarded as aloof from normal everyday behaviours, even eating. Monks do not merely eat food (*kanavā*), they consume food (*valandinavā*). The notion of *eating* food entails a whole range of worldly implications – first amongst them being the *desire* to eat. Desire, however, is rejected by Buddhist doctrine. *Consumption*, on the other hand, is a more ambiguous act that conveys an air of indifference and such indifference speaks to the intended character of the monks.

In due course, the monks slowly file into the room. Their casual, almost laconic, disposition is considered proper monastic decorum. Since the monk is detached from worldly affairs he has gained control of his emotional state and is no longer subject to the fickle ebb and flow of desires and impulses. This, at least, is how the monk is to be ideally perceived. This detachment and control is exemplified by his initial lack of interest in the laity. This lack of interest can be observed even in apparently inappropriate circumstances. At televised government events invited monks can sometimes be seen apparently sound asleep in the audience. Still, this religious detachment need not imply total social disconnection and monks usually comport themselves in a kindly fashion to their lay audience.

Once seated, the Māligāva alms ceremony can begin. In general, the ceremony concerns the celebration of a life event and the merit produced by the ceremony is shared by the alms giver with another recipient.[1] Food offering is critical in such circumstances. Food nourishes and sustains the clergy and therefore the Dharma. In this sense, supplying the *sangha* with food is perhaps one of the most effective ways of generating good karma (*pin*).

At one Māligāva alms ceremony I attended the *dāna* (offering) was dedicated to a 90-year-old family matriarch. The intention was to transfer the merit produced by the ceremony directly to her so that she might be protected from illness and harm in her old age. A famous and revered elderly monk was responsible for delivering *baṇa* (the sermon).

The ceremony unfolded in the following way: he was given a notebook where the name of the grandmother was written along with the names of her closest relatives and the region where she live. He first announce that the alms giving ceremony is being conducted in her honour. He then sermonise on the importance of *mettā* (loving kindness).[2] He discussed how alms giving is an opportunity to create great karma – provided, of course, that the intention is right. This, of course, is an implicit criticism of lay people that give food to monks with the object of glorifying themselves in the eyes of others.

At the end of the monk's *baṇa* the alms are distributed. This is the usual order in any alms giving ceremony. Each layperson carries a dish of food and systematically ladles a spoonful of food onto each monk's plate. Monks routinely refuse certain foods for medical or personal reasons. Some types of food are unpopular. Sometimes monks refuse certain foods because they have enough of that type on their plate. Furthermore, some monks are vegetarian, though the vast majority accept any type of meat or fish.

Once the monks have finished eating, the lay people begin to distribute parcels of material requisites called *aṭa pirikara* (see Chapter 2). They then move amongst the monks and worship at their feet. In return for this worship the laity are blessed by the monks who say '*suvapat vevā*' (may you be happy) and gesture towards the crown of the head (generally, monks do not actually make physical contact with laity, and certainly never with women).

Once our ceremony had concluded there was a mad rush for the elderly monk as he was the most senior and therefore his blessings the most auspicious.[3] In an idiosyncratic fashion, he haphazardly strike worshipers with his bamboo fan whilst uttering the words *suvapat vēvā*.

This distinctive behaviour is indicative of the way that monk cults can arise. The personality of a monk provides the basis for a growth in individual popularity. Some lay people gravitate towards certain monks and are therefore more likely to furnish their temple with alms and other resources. The Māligāva is itself a unique celebrity space due to its intrinsic religious significance. Yet in smaller more local temples monk cults are an important way of sustaining and growing the temple. Unpopular monks who supply tedious and rote sermons risk endangering the existence of the temple as lay supporters begin to wane. Monk cults may form around monks with charismatic personalities, such as the old monk at the Māligāva alms giving ceremony, or they may form around individual monks who possess special powers, such as Magalkande Sudātta Himi Thēra, who is renowned for his ability to inspire faith in animals such as cows.

This distinction between the conventional and non-conventional monks is an important distinction in our investigation of food practices amongst the clergy. As we shall see, in the case of vegetarianism and other special dietary practices, the majority of monks strictly obey minimal monastic allowances and thus consume fish and meat. A few renegade monks interpret the Buddhist doctrine differently and elect to abstain from meat and fish. For the most part, these monks are very much in the minority however. This is in contrast to the lay people discussed in the previous chapter, many of whom quite enthusiastically embraced vegetarianism and regarded it as a vital part of Buddhist ethics.

The standard view

It is important to distinguish between two motives for vegetarianism. The first motive is an ethical one: meat should be abstained from because it is immoral.

Usually the reason for this is that meat consumption directly and indirectly harms animals. However, there may be other ethical reasons for abstaining from meat such as a concern for the impact animal farming has on the natural environment. Alternatively, meat consumption might be regarded as morally polluting regardless of the harm done to the animal and the environment.

A second motive for abstaining from meat is non-ethical or prudential. One might abstain from meat out of concern for one's health. For example, vegetarianism is sometimes regarded as a healthier alternative to a meat-based diet. Another similarly prudential reason for abstaining from meat might be to conform to social expectations. It is clear from the previous chapter that there is a mix of prudence and ethics in lay considerations about vegetarianism.

In societies where meat abstinence is mandatory, it might be regarded as imprudent to consume flesh because it could lead to social sanction or even exclusion. In Western societies, the opposite is usually the case – it is the vegetarian or vegan that is considered the outsider. In any case, this distinction between ethical and non-ethical reasons for abstaining from meat is a critical distinction in understanding the attitudes many monks had towards vegetarianism. We have already seen this distinction being drawn in Chapter 2, where we have examined some of the vegetarian literature. There this distinction was made in terms of moral justifications for vegetarianism versus prudential justifications for vegetarianism, especially justifications based around health concerns. In what follows we will find that many of the views expressed by those vegetarian and non-vegetarian authors are repeated by the informants.

Monks interviewed routinely reject ethical vegetarianism outright or are otherwise indifferent to it to the point where it cannot be correctly said that they support it. For them, it is not – and should not be – a question of morality. They do not, however, necessarily oppose vegetarianism born from non-ethical motives, such as from concern over health. This attitude will become clear in the following.

It is instructive to consider the attitude some monks had towards the question of vegetarianism when they were approached for interview. Some refused to participate in the research outright because they believed that vegetarianism could never be endorsed by any Buddhist monk. Such views originated from a strict reading of the Buddha's statements in the Pāli texts.

This is the attitude, for example, of the head monk (*nāyaka hāmuduruwa*) of a famous and large monastery called Lakmal Vihāra,[4] who claims that there is no point in conducting the research since all monks would answer these questions identically: vegetarianism is not endorsed by the Buddha and therefore the question is irrelevant.

This expectation turned out to be false as some monks defied this prediction, but this attitude does betray the fundamentalism present in some quarters of the clergy and the fact that some monks simply believe that there are some questions not worth asking. Another temple that was approached, Tusita Vihāra, was similarly antagonistic to the question of vegetarianism. As with Lakmal, Tusita Vihāra was a famous and politically active temple. The two monks interviewed believe that vegetarianism is a non-issue in Buddhism and that it is of no moral consequence whatsoever.

This outlook is shared by one monk at a prosperous Colombo temple, Manik Vihāra, who wishes to participate in the research but not be recorded. Like the head monk at the Lakmal, he wants to set the record straight about Buddhism and vegetarianism. He believes that there is no legitimate question to be had about vegetarianism and Buddhism. Indeed, he strongly believes that other monks will answer uniformly on this point.

First, he regards vegetarianism as a position that was a defining feature of Jainism, a religious movement rejected by the Buddha. According to this monk, the Buddha rejected Jain dietary stipulations on the basis that it was an extreme philosophical outlook. From a doctrinal perspective, the Buddha experimented with such ascetic diets prior to his enlightenment and found them wanting.[5] The Pāli texts provide us with the following chilling report of the Buddha's experimentation. The Buddha says that, 'Because of eating so little my belly skin adhered to my backbone; thus if I touched my belly skin I encountered my backbone and if I touched my backbone I encountered my belly skin.'[6]

For this monk, vegetarianism is similar to extreme ascetic practices and behaviours advocated by Jains and other rival religious groups of the Buddha's day. Since the Buddha rejected extremes such as physical starvation he would reject vegetarianism as well.

We have already encountered similar arguments to this in Chapter 2 when the Pāli literature was considered. Also in that chapter, Gñanananda Thera, the author of *The Question of Vegetarianism*, made the complaint that vegetarians are overly extreme in their dietary decisions and thus act against the Buddha's middle-path principles.

The monk also mentions the *Jīvaka Sutta*, a *sūtra* that we have encountered already.[7] This *sūtra* discusses a case where the Buddha is accused by his Jain opponents of eating flesh knowing that it had been slaughtered on his behalf, something that would be regarded by Jains and Buddhists alike as cruel to the animal. The Buddha rejects this accusation saying that monks may eat flesh food if the animal has not been known, heard, or suspected that it was killed on their behalf. Such allowances have already been discussed in Chapter 2 and I direct the reader there for further details.

This principle now forms the basis for the justification of meat consumption amongst monks and is a central ethical difference between Jainism and Buddhism. For the Jains, of course, this principle is a fundamental betrayal of the non-violence principle. It is this point of difference that the Manik Vihāra monk regards as crucial in undercutting the question of vegetarianism in Buddhism. Despite the Jains' criticisms, it is this principle that allows this monk to regard ethical vegetarianism as doctrinally unsound.

The monastic stipulation that allows for the consumption of flesh foods was repeatedly mentioned by many of the monks interviewed. These dietary allowances led many monks to reject ethical vegetarianism as a moral necessity and regarded any adoption of ethical vegetarianism as doctrinally deviant. Because the majority of monks overwhelmingly supported this critical attitude I have referred to this as the 'standard view'.

It is perhaps unsurprising that monks adopted this attitude given these statements issued by the Buddha. Nonetheless, the details of their view are intriguing, not to mention the extent to which this view contrasts with the lay perspective discussed in Chapter 3. It may be recalled that there was widespread support for ethical vegetarianism from a Buddhist perspective amongst laity. In the following I will explore in more detail why monks are so critical of ethical vegetarianism and under what conditions they might accept it. Some unusual, or otherwise idiosyncratic, monks adopted a more favourable attitude towards vegetarianism. These individuals were outlier cases.

The permissibility to eat meat

Despite the protests from the monks at Lakmal and Tusita Vihāra, even the monks who maintain a negative attitude towards the idea of ethical vegetarianism nonetheless express complex ideas about why that is the case, and to what degree. The monk at Manik Vihāra mentioned previously is, of course, strongly against ethical vegetarianism. Yet although his colleagues tend to agree with him, the forcefulness by which they agree varies greatly.

The head monk at Manik Vihāra repeats the fact that the Buddha allowed meat consumption. He says, 'The Buddha has said *kæpa mahansha*. *Kæpa mahansha* means: if someone didn't kill on your behalf, if you don't suspect someone killed on your behalf, and if it is not said [that a creature was killed on your behalf] then that *mansha* (flesh) is *kæpa mansha*.'

Kæpa, in Sinhala, simply means 'acceptable'. In this way, and like his more assertive junior, the head monk follows the monastic regulations laid down by the Buddha in a very faithful manner. Yet the head monk does allow for the fact that this monastic regulation was historical and contextual. Just because it was easy to identify whether an animal had been slaughtered for you in the Buddha's day does not mean it is so easy in contemporary times: 'So let's think that an animal has been killed – there is meat lying there. Long ago, that was what life was like – it was a nomadic life. It's not like that today. So that kind of meat…you know for certain it wasn't for you.' Although the head monk of Manik Vihāra believes that meat eating is allowable according to Buddhism he also accepts that following this rule in a strict and sincere way is not always easy.

Venerable Lankatilaka was also affiliated with Manik Vihāra. He is a young monk who sincerely hopes to become a forest renunciant. This desire is illustrative of how dedicated he is to his Buddhist practice.[8] His dietary decisions are determined largely by this objective. Ven. Lankatilaka explained, that in his childhood he avoided eating fish. This decision was not born from any moral compunction, but was rather born from his dislike of the smell. He claims that he had an aversion (*piḷihuḍak*) to the smell of flesh foods. Eventually he stopped eating meat altogether and became a vegetarian. He carried on with this diet for some time until he decided he needed to begin eating meat again in preparation for his plans to become a forest renunciate. He says, 'If I have something like meat and fish, the nutrition that I need – the strength – for my existence as a recluse, then that is something that I need to have.' Again, the connection between meat eating and energy has wider support as we saw in Chapter 1 and Chapter 3. There we discovered that meat is considered a vital way to improve not only one's martial skills, but also one's virility and energy.

Ven. Lankatilaka believes that he needs to do whatever he can to 'get to the other shore' – a metaphor for enlightenment or Nirvana. Having the strength to eradicate mental defilements (*kileṣa*) is paramount in realising this goal, but Ven. Lankatilaka does not view meat eating as itself defilement producing. Rather, vegetarianism is something he chose to participate in for non-ethical reasons. In his youth, he simply found meat unpalatable. This ambivalence towards ethical vegetarianism is clear from the way he addresses the question of whether Buddhism encourages vegetarianism at all. He answers that the Buddha's teaching condemns animal killing but, as mentioned by both his colleagues at Manik Vihāra, meat consumption is permitted by the Buddha. The only danger in eating meat, Ven. Lankatilaka says, is that it might lead to the formation of mental defilements through the production of desires: 'If we think 'That is meat and fish' with a desiring thought, with a lustful thought, if you take it with a greedy thought...that is also wrong because it causes defilements.' Such defilements accrue from the formation of desires that are, as already mentioned, the root cause of suffering and rebirth.

It is through the production of these defilements that liberation and enlightenment is obstructed. The avoidance of defilements is therefore very much at the forefront of Ven. Lankatilaka's concerns since it is apparent that he wants to achieve the ultimate goal of release from rebirth. Ven. Lankatilaka's view is that food should be taken without craving and without desire. What is important is the attitude and mental disposition of the monk, not the actual food that he consumes. In this respect, he does not favour or disfavour vegetarianism as such, but at the same time it is apparent that he does not regard Buddhism as encouraging vegetarianism either.

This critical attitude towards ethical vegetarianism continued at Swarna Vihāra, a small hermitage located in near Kegalle town. The head monk there, Venerable Allagoda, is a professor at a large secular university, but he is also the chief instructor and curriculum coordinator at a large rural *piriveṇa* or monastic university, also located in Kegalle.

This *piriveṇa* is called Nuwan Piriveṇa and the views of some of the monks there will be discussed presently. Ven. Allagoda's hermitage is located in the hilly country overlooking Kegalle and is surrounded by thick jungle. Such temples are considered ideal retreats for scholarly monks who wish to reflect on the Buddha's teachings and refine their meditative practice.

Ven. Allagoda has this view: 'At the end of the Buddha's life when he was attaining *parinibbāna* someone asked him this question and the Buddha

answered like this "As a hard and fast rule (in English) it is not accepted".'
Ven. Allagoda maintains the view that the Buddha did not make vegetarianism mandatory, which, as discussed already, is perfectly in accord with the *Jīvaka Sūtta* and the *Vinaya*. Ven. Allagoda repeats the fact that the Buddha allowed meat to be consumed if it was 'pure' in one of three ways. He also adds that mandatory vegetarianism is doctrinally deviant because it was associated with Devadatta – the Buddha's nemesis and the archenemy of the Buddhist religion. Ven. Allagoda says, 'Devadatta asked the Buddha for five requisites; one of the requirements was to remove yourself from meat and fish for the duration of your life. The Buddha did not give permission for that.' Allagoda is clear that ethical vegetarianism is a potentially deviant activity by associating it with the heretic Devadatta.[9]

Be that as it may, Ven. Allagoda does regard lay people who offer vegetarian *dāna* to be especially pious: 'They are people who have an understanding of the Dhamma. The other thing is (in English) they are truly following the principle of non-violence.' Vegetarianism, then, is a practice that follows from the first precept of non-violence. This was, as we found in Chapter 3, a point made by a number of lay informants. On the face of it, such a comment does seem to conflict with Ven. Allagoda's criticism of ethical vegetarianism because he does also suggest that vegetarianism is doctrinally deviant. This conflict deepens when Ven. Allagoda goes onto say that the original position for human beings is vegetarianism and it is only because of the adoption of social norms that people come to eat meat: 'There are children in some houses. What do they eat? They don't eat [meat and fish]. They haven't gotten used to it. The mother and father eat it, but the child doesn't eat it…They say, 'You need protein, you need this, you need that, so eat meat and eat fish.' That is the influence under which most people refer to.'

Although Ven. Allagoda is critical of ethical vegetarianism, he is conflicted on this issue. A senior monk of the same hermitage, Ven. Galvihara, is similarly critical of vegetarianism. Like the other monks already mentioned, he explains that meat is can be eaten if it is pure in three respects. As with Ven. Allagoda, he also mentions the case of Devadatta. Furthermore, Ven. Galvihara regards food as a kind of fuel: 'The Buddha said, 'Protect all creatures' but having said that, it's not about this or that taste. There's nothing like that. Food is necessary for the survival of the human race.' As we have seen, this position is consistent with the *Sūtra Piṭaka*. There, the Buddha repeatedly states that food should be regarded only as a fuel and should not be unduly discriminated over.[10]

Ven. Galvihara insists that sincere vegetarianism is impossible anyway because traditional medicine often demands that meat be consumed: 'Now let's say somebody tells a monk, a doctor, "For this monk's ailment he must take liver." It's a problem. Either the monk accepts it or rejects it.' Nonetheless, a number of traditional doctors interviewed accommodate vegetarian diets, and at least one exclusively practices vegetarian friendly medicine. So although traditional medicine, especially *āyurvedic* medicine, does sometimes

106 *The disciple's diet*

require that meat be used, it is clearly not an absolute necessity. This issue will be discussed at greater length in Chapter 6.

Like Ven. Allagoda, Ven. Galvihara is sensitive to the fact that animals are in need of protection and is aware of the impact diet has on animal welfare. 'An animal that has a long time to live is something we eat in one meal, not for a life time. We kill it for that meal. Let's think about a cow. Let's say his lifetime is five years. We kill him before that time and so that is where the problem is.'

As it so happens, Ven. Galvihara is himself a vegetarian, but his decision is born out of prudence not ethics. Like some of the other monks, he rejects ethical vegetarianism whilst accepting the importance of vegetarianism as a way of avoiding ill health: 'So let's think, when we eat an animal it's possible that the animal had an illness, a problem with the body, so if we use that it's possible that additional ailments will be created for us. The best thing is vegetables. With meat and fish you can't tell for sure [i.e. whether there are contagions].' Again, as with Ven. Allagoda, his opinion on vegetarianism is complicated. On the one hand he accepts that it is a practice that is not endorsed by the Buddha, but he does see some prudential advantages in adopting it from a non-Buddhist point of view.

Ven. Galvihara's focus on prudence as a deciding factor in adopting vegetarianism can also be compared with Ven. Lankatilaka decision to *reject* vegetarianism out of prudence. In fact, prudence is the main consideration that governs the rejection or adoption of vegetarianism amongst the sampled clergy. This can be contrasted with the laity who largely endorse ethical vegetarianism and regard it as a manifestation of Buddhism properly understood.

The Nuwan Piriveṇa is associated with Swarna Vihāra by way of Ven. Allagoda. I interviewed four monks at Nuwan Piriveṇa and none of them strictly endorsed ethical vegetarianism. A *piriveṇa* is a monastic university that monks attend to study the more theoretical aspects of Buddhism.[11] It is at these institutions that Pāli and Sanskrit are studied, and it is here that monks become fully acquainted with the Buddhist sacred literature.

Unlike large and famous *piriveṇa* such as Vidyalankara in Peliyagoda or Vidyodaya in Maligikanda, this *piriveṇa* is relatively isolated and rural. The location and context of the temple is relevant as it has some impact on what alms disadvantaged rural *dāyaka* (donors) are able to give.

One of the monks, Ven. Ratutilaka, is young, apparently in his late teens, and has therefore not taken the higher ordination. Ratutilaka is not aware of any issue associated with meat consumption whatsoever. For him, vegetarianism is something people adopted for seemingly arbitrary reasons. The only significant issue for him is whether vegetarianism is medically feasible: 'Even if you take a part of vegetables the necessary vitamins are received. There *are* vegetarians. They *are* alive, right? They're not dead. So if you are a vegetarian it's alright.' Again, this reply echoes the pragmatic attitude monks take to the real practice of vegetarianism. It is not interpreted as a moral issue, but is rather a question of practical efficacy. The only relevant question is this: is vegetarianism a medical benefit or is it harmful?

The question of whether ethical vegetarianism is a necessity was again answered in the negative by a fellow monk of a similar age to Ven. Rathutilaka, Ven. Haputale. Ven. Haputale says, 'No, the Buddha hasn't allowed that [i.e. vegetarianism]. Like Ven. Allagoda and Ven. Galvihara, he mentions the case of Devadatta as a case study in why vegetarianism is not mandatory. He also adds that, 'By allowing the consumption of meat and fish there is no demerit (*pav*) because what is given for the offering at a *dāna* is what we accept.'

The idea that a monk should accept any food offered to them is consistent with claims made by many Buddhist Studies scholars.[12] Many of these scholars argue that this makes vegetarianism practically impossible.[13] In reality, however, many monks are vegetarian – either for health reasons or because of moral scruples. These monks have no problem rejecting unsuitable food.

Like Ven. Lankatilaka at Manik Vihāra in Colombo, Ven. Haputale regards the intention of the eater to be more important than the actual act of eating: 'The Buddha said "intention, monk, is karma" [said in Pāli]. Mainly what was preached, the important part of what was preached, is about our thoughts. When we eat, our thoughts are not about killing an animal.' No harm is done in eating an animal because the monk never intended that the animal be killed. The fact that the industry that is responsible for the animal slaughter is being supported by the consumption of flesh is not relevant here, it would seem, though it should be noted that boycotts of cattle abattoirs are routinely carried out throughout Sri Lanka (to be discussed in Chapter 5).

Kaha Vihāra is a temple frequented by many of the lay informants from the Colombo sample. The head monk, Ven. Panadura, is extremely popular and is viewed as a pious monk with considerable scholarly credentials. It should not be assumed that monks were automatically regarded in this way. For example, several of the Colombo informants lived very close to a reasonably well-resourced temple. Nonetheless, they typically avoided visiting it because the head monk there is viewed as impious and prone to consuming alcohol. One informant recounted a rumour that he kept a mistress on temple property. This illustrates how monks can fall out of favour as much as they can fall into favour. Ven. Panadura, in contrast, is viewed as exemplary and so his worship is not only considered legitimate, it is considered an efficient way to produce merit. Nonetheless, Ven. Panadura's ambivalent attitude to vegetarianism does not match the lay people's acceptance of ethical vegetarianism. This illustrates that there can be a break between monastic beliefs and lay beliefs about certain moral issues.

Ven. Panadura, in accordance with expectation, recounts the standard view that the Buddha allowed the consumption of meat. Like the monks before him, he also raises the case of Devadatta. In this regard, he rejects ethical vegetarianism as a necessity from a Buddhist point of view. Like other monks, however, he does believe that vegetarianism might be necessary from a prudential health perspective. For example, Ven. Panadura observes that some families who came to Kaha Vihāra prefer to give vegetarian *dāna*. He regards this as practically possible because there are soya substitutes for meat.

When asked why people might give soya he replies, 'There are things such as cholesterol and heart attacks ... because of those problems some people abstain from meat and fish. For that reason people don't eat meat or fish.' In this case we can see that Ven. Panadura does not even entertain the notion that meat and fish might be rejected for ethical reasons. It occurs to him only that people might not eat it for health reasons.

Ven. Panadura's deputy took a different view on the healthiness of meat. He believes that vegetarianism is fundamentally problematic because meat is needed as a medical treatment for many diseases: 'Because of some diseases meat eating is necessary for people. At those times, the Buddha hasn't prohibited it and for some things it becomes necessary, right? Depending on your illness you might need it. When you have fertility problems you are told to eat meat, fish, and eggs. So it's okay to eat it.' In general, the consensus of the three monks at Kaha Vihāra is that vegetarianism could not be regarded as a moral necessity. They could not even agree that it made for a healthy diet. (As a side note, *āyurvedic* treatments do not absolutely require meat – this is discussed in Chapter 6).

In the end, the third and final monk interviewed at Kaha Vihāra put things like this: 'There is no preaching like that. [The Buddha] didn't say "no." That's the individual's thought. It's your desire.' In short, whether vegetarianism is right or wrong is not a doctrinal matter for Buddhism to decide. Rather, it is an issue that stands outside of Buddhism altogether.

The remarks of all these monks is roughly consistent with the views already articulated by Gñanananda Thēra in, *The Question of Vegetarianism* (2010). As such Gñanananda Thēra should be viewed as a proponent of the standard view, though he has engaged in a much more lengthy and detailed discussion of this issue and is perhaps the most hostile to the notion that vegetarianism is in any way doctrinally justified.

Monastic responsibilities

One may inevitably conclude from these discussions that even in cases where monks did not reject ethical vegetarianism outright, they were at least ambivalent to it.

In cases where vegetarianism was supported, it was generally done so only out of prudence. Monks sometimes endorsed vegetarianism, but this was because it was viewed as a healthy dietary alternative. The welfare of the animal was not considered an important factor.

Ultimately, ethical vegetarianism was regarded as a non-Buddhist matter that was the exclusive purview of the laity. This point is made explicitly by Ven. Gampola, a monk at Nuwan Piriveṇa. When pressed about the connection between animal slaughter and meat consumption, and the fact that the eating of animals supports animal slaughter industries, Ven. Gampola states that, 'That's something that happens in society.' From his perspective, immoral activities that arise in ordinary society cannot be explicitly avoided. All monks can do is try to steer the laity in the right direction, but they otherwise have no authority over lay activities, including the existence of animal slaughter.

This view is likely shared by many monks. Ven. Haputale adds the following remark: 'That depends on who you are looking at it. If you are looking at the monks' side or the givers' side. From the givers' side it is a difficulty, but from the monks' side it is not a difficulty. The side that it has to develop on is the givers' side.' These comments are especially enlightening because they reveal an underlying assumption implicit amongst the clergy, namely that the clergy have no obligation to consider certain ethical questions and that responsibility for such concerns are surrendered upon entered the *saṅgha*. This position may also explain why monks at Lakmal and Tusita Vihāra were so completely against ethical vegetarianism: it did not even register as a matter for clergy to deal with.

The issue of animal welfare, and the correct way to reduce the mistreatment of animals, is one such issue. For Ven. Haputale, and perhaps for other monks, the issue of what constitutes an *ethical* diet in relation to animal welfare is a worldly matter and is therefore not a concern of the clergy. The reason for this relates back to a point already posited by Ven. Haputale; monks should accept whatever food is given to them without discrimination. Given this assumption, what food they eat is not ultimately the clergy's responsibility but is instead the layperson's. It is plausible that the laity themselves are conscious of this. As established in Chapter 3, the sampled laity are very concerned about what foods were appropriate to give to monks. Many believe that vegetarian food is ideal but nonetheless do not supply it at a *dāna* because there was a fear that they might be characterised as miserly by their peers.

The monks at Nuwan Piriveṇa are nonetheless routinely given vegetarian food at their *dāna* ceremonies. The head monk there states that, 'Around 80% of the people give a vegetarian *dāna*.'

Yet this frequency of giving only vegetarian food at a *dāna* is not due to the local villagers being especially pious. Rather, because the *piriveṇa* is located in a rural area populated by people of a low socio-economic background, it is simply the case that the local *dāyaka* could not *afford* to give meat. Meat is a luxury item and the meals most often eaten by the villagers in the area is very basic by Sri Lankan standards: *bat* (rice), *parippu* (lentils), and *kŏs* (jackfruit) would be considered a perfectly conventional meal. The head monk explains it like this: 'A lot of people are labourers [and therefore poor] and they eat mostly vegetables.' Like their wealthier city counterparts, these *dāyaka* would probably give meat if they could, for the reasons discussed earlier, but it is simply the case that they cannot afford to do so.

Another reason why monks may be eager to defer responsibility for their diet is because the active adoption of ethical vegetarianism seems to demand certain political commitments. Participating in politics in Sri Lanka is a risky affair that can either bring glory or an ignominious demise. Historically, monks have participated in Sri Lankan politics,[14] but these individuals may be regarded as outliers. Most monks might discuss politics in private, but their main concern is participating in their spiritual development. Being involved in politics interferes with this objective. For these monks being involved in political matters is not their responsibility or role. This is the case for seemingly innocuous political activities such as animal welfarism.

The monk's responsibility is simply to better themselves spiritually and communicate the Dharma to the masses, nothing more. The reluctance of monks to get involved in animal welfare for fear of its political implications is not without warrant as we shall see in Chapter 7.

Animal welfarism amongst the clergy

This is not to say that all monks uniformly rejected ethical vegetarianism. Several of the monks interviewed enthusiastically promoted it. As mentioned earlier these monks might be viewed as outlier cases and idiosyncratic in their own right. There were three principle cases that I will discuss here, though the last one, the monk who ran the *Organisation for the Preservation of Life* (*sangvidānaye pani vudayaki*), will be discussed at length in a separate section.

Ven. Hambantota is temporarily staying at Manik Vihāra. He explains that he is new to the temple and had previously been affiliated with a different monastery. Ven. Hambantota differs from his other monastic colleagues in that he is a European monk who originated from the United Kingdom. He says that he had been ordained into the *sangha* from an early age and had travelled to Sri Lanka for the purpose of entering the order. Consequently, like his colleagues, he knows perfect Sinhala. Unlike many of his other colleagues, however, he views vegetarianism as an implicit imperative of the Buddha's Dharma.

For example, he says, 'It's connected with the Dharma, yes. The teaching of truth. I personally don't feel that it's necessary nowadays to consume meat or fish. It might have been useful in certain circumstances if monks were offered meat and fish in very austere circumstances, in certain regions, in ancient India where no food was available.'

Ven. Hanbantota goes on to add that because he is a vegetarian he feels comfortable rejecting meat and fish when it is offered to him: 'Other things, unless it was for medical reasons…I would personally accept whatever is offered. If I didn't want to consume that I would put it aside. But I have stronger feelings about the consumption of meat, fish, and eggs … and I'm to some degree repulsed by that, and so I feel personally that it's alright for monks to politely refuse that, even on alms round. We just, without saying a word, cover the bowl with our hand.'

Interestingly, though Ven. Hambantota is himself a vegetarian and believes that others should be vegetarian, he nonetheless echoes an idea already made by other monks that did not agree with ethical vegetarianism: 'I personally believe that it's wrong for people to purchase meat, fish, and eggs – as Buddhists. I personally don't think that it's wrong for monks to consume meat, fish, and eggs in certain circumstances if their intention is to sustain life. But I do believe that it is wrong to purchase those things, because in purchasing meat, fish, and eggs they are directly contributing towards the continuance of that trade, whereas we haven't asked for it, we haven't sought for it, you know, and our intention would simply be to sustain life.'

There is a clear distinction being made here between the responsibilities of the monk and the responsibilities of the layperson. Ven. Hambantota believes that people should be vegetarians in general, but there is an implication that ultimately the onus lies most on the laypeople since they are the ones engaged in the worldly activity of sale and purchase.

In the end, Ven. Hambantota believes that Buddhism does encourage vegetarianism. In this regard he is one of the few monks sampled who is actually committed to such a position. 'The entire teachings and their emphasis on harmlessness, by definition, encourages [that practice].' He added that, 'Because of the mass availability of various highly nutritious foods, it seems to me personally that nowadays vegetarianism is in keeping with the times. ... I follow the Buddha's admonition – if that's the word – to use one's own intelligence and to make one's own independent decisions about the given issue.'

Ven. Hambantota is one of the few monks to clearly utilise the principle of non-violence as a reason for why vegetarianism is necessary. It is interesting to observe that the first precept plays a significant role in determining appropriate diet amongst the lay informants. But amongst the monks, what is usually the most important factor when considering diet is prudence.

Another monk of some importance, Ven. Gampaha (from Dambura Vihāra), resided in Kandy and is affiliated closely with the Māligāva. His views have already been mentioned in chapter two. Ven. Gampaha is impressed by vegetarianism and regarded it as an exemplary diet that is encouraged by Buddhism. Like his other colleagues, his reasoning is in part prudential and concerned with the fact that he perceives vegetarianism to be exceptionally healthy.

He claims that Buddhism encourages vegetarianism because, 'the nutrients that you get from meat come from vegetables.' The non-eating of meat also entails other cosmetic benefits. For example, 'One experience I have had is that even when you raise a dog without meat or fish, even after a week of not bathing it doesn't smell. A dog that eats meat and fish, if not bathed for a couple of days, [it smells].' The connection between meat eating and body odour is made in another Buddhist text, the *Laṅkāvatāra Sūtra*, though this *sūtra* is a notable Mahāyāna *sūtra*. The *Laṅkāvatāra Sūtra* is well known for containing a chapter that claims that the Buddha himself preached vegetarianism and one of the reasons supplied is that it vegetarianism creates a neutral odour, while meat eating leads to one omitting a foul stench.[15]

These reasons were all prudential of course. Yet, Ven. Gampaha does imply that vegetarianism is connected with improved care of animals and that those who treat animals well are karmically rewarded. Contrary to the views espoused by other monks, these observations suggest that vegetarianism is connected to the Buddhist moral world after all.

To illustrate his point, Ven. Gampaha tells the following story: 'I have experienced this and because of that I have received no harm from animals. Not on any day have I been harmed by a serpent, for example. One day, soon after the passing of [a colleague] I had this experience. We had to make a [fire] so we cut a tree in a small forest. There was Saratuvi, Gunana, Yasitha, Nilamayi and myself. Nilamayi was the one that cut the tree, the others were clearing the leaves. Nilamayi is a person who doesn't even eat Maldive fish. After the tree was cut, I walked away. I felt a great coldness over my foot. A python was going over my foot! I called Nilamayi and told him about it. It went over Nilamayi and my feet! I have never done any harm. On any given night I don't go out with a light [because he is not afraid of snakes]. I've never harmed an animal or a serpent. I am convinced that this is because I don't kill animals. I will never even kill an ant.'

Ven. Gampaha and his friend Nilamayi are both concerned with the welfare of animals. Ven. Gampaha is scrupulous in avoiding the death of animals while Nilamayi, on the other hand, is also a vegetarian.

According to Ven. Gampaha, it is through their shared moral prowess that they avoided being attacked by the python. This indicates that Ven. Gampaha accepts that there is moral efficacy in avoiding the killing of animals and also in avoiding institutions that support that killing. The acceptance of the latter principle is something that is actively avoided by most of the other monks. This is what sets Ven. Gampaha and Ven. Hambantota apart from the others; they both believe that vegetarianism is a facet of animal welfarism and therefore connected intimately to the first precept of nonviolence.

This, of course, did not mean that Ven. Gampaha is himself a vegetarian. Indeed, Ven. Gampaha is sceptical of lay people who give vegetarian food at *dāna* ceremonies because he believes that sometimes their motives are wrong: 'The problem is this: today I think that people sometimes make a *dāna* and say, "We don't put meat and fish, unholy foods, [in this meal]" and they say this for the world to see (*lōkiyaṭa pennā*).' He goes on to add that, 'We can talk about people who give vegetarian food as being better Buddhists. But if you only offer vegetables over the *sīl* gown [the white clothing worn by laity] …we cannot accept people doing bad deeds. People who offer meat and fish sometimes could be more a more virtuous person. [Those vegetarians] do it to show it to the world.'

His concern is that such *dāyaka* might give a vegetarian *dāna* only with the objective of glorifying themselves by presenting themselves as pious Buddhists. This complaint contrasts with the concern of Nawanga, mentioned in chapter two, who maintains that giving a vegetarian *dāna* might lead to accusations of miserliness or thriftiness. What we learn, therefore, is that providing a vegetarian *dāna* is fraught with many social perils. Small wonder, then, that *dāyaka* typically refrain from giving them.

The Organisation for the Preservation of Life

Perhaps one of the most public and well-coordinated animal welfare groups in Sri Lanka is the Organisation for the Preservation of Life (hereafter, 'Organisation'). The group is ostensibly an animal welfare organisation that promotes vegetarianism, but it is also deeply invested in cow protectionism. The relationship between vegetarianism and cow protectionism is intertwined in complex ways. The next chapter will be reserved for a detailed discussion of cow protectionism in Sri Lanka, but in this section cow protectionism will inevitably be discussed in elucidating the Organisation's views on vegetarianism and animal welfare.

The Organisation is operated almost exclusively by a lone monk who remains somewhat idiosyncratic, not only in terms of his chosen extracurricular activities, but also in terms of his general demeanour. Ven. Koswatte, unlike the other monks interviewed, is a politically savvy monk who is engaged in public animal welfare activism. This would likely be considered unmonkly by some members of the laity and certainly by a reasonable number of clergy. The unusual characteristics of this monk should be made clear in part because it highlights a point made earlier, namely, that charismatic and idiosyncratic monks are sometimes involved in unusual fringe activities such as animal welfarism or other political activities. Indeed, Ven. Koswatte is holistically involved in other social welfare activities. The building in which the Organisation is based doubles as a school for disadvantaged children and also backs onto a Hindu shrine room. The reason the temple is dedicated to Shiva is important will be apparent when Sri Lankan cow veneration is discussed in more detail in the next chapter.

Ven. Koswatte, favours vegetarianism: 'Eating the flesh of another animal is not good. We love our own lives. ... If we don't like dying and we don't like suffering, if we don't like being beaten, if we don't like facing pain, well, the way we love our bodies is the same as every animal. Only they are not able to say so. Whether it be a fish, a wild animal, or even the worm in our stomachs, they really love their lives. We don't have the right to take away that life. The Buddha Dharma states that wisdom.'

Unlike many of the other monastic informants Ven. Koswatte recognises a connection between the slaughter of animals and meat consumption. Moreover, he adopts an argument based on a sympathetic understanding of the animal's circumstance in order to motivate his general view on vegetarianism. This argument is very similar to pro-vegetarianism arguments propagated by the lay vegetarian Nawanga and the author Sudasinha. Humans and animals are similar in that they both want to live and want to avoid suffering. This shared understanding should lead us to avoid practices that hurt animals.

Protecting the first precept of nonviolence is critical because it ensures that we will be reborn well: 'We travel to the next life like this, like a train moving along the tracks. If you think in a bad way, only bad things will come into one's mind anyway ... When this cage that is a body departs, where it goes, what happens to it, we can't say. We get together, we lose each other, we become a human, we become a demi-god, we go to hell...we don't know. ... Now if we protect the goodness of the precepts then we'll ensure a good rebirth from generation to generation.' For Ven. Kosgoda it goes without saying that protecting the first precept necessarily involves the adoption of vegetarianism, if for no other reason that it helps cultivate the right mental state and the right disposition towards animalkind. This, in turn, has certain prudential advantages – such as a good rebirth.

Ven. Kosgoda is quite clear that the Organisation's media campaigns are mainly concerned with the protection of cows and the promotion of milk drinking. Nonetheless, underlying this concern is an interest in propagating vegetarianism. He is also involved in other political measures such as petitioning the police to take action against abattoirs and animal abusers. His organisation is also involved in rescuing cows from slaughterhouses.

I will discuss the politicisation and militarisation of the cow protection movement in Chapter 5.

The Organisation's literature is considerable. They run adverts in newspapers, have billboards located around the city, produce posters, and even have bumper stickers. The bumper sticker, for example, features an image of Śiva, Pārvatī, and Kāmadhenu the mother of all cows. Milk flows from Kāmadhenu's teats. The text reads: 'Mine: From the five products of the cow there is a prosperous nation. Yours: The cow mother is treasured by every Sinhalese. Theirs: The empty and cruel people who kill her and consume her meat. Mother's: It's like consuming the flesh of the mother who gave you birth.'[16] This promotional material helps demonstrate a key tactic in the *Organisation's* media campaign: the cross-fertilisation of cow protectionism rhetoric with anti-meat-eating discourse. It is already widely accepted – for reasons discussed in the next chapter – that cows are sacred, but by referring to the rejection of meat eating in general the *Organisation* is able to draw a parallel between these the abstention of cow flesh and the abstention from meat more generally.

The Organisation's position on vegetarianism, the consumption of milk and the respect we owe to cows is highlighted by one of their promotional posters. It is a design decorated with bright colours and features the image of a grazing cow accompanied by her calf. It reads:

> Let us protect cows as if they were our mothers.
>   You are a Sri Lankan. A glass of milk is the first food consumed by people young and old when they get up in the morning.
>   Your body wakes up and the milk energises you. A brain as developed as ours tells us not to give an animal's blood, flesh, nerves, and everything in between.
>   All milk is made from blood, flesh, and nerves. When we eat these tasty things who are we? Are we human?
>   Concerning that, it's the right time for Sri Lankans to give this a lot of thought and take action about what's going on.

Let's ensure that cows in this country receive a natural death instead of being cruelly murdered by the hands of human beings.

To satisfy that end, let all people unite in this name. Concerning that, call the telephone number or address below. Provide your name, address, and telephone number.

[Contact details provided].[17]

The poster makes it clear that meat consumption is wrong. Indeed, it is downright inhumane. It is simply a matter of moral intuition that we should not consume animal flesh. This is all tied up with a cow protectionist discourse, but it is also apparent that, for the Organisation, cow protectionism and vegetarianism fundamentally intersect.

One other notable aspect of these documents is the role that nationality and ethnicity play. The bumper sticker states that the cow is treasured by 'every Sinhalese.'

Under such a nationalist discourse to be Sinhalese, properly speaking, is to be a Buddhist. Even Christian Sinhalese are excluded from such an account because these Sinhalese are often considered to be traitors to their race. In this way, there is an ethno-political element that is being introduced in these documents. It is the Buddhist Sinhalese that protect cows in Sri Lanka – not the Muslims or Tamils. This is also reflected in the poster where we find statements such as 'you are Sri Lankan.' This might be assumed to be an inclusivist statement intended to gather all the different religions and ethnicities of the island. But this would likely be a misinterpretation. As we learn in Chapter 7 the cow protectionist movement is highly invested in a pro-Sinhala political agenda.

This was actually made clear by Ven. Kosgoda. He believes that Buddhists care about animals more than other religions. He says that this was, 'Because Sinhala Buddhists, more than other religions, feel that Sri Lanka is a Buddhist country. This is our country. There's that philosophy and that's the first thing. ... Other religions, Christians, Muslims, Hindus – there *are* very devoted Hindus – but with Muslims, they don't really think about animals, they don't think about compassion or love, they don't think about people. The people in our country think about people, they protect the first precept of nonviolence.'

This special animosity towards Muslims in regards to their treatment of animals become increasingly clear and reaches a fever pitch when it comes to the subject of *halāl*. This will be addressed in greater detail in Chapter 7. That chapter is exclusively concerned with the intersection of politics and the animal welfare movement of Sri Lanka. To a lesser extent this will also be addressed in Chapter 5, which is concerned with cow protectionism. However, Ven. Kosgoda's views serve as a primer to this complex discussion.

This, of course, harks back to an issue raised earlier: many monks are, presumably, resistant to participating in animal welfarism because it is not their responsibility. This is obviously not the case for all monks, as we learn with Ven. Kosgoda. Likewise, the monks that found nationalist political organisations like Bŏdu Bala Sēnā and Jātika Hĕḷa Urumaya are also apparently immune from such concerns. Moreover, it is important to note that there is a clear break between what is expected of the clergy themselves and what is expected of them by the laity when it comes to the question of whether ethical vegetarianism is considered a warranted dietary practice. It is this issue that will be addressed in the next section.

Protestant Buddhism

The laity that were interviewed in this study are generally supportive of ethical vegetarianism and regard it as a critical implication of Buddhism. This is the case even in instances where a layperson did not themselves practice vegetarianism. Many people regarded vegetarianism as a necessary result of any serious understanding of the first precept.

On the other hand, the clergy, barring certain cases, were largely indifferent to ethical vegetarianism if not downright hostile. Why is there such a split between the opinions of the clergy and the opinions of the laity? Wouldn't one expect the clergy's opinions, who are supposedly an authority on matters of Buddhist doctrine, to be reflected in the opinions of the laity? This break between the views expressed by the clergy and the views of the laity requires some explanation. The break can in part be explained through so-called Protestant Buddhism.

Protestant Buddhism is a label applied to Buddhism as it developed in Sri Lanka (then Ceylon) leading up to Sri Lanka's independence. Heinz Bechert originally called this movement Buddhist Modernism, but Obeyesekere later argued that a better term is Protestant Buddhism and this term has since become a popular way of describing this period of Buddhist history in Sri Lanka and elsewhere.[18] In his article introducing this terminology, Obeyesekere writes: 'The term 'Protestant Buddhism' in my usage has two meanings. (1) As we have pointed out many of its norms and organizational forms are historical derivatives from Protestant Christianity. (2) More importantly, from the contemporary point of view, it is a protest *against* Christianity and its associated Western political dominance prior to independence.'[19]

Gombrich and Obeyeskere claim that the rise of Protestant Buddhism occurs in the latter part of the nineteenth century and found its roots especially within the educated middle class.[20]

Protestant Buddhism is in part a way Buddhism shifted from a primarily clerically driven religious movement with little lay input, to a form of Buddhism that is uniquely characterised by a vibrant lay community. Malalgoda notes that Olcott was pleased with transformation the lay community had undergone. During the revivalist period, the laity became more organised and unified.[21] There was a shift towards private ritual and individually accessible forms of the Buddhist religion.[22]

According to Obeyesekere these structural changes were modelled directly on Protestant missionaries active in Sri Lanka. The result was that the Sri Lankan Buddhist movement during the burgeoning modernist period of the 1890s increasingly began to adopt proselytising and adversarial methods to deal with European missionaries. As we saw in Chapter 1, there is evidence of such aggressiveness even earlier than this period (take for example, the *Carpenter Prēta Tale*).

As Obeyeskere points out, this involved the adoption of more overt symbols of Buddhism such as the erection of shrines on public roads, the creation of a Buddhist flag and the implementation of a so-called Buddhist catechism.[23] This overt way of displaying Buddhism was an explicit attempt to model, and thus combat, missionary practices. These modifications are why it is (controversially) called Protestant Buddhism by Obeyesekere and others. As with the case in Europe, this reformation was an organic process in which lay people began to have more direct involvement in shaping Sinhala Buddhism.

The concept of Protestant Buddhism, however, has been subject to some criticism. John Holt, for example, believes that the term is a misnomer because there is not sufficient commonality between Protestantism and Buddhism.[24] He argues that a better way of conceiving modern Buddhism might instead be as a kind of militant Buddhism.[25] Prothero's objection in part stems from his observation that the Protestant movement in Sri Lanka was not a unified movement and should not be treated as such.[26]

Despite these valid objections I have continued to use this term simply because it is the standard description in much of the literature. Furthermore, although the label is problematic, it is not totally unviable and it seems to me that the term should be understood as a kind of short-hand for an analogy which points towards some particular similarities between Buddhist modernism and Protestantism.

There is also a problem where Protestant Buddhism might be incorrectly construed as an exclusive product of Western influences. Richard King notes, however, that Buddhist revivalism was a direct response to engagement with the West – and was sometimes inspired by Western ideas – but was ultimately a response initiated by colonial subjects as a way to respond to Western cultural imperialism.[27] In this way, it was not only a reformation of how Buddhists themselves understood and reorganised their own conception of what Buddhism meant, but was also a way to respond to external forces that threatened the viability of Buddhism as a religion.

These methods were adopted as a way to counter European conversion attempts and roll back the tide of Christian and Western influence. As Gombrich shows, however, Christian missionary work was remarkably unsuccessful.[28] Colonial religious authorities were routinely puzzled and sometimes frustrated by the Buddhist clergy's initial liberality and willingness to engage with alternative religious traditions.[29] Regardless, missionaries began to more aggressively attack Buddhism and this led to an increase in animosity between Buddhists and Christian missionaries. Protestant Buddhism has remained an important way to understand Buddhism in contemporary Sri Lanka.

One of the features of this so-called Protestant Buddhism is a move towards a private religion that is less affected by monastic mores. This is apparent from the material presented here: some lay Buddhists regard the Buddha's teachings, when properly understood, to demand ethical vegetarianism. The fact that most monks may not agree entirely with this sentiment does not seem to impact lay opinion greatly. Some lay people believe that vegetarianism is an important feature of Buddhism and this is the case regardless – and sometimes precisely in spite of – how monks behave.

During the revivalist period, as Malalgoda observes, lay organisations were heavily influenced by the Theosophists. It may be recalled that one of the tenets of Olcott's Buddhism is a refusal to consume meat. This was laid out in his *Buddhist Catechisms*. It is possible that modern laity have inherited these general assumptions about the virtues of vegetarianism from Olcott and other Theosophists. On the other hand, the clergy ultimately became divorced from Theosophist influence. This split may explain some of these differences observed above.

Of course, there are some other important factors that may influence the difference in opinion between monks and lay people.

One, it is plausible that lay people and monks are simply unaware of each other's opinion. Indeed, monks may not even be aware of their brethren's opinion. This is indicated by one monk who was quite curious as to what other monks' opinions were on the question of vegetarianism since, as he put it, it was not a question that they ever discussed.

Two, it is likely that the different literature that lay people and monks are exposed to has some bearing on their general attitudes towards animals and vegetarianism. As mentioned in chapter one, monks spend a great deal of time studying the *Vinaya Piṭaka* and take its contents very seriously. The *Vinaya Piṭaka* of course, not only allows monks to eat meat, it also regards the killing of animals as only a minor offence. The laity, on the other hand, are exposed primarily to *Jātaka* tales and selections from the *Sūtra Piṭaka*. As argued previously, however, the *Jātakas* and *Sūtra Piṭaka* take animal violence much more seriously and generally treat animals as being on a moral and intellectual par with human beings. Lay people may pick up on these subtleties and may be more likely to cultivate a sensitive attitude towards animal life.

Another element of Protestant Buddhism is a strong lay activist tradition. Holt characterises this as a type of militancy. For him, modern Buddhism differs from pre-colonial Buddhism in that it is much more intolerant of difference.[30] As we shall see, especially in Chapter 7, modern lay animal activism is often expressed through the *hālal* abolitionism movement. Ethical vegetarianism, as a protest against animal killing, is another part of the animal welfare movement. The Organisation was well supported by the lay community and ethical vegetarianism, as a moral and political activity, was much more commonly supported by the laity than the monks.

However, as suggested earlier, charismatic monk leaders are very important in rallying support amongst the laity. These charismatic monks are often instrumental in developing lay activist initiatives. This is clear in the case of the *hālal* abolitionism movement, but also with the Organisation's cow protectionist activism. But these radical monks also tend to straddle the worldliness of the lay person and the monasticism of the clergy in a way that is not necessarily traditional.

Ven. Kosgoda, though a monk, is the very definition of a Protestant Buddhist leader. He was a non-typical Buddhist monk: he has a personal style, he is charismatic, and takes on the preaching style of a missionary or politician. This can be compared with the more traditional Buddhist monks who are much more withdrawn in their approach, are more reserved, and are unlikely to express themselves in overly emotional ways.

Gombrich explains the difference between modernist monks and traditional monks by comparing traditional monastic preaching behaviours to one of the founders of Protestant Buddhism, a monk called Guṇānanda: 'Traditionally Buddhist monks preach seated, and often hold a fan in front of their faces, in order to render the sermon as impersonal as possible. We know that Guṇānanda, at least in public debate, adopted the Christian style of preaching; he spoke standing, gesticulating, and generally acted the orator.'[31] Ven. Kosgoda's style was much more in the style of Guṇānanda's. Similarly, monks affiliated with Bŏdu Baḷa Sēnā and other political groups tended to be quite fiery and unmonkish in their public comportment.

This leads onto another element of Protestant Buddhism: Western influences on Buddhist activism. Protestant Buddhism is not only characterised by lay activism (and the activism of sympathetic monks), it is also characterised by a particular sort of activism: aggressive proselytising and adversarial politics. This is quite clear when we look especially at Ven. Kosgoda's comments and his view that Buddhism uniquely friendly towards animals while other religions, especially Islam, adopt a cruel attitude towards animal welfare. This adversarial approach is especially obvious in the case of the *hālal* abolitionism movement that will be discussed presently. In many ways, the *hālal* abolitionism movement is partly a product of long-standing Protestant Buddhist tendencies.

Protestant Buddhism also has a presence in the Sinhala Buddhist vegetarian movement which, as suggested in Chapter 1, is historically linked to anti-Christian (especially anti-Catholic) discourses. Vegetarianism is therefore an opportunity to protest against the inhumane and cruel practices of non-Buddhists. This shrill and hypercritical approach to non-Buddhist practices, conceived of as a way of protecting Buddhism, is much more common amongst the laity and more widely resisted amongst the clergy (which, as we see, is not to say that it is never adopted by them).

Conclusion

These differences between the clergy and the laity are already evident from the study of Sinhala literary works undertaken in Chapter 2. Gñanananda Thēra, for example, was aggressively against ethical vegetarianism. He allows for vegetarianism only as a 'private' activity and believes that monks should not justify it on doctrinal ground. Gñanananda Thēra, of course, is a monk. On the other hand, lay writers – such as Sudasinha and Ratnakāra – maintain that ethical vegetarianism is entirely justified by Buddhism and go to great lengths to show that it is not contrary to Buddhist doctrine.

This divide in the Sinhala literature between laity who are pro-vegetarian and monks that are anti-vegetarian again reinforces the significance of the Protestant Buddhist impulse, an impulse that tends to ally itself with the laity who seek to reform Buddhism. Monks, on the other hand, prefer traditions to be maintained.

Of course, we have also seen in this chapter that some monks buck against this traditionalist trend. Ven. Kosgoda is an obvious example here. There are other examples too, however. In Chapter 6 we will encounter another monk – Ven. Māhimipāṇan – who endorses vegetarianism for a range of reasons, though he chiefly supports it because he considers it to be a matter of health. While this would seem to satisfy some of the monks interviewed above, his proselytizing behaviour – and his tendency to allow his Buddhist convictions influence his views, would certainly be at odds with many of his colleague's restrictive views on proper monastic decorum.

Finally, Protestant Buddhism may at first appearance be a force for good as far as the vegetarian agenda is concerned. But as we shall see, Protestant Buddhism – as a force for change – also becomes caught up in political manoeuvring and therefore easily becomes entangled in the ethnic violence that sadly tends to consume Sri Lanka. We have already seen hints of this in the above discussion of Ven. Kosgoda. Animal welfarism, however innocent it may at first appear, also has a dark and violent side.

Notes

1 The practice of merit sharing has been well studied in the anthropological literature, though its doctrinal basis has often been questioned. See Gombrich (1991: 267, 378; 2008: 125–128), Gombrich (1991: 203–219). The reader may also like to consult Melford Spiro's work *Buddhism and Society* for information on merit sharing in Burma (124–128).
2 According to Gombrich's classification this type of *baṇa* is known as *dharma saṃvāda* or discourse on a doctrinal subject (1991: 321). Consistent with Gombrich's observation, the nature of such *baṇa* is usually informal in its manner of communication.
3 There are many reasons why laity might view particular monks as being more merit producing. For example, worshiping ascetic monks is considered especially merit producing. See Gombrich (1991: 326).
4 In accordance with the requirements of my ethics approval guidelines all temple and monk names are pseudonyms.
5 See for example: MN, 12.52, 175; MN, 36.6, 333; MN, 12.52, 176.
6 MN, 36.28–30, 339–340.
7 MN, 55.5: 474.
8 The sort of ascetic practice often takes the form of forest renunciation in Buddhism both historically and in modern times. The practice is widely discussed in the anthropology literature (Carrithers, 1983; Gombrich, 2008: 156–157; Bond, 1992: 68–69)

The disciple's diet 121

9   For full details of Devadatta as an object of criticism, and sometimes veneration, see Ray (162–173).
10 See for example: SN (46.49, 1620) and AN (22.8, 199). In the *Itivuttaka* it is claimed that excessive enjoyment of food can lead to cravings (Iti, 4.1.16, 192). In general, the texts encourage monks to regard food only as a fuel.
11 Gombrich (1971: 316–317) discusses the development and educational purpose of the *pirivena* in some detail. Also see De Silva (2005: 429) and Bond (1992: 69–70) for details on the political influence the *pirivena* has had.
12 This sort of argument is made by the following authors: Harvey (2000: 160), Horner (1967: 11), Keown (2005: 49), Seyfort-Ruegg (1980: 239). R.S. Khare also puts this idea in terms of the Hindu concept of *guna* (essence) and *rasa* (aesthetics): monks consume food only for the nutritional or essential content, not its cosmetic or aesthetic, i.e. taste, aspect (1992: 189).
13 One exception to this rule is Gombrich who writes, "In accordance with the principle that any Buddhist must avoid life, a monk must refuse to eat an animal which has been killed especially for him. Clearly, once the laity learn of this rule they will not slaughter an animal to feed the Sangha. In practice (though the *Vinaya* says nothing of this) it is feasible for a monk to let it be known the he would prefer not to eat meat" (2008: 102). This, of course, is precisely what happens. Moreover, it would be incoherent for this not to be the case, as I argue elsewhere, because monks are simply required to refuse certain types of food (Stewart, 2010: 111). Refusal as such is not necessarily prohibited in Buddhism.
14 See for example the following: Tambiah (96–101), Deegalle (3, 8) and Bartholomeusz (147–148).
15 Suzuki, 214.
16 *pas gorasin pubadana raṭa dæya – māge. vas thuva gava mavayi kavadat hĕḷa – yāge. his minisun marā mas kathinam – æge. mas kanavā væniya bihikaḷa – ammāge.*
17 *gava sampatha rakimu ape mava vage. srī lānkika oba. apa ude nægiṭa bŏna kirigiduraĕva lŏku kuḍā saĕmage paḷamu āhārayayi. oba sirura avadi karana ema kiri nipadavanne oba, apa tharam mōḷaya nŏdiyunu satekuge le, mas, nahara atarini. ese kiri nipaduvū le, mas, nahara api rasakara kanne nam, api kavuda? api minisun da? ĕ piḷibandava srī lānkika minisun api hŏndin sitā bæliya yutu kālaya eḷamba aĕta. apa rate upadina gavayanṭa – svābhāvika maranayak uruma karadĕnnaṭa minisun vana apa atin nŏmaĕrĕnnaṭa eyaṭa magak salasannaṭa api ekvĕmu minisatkame nāmayĕn, e sandahā pahata durakathana ankayanṭa amatanna. obe nam, lipinaya, durakathana ankaya labādĕnna.*
18 Obeyesekere, 1970.
19 Obeyesekere in Holt, 1991: 307.
20 Gombrich and Obeyesekere, 202.
21 Malalgoda, 247–248.
22 Holt does object even to this claim (1991: 309).
23 Holt, 1991: 307.
24 Holt, 309.
25 Holt, 1991: 307, 310.
26 Prothero, 298.
27 King, 152.
28 Gombrich, 2008: 176–177.
29 Holt, 310.
30 Holt, 310–311.
31 Gombrich, 2008: 181.

5 Milk of life

Cow veneration and milk consumption in Sinhala Buddhist society

It is difficult to miss the large animal welfare billboards displayed at key intersections throughout Colombo. One such billboard, located on Galle Road, shows a monk bending over and touching a grazing calf.

This act should be considered in context to other monkly behaviours. In particular, monks often touch the crown of the head of a worshipper whilst uttering the words '*suvapat vēvā*' or 'may you be happy.' Such actions are almost always reserved, however, for human beings. To find this physical interaction between a monk and a cow is a considerable statement that exemplifies the Buddhist virtue of compassion and loving kindness being supplied to all living creatures, not just the human ones.

The text that accompanies this peaceful image is even more striking. It asks, 'how can we humans look at this playful face which mother nature has given this animal and then consume its flesh?'[1] This rhetorical question excites a genuine feeling of sympathy in many Sinhala Buddhists. Cows are held in very high regard in Sri Lanka, not only amongst the Hindu Tamil community but also, and perhaps more surprisingly, amongst the Sinhalese. A second billboard, this time located in Dehiwala, has the image of a cow emblazoned on it. The text reads, 'Don't eat the milk mother's flesh' and 'Let's protect the cow as we would our mothers.'[2] Again, the billboard encourages observers not to eat cow meat. Talk of other animals is noticeably absent. Furthermore, the billboard connects the protection of cows to the protection of our own mothers.

A more recent billboard (2015) shows the image of a mother nursing a baby with the text, 'The mother's milk is for six months.' Next to that is a family surrounding a cow. The text above it reads: 'The cow's milk lasts throughout your entire life.'[3] It ends with the same refrain 'Let's protect the cow as we would our mother.'

It is clear from such billboards that there is a concerted campaign in Sri Lanka to promote the protection of cows. This cow protection movement is fundamentally related to two other movements: (1) the vegetarian and animal welfare movement more generally understood; and also (2) the *halāl* abolitionism movement. The vegetarian and animal welfare movement is much less politically organised and is present in pamphlets and booklets authored by individual crusaders. Though as we saw in Chapter 2, there is a Vegetarian Society of Sri Lanka and this organisation does avoid the obvious militancy of the other movements. Nonetheless, vegetarian organisations are also preoccupied with the better treatment of cows and often discuss their virtues.

The *hālal* abolitionism movement, which is essentially a more outspoken extension of the cow protection movement, is much more radical and politically active. Unlike the vegetarian and animal welfare movement, the *hālal* abolitionist movement is not composed primarily of lone activists and loose collectives but is a highly visible movement with considerable presence in the Sri Lankan, and even international, media.

These groups engage in activities that especially target the religion of Islam and the wider Sri Lankan Muslim community. This is based around the idea that Islamic religious practices are especially harmful to cows. The *hālal* abolitionism movement only makes sense, however, in connection to the wider cow protection movement. *Hālal* abolitionism will therefore be covered in considerable detail in Chapter 7.

Why are cows so special?

Many Sinhalese are incensed by Islamic practices in particular because many Sinhalese favour the cow over other animals. This oddity requires explanation, especially in light of earlier observations that Buddhism regards all animals as having equal moral worth.

In Chapter 2 it was argued that the Buddha preached that all sentient creatures – and therefore most animals – should not be harmed and this is enshrined in the first precept of non-violence. It is clear that this has led a number of Buddhists to adopt vegetarian practices as a way to express their rejection of violence conducted in the animal slaughter trade. Given this egalitarian perspective, how is it that cows are treated with special veneration and respect? This chapter is concerned with addressing this basic question.

This brings us back to the billboards previously mentioned. These billboards were designed and funded by the Organisation for the Preservation of Life, an organisation discussed in Chapter 4. This group, run by a charismatic and politically active monk called Ven. Kosgoda, produces a large amount of marketing material to prosecute the argument that people should not eat beef and should be respectful of cows.

In order to contextualise these cow protectionist cases, a more general understanding of Sri Lankan cow protectionism is required. For example, there are also notable similarities between cow protectionism in Sri Lanka and cow protectionism in India. I will argue that the origins of Sri Lankan cow protectionism are in part owed to Indian influences. Consequently, examining the history of cow protectionism in India is vital.

Cow protection in India

The following statement by Mohandas Gandhi gives us some idea of at least one strand of thought present in India concerning the value of the cow and its place as an objection of veneration: 'Our mother gives us milk for a couple of years and then expects us to serve her when we grow up. Mother cow expects from us nothing but grass and grain. Our mother often falls ill and expects service from us. Mother cow rarely falls ill. Our mother when she dies means expenses of burial or cremation. Mother cow is as useful dead as when alive.'[4]

This rather severe review does show us just how highly regarded the cow is in India during the period of the Indian independence movement. Things have changed little today, and the cow is still regarded with a level of unprecedented respect. This observation has been confirmed by various Indologists. In 1912 Crooke wrote that Hindus feel 'passionate devotion' towards the cow[5] while the more contemporaneous Gabriella Eichinger Ferro-Luzzi observes that, 'In the animal realm, the bovines enjoy the widest worship. The Hindu veneration of the cow has taken root among tribal communities and is still spreading.'[6] Cow protection is sometimes even extended to buffalo and other bovine animals.[7]

This non-violent attitude towards cows in India has not always been the norm, however. As Alsdorf (2010) and Jha (2004) both illustrate, special protection towards cows was not afforded in the Vedic and post-Vedic literature. This literature forms the basis of Hinduism as we know it today, and yet despite the fact that Hindus lean heavily on their religion as a way to support their non-violent position towards cows, the *Vedas* are actually quite encouraging of cow slaughter. The *Vedas* specify that the cow can be sacrificed to the gods[8] and, in fact, it is considered an especially auspicious animal to sacrifice. This slaughter ultimately led to the ritual consumption of beef as a way to imbibe the blessing of the gods. Cow slaughter was therefore critical in the early Vedic tradition.

This is, in fact, the origin of contemporary cow veneration in India, though the practice has been completely transformed such that cows are protected rather than killed. There is a commonality in both activities insofar that, in both cases, cows are uniquely venerated and considered animals of value. In the Vedic case, cows are highly valued because they confer great merit when they are sacrificed; in modern Hinduism, on the other hand, the cow is regarded as being intrinsically valuable and for that reason should not be scarificed.

Yet the straightforward historical observation that the cow has not always been subject to modern principles of non-violence does not sit well with Hindu nationalist groups. When Jha released his book *The Holy Cow* (2004) there was widespread protest in India because it denied the presumption that the cow has always been unkillable. This protest was led by Hindu nationalist groups who maintained that such claims were blasphemous and a slight to the Hindu religion. Ultimately, *The Holy Cow* was discontinued in India.[9] This remarkable turn of events shows just how politicised cow protectionism is in

India and how the cow protection movement is tied up with nationalist agendas. As we shall see in Chapter 7, the same is true in Sri Lanka where cow protectionism is also connected to nationalist ideology.

Why is the modern cow so important in modern India? One point is that cow protectionism was a rallying point for Indians during the independence movement. Hindus were already opposed to the consumption of cow flesh while British imperialists aggressively killed and consumed beef. This point of difference was something that could be readily exploited by Hindu independence leaders in order to raise passions amongst the general population.

This historical difference between the British and the Indians over the sacredness of the cow was something that also came between the Sinhalese Buddhists and European colonists as will be discussed shortly. Similarly, the cow has been used as a rallying point for patriotic Sinhalese in modern Sri Lanka too. This will be made clear in Chapter 7.

Yet this point of difference still does not explain their apparent sacredness. Perhaps the most important cause of this perceived sacredness is the rise of the deity Kāmadhenu, the endlessly lactating cow. Kāmadhenu is critically connected to the role of the nursing mother, and the feminine more generally. To worship and respect Kāmadhenu is to respect and worship one's own mother as is clear from the Gandhi passage mentioned above.

There are various myths related to the origin of Kāmadhenu, who is generally depicted as a cow. One myth is that she arose from a great ocean of milk after it was churned by the gods.[10] Another story says that she was born from the side of Krishna.[11] Kāmadhenu is significant because she is connected to, and represents, the action of oblations where milk and its derivatives are poured.[12] In this way, Kāmadhenu is an important background deity that plays a critical supporting role in any devotional act of sacrifice. This significance is projected onto cows in general and they are consequently regarded as lifegivers who are deeply tied up with the fundamentals of Hindu religious life.

In the case of Sri Lanka, Kāmadhenu arises as an important figure both in the Tamil and the Sinhalese context. This is somewhat unexpected given that the Sinhalese are predominately Buddhist. In Sri Lanka, however, it is not Kāmadhenu who is directly venerated, but a different manifestation of her, namely Kiri Ammā (Milk Mother).

The Kiri Ammā cult critically underpins the entire cow protectionist movement in Sri Lanka and features, in explicit and implicit ways, in much of their literature. Despite the obvious fact that the Kiri Ammā cult has its origins in the worship of Kāmadhenu, the latter god is hardly known in Sri Lanka. Kiri Ammā, however, is an entirely ubiquitous name.

Cow protection in Sri Lanka

As mentioned, it is remarkable just how significant cows are to the Sinhalese given that (1) the majority of Sinhalese are Buddhists and therefore perhaps wouldn't, *prima facie*, share the Hindu enthusiasm for cows; and (2) Buddhism encourages non-violence to all animals equally. Nonetheless, the origin of Sinhalese Buddhist cow protectionism shares a commonality with the Indian cow protection movement, albeit with a unique Sinhala Buddhist angle. The cow protectionism movement has spread to other Buddhist nations too, and the most obvious case here is Burma.[13]

There is another important ethnic group in Sri Lanka that has a vested interest in the protection of cows: the Hindu Tamils. Their connection to the welfare of cows is more obvious given the Sri Lankan Hindu Tamil's common cultural and religious connection to mainland India. As with Indian Hindu Tamils, Sri Lankan Hindu Tamils hold the cow in high regard. One deviation is that unlike their Indian brethren they recognise Kāmadhenu as Kiri Ammā just like their Sinhalese counterparts.

Hindu Tamils also participate in festivals and rituals that are not otherwise engaged in by the Sinhalese. For example, the festival of Thai Pongal is an important celebration for Hindu Tamils in India and Sri Lanka. Thai Pongal is a harvest festival in which food is shared within the community and it is an opportunity for people to come together regardless – or even in spite of – caste and economic differences.[14] It is also a time where cattle are subject to special treatment and acts of worship. Gough describes these events: 'In Thanjāvūr the day after Pongal was even more important than Pongal proper. This day, called Māṭṭu Pongal, or 'Bullock Pongal,' marked the worship of cattle. *Paṇaiyāls* bathed their landlords' cattle in the early morning, painted their horns gay colors, garlanded them with flowers, and adorned them with yellow saffron powder and red *kungumam*. Tenant cultivators washed and decorated their own cattle and prostrated themselves before them in worship and thanksgiving for the harvest.'[15]

Thai Pongal is therefore a time when cows are explicitly recognised as being unique and important animals in Hindu Tamil society.[16] Thai Pongal is a festival of importance also for Hindu Tamil Sri Lankans.

The importance of the cow during Thai Pongal is also illustrated by activities involving the preparation of milk rice (*kiri bat*). Milk rice is a food eaten at special times both amongst Hindu Tamils (India and Sri Lanka) and Sinhalese Sri Lankans. It is a celebratory food that highlights the two most important sources of nourishment in Sri Lankan society: milk and rice.[17] Although milk rice is the first food to be prepared and eaten on almost any auspicious day (such as birthdays and New Year) it is especially important for Tamil Thai Pongal festivities. It is fundamentally connected to the entire purpose of the festival, namely to celebrate the harvest and to promote a bountiful crop of food in the coming year. Milk rice, in this context, refers to the hope for bountiful food and widespread prosperity. This is also reflected in the importance of the cow, an animal that is a key source of food and is therefore recognised and worshiped as such.

Hindu Tamils recognise the importance of the cow in other ways, however. Cow dung, for example, is regarded as sacred and its ash is used in various

Hindu rituals. This is the case both in India and Sri Lanka. Rowan Bastin observes that cow dung is a central aspect of rituals conducted at the Munnesvaram Temples in Eastern Sri Lanka and, in particular, is used for the sacred markings of deity images.[18] Bastin also notes that other cow products – milk, curd, ghee, dung, and urine – that is, the five products of the cow as it is known, are used regularly in various rituals. The recognition of these five products, as we will see, is also clear in the case of the Sinhala Buddhist worship of the cow. Cow milk is also critical. Not only is it a central ingredient of milk rice, it is used unsparingly in Hindu rituals amongst Tamil Saivites in the course of celebrations at the Munnesvaram temple.[19] This is most obvious during the so-called flag hoisting ceremony. As Bastin describes it, the ceremony involves hundreds of litres of milk being spilt as the temple flag is raised. The action is meant to illustrate the possibility of bountiful prosperity and milk is central in this imagery.

The spilling of milk in this way is present in other rituals, however, and this brings us back to the case under specific examination here: the Sinhalese Buddhist community. At the start of the Sri Lankan New Year the household engages in a number of rituals perhaps the most indispensible of all being the milk boiling ceremony. In the morning, the family assembles together – usually in the kitchen. There, a small clay pot is placed over an open flame and milk poured inside. In due course, the milk boils over the lip of the pot and the direction from where this happens will determine the fortune of the family in the coming year.

At the ceremony I attended, the milk boiled in an inauspicious direction but no one paid this any heed. An unfortunate result does not seem to warrant much attention. The significance of this act is more to do with the symbolism of the ceremony. Like Thai Pongal, it is essentially a harvest ritual in which it is hoped that food will be plentiful, and wealth easy to come by, in the coming year. The milk boiling over the side is a symbol of fertility and a bountiful harvest. Milk is therefore an important symbol in Sinhala culture. Likewise, the cow is also critical as it is responsible for the production of the milk.

These various rituals and celebrations all show just how important the cow is throughout Sri Lankan society. As is clear from the previous section, it is perhaps unremarkable that Hindu Tamils venerate the cow and hold it in high regard. After all, a combination of religious and nationalist factors has led to the special recognition of the cow in India.

What is unusual, will soon be apparent, is the way in which the cow is so fundamentally respected in Sinhala Buddhist society. This special reverence for the cow amongst the Sinhalese has historic roots, however. Peiris, writing about the Portuguese occupation, notes that, 'They [the Sinhalese] had inherited the Hindu reverence for the cow, and none would eat beef save the outcaste.'[20]

As we saw in Chapter 1, Robert Knox, whilst imprisoned in the Kandyan Kingdom in the seventeenth century, similarly notes that beef eating was considered 'abominable' and that foreign colonists were repudiated for their purported consumption of cows.[21] Robert Percival, writing in 1803, makes similar observations. He writes, 'The Cinglese supply our garrisons plentifully with beef, fowls, eggs, and other articles of the same sort, at a very moderate rate, as they seldom make use of them for their own consumption: *beef in particular they never taste, as the cow is an object of their worship*' (my italics).[22]

In more recent times this cow protectionism has been reinforced by modern Sri Lankan groups such as the All Ceylon Buddhist Congress that, as we saw in Chapter 1, urged all Sri Lankan's to give up the consumption of beef on the grounds that it is disrespects the importance of rice cultivation since the cow is fundamental in the development of rice crops.[23] This organisation has consequently sought to ban the slaughter of cattle completely in Sri Lanka. As we shall see, other organisations with a more nationalist anti-Muslim agenda have adopted this goal as well. We will discuss these groups and their views in more detail in the final chapter of this book.

This unusual respect for cows may be regarded as unexpected as Buddhism tends to regard all animals as being of equal moral worth. Doctrinally, even killing small insects is not allowed. While it is true that there is a ranking of some animals above others, it is also the case that killing animals as such is forbidden and this is quite unlike the Hindu case where some animals are simply born to be slaughtered. Yet modern Hindu Indians and modern Sinhala Buddhists seem to both share a special respect for the cow. We can understand why this is the case for Hindu Indians and Hindu Sri Lankan Tamils, but why is this the case for Sinhalese Buddhists? Let us begin by examining the extent of this cow veneration amongst the Sinhalese.

Cow protection in the media

Sinhala newspapers and media are full of stories that concern the welfare of cows. The frequency of these stories illustrates the popularity of cow welfarism amongst the Sinhalese and there is a shared sense of justice when the antagonist in these stories suffers a miserable fate as a result of their cruel actions towards cows. As discussed in Chapter 2, *Lankadīpa's Taksalāva* collects letters sent by readers that detail the stories of evil deeds done by immoral individuals towards animals and humans alike. The stories always include vivid descriptions of their karmic punishment. Often these stories involve cows.

For example, one submitted story tells of a man who works as a caretaker on a pineapple plantation. 'With his intense love of flesh, he shot dead and consumed the flesh of monitor lizards, porcupines, rabbits, and small deer. In addition, his love of meat resulted in animals such as bats and monkeys becoming his morning meal.'[24]

The type of animals that this individual eats is already indicative of his gross moral incompetence. The consumption of animals like monitor lizards and monkeys is considered completely unpalatable, and especially immoral, to the majority of Sri Lankans regardless of ethnicity. The article continues: 'His most sinful action was that he killed a cow for its flesh.'[25]

As discussed in Chapter 2, articles like this often relish in the details and method of the animal's death as it adds to the sensationalism of the piece and tugs at the emotional heart-strings of the reader who feels great compassion for the suffering of the animal.

Hence the following, 'The specialty of this man was that he used a method that was unique to him. It involves using a thick rope. Initially he would tie a knot in the middle of the rope and put this knot around the animal's neck. Afterwards he would tie the loose ends of this rope onto two adjacent trees. When the animal realizes that it is getting choked by the knot it tries to flee but only ends up tightening the knot further. Once the animal starts choking the man leaves the location and heads home. The cow will continue to struggle resulting in further strangulation and eventually after a significant amount of suffering the animal finally dies with its tongue sticking out. The man revisits the location the next morning in order to harvest the flesh of the dead cow.'[26]

This graphic account allows the reader to feel especially justified when the perpetrator subsequently perishes after being dragged through the pineapple plantation by a panicked cow. This results in his arms and legs being broken and ultimately receiving fatal injuries.

Another story from the *Taksalāva* series further illustrates the market for sensational tales of animal cruelty that reinforces the prevailing idea that justice will be reached through the operation of karma. The story is titled, *'The man who ate the cow's tongues'* (*harakungē diva kæ minihā*) and the story begins, 'There was a man who was engaged in the killing of cows. He loved eating cows tongues. He would pull their tongue out while being slaughtered and slice it off. His wife got the tongues and seasoned and cooked them.'[27]

As is commonly the case with stories of this type, the author takes some time to express in detail the suffering and hardship the animal is forced to undergo. These descriptive accounts further illustrate the cruelty and depravity of the antagonist who usually takes special effort to ensure the animal's prolonged misery: 'He would first open the cow's mouth and then bind its neck [with a rope] to two columns in order to stop the animal's head from moving around. Afterwards he would use a sharp knife to expertly slice off the tongue. He is so quick in doing this that often the animal has no clue as to what is happening.'[28]

The story goes onto add that the man especially enjoyed the taste of young calves as their flesh is sweeter. The horror of torturing calves is of course especially repugnant to many Sinhala Buddhists.

As with story above, the antagonist comes to an unpleasant end when a blister begins to appear on his tongue. It is not by accident that it is his tongue that is afflicted. As already discussed, karmic results are often thought to reflect – in very precise ways – the crimes that caused them. Therefore, because the man tortured cows by abusing their mouth and tongue, it is his mouth and tongue that will ultimately cause him to suffer and lead to his downfall. Even after visiting a hospital and taking medicine, his affliction did not end (thus also showing that medicine is no match for the laws of karma which effectively violate natural laws relating to biology confirming that karma is a supernatural process). 'Because of the difficulty of his tongue and taking medication he didn't stop eating the tongues of cows. Even though a slaughterer friend said, 'You have to let it go,' but it was difficult for him to stop eating cow tongue knowing how delicious it was.'[29] Again, a Buddhist theme emerges in his consumption of cow flesh: craving. His craving for cow tongue, even after it is obvious that it is the cause of his suffering, continues to steer him on a path towards death. The end results are disastrous: 'During this time blisters spread all over his tongue. His doctors decided to cut his tongue off.'[30] The story tells us that the tongue was cancerous. But even after his tongue was removed the man continues to harbour an obsession for cows' tongues – in other words, he still has a craving for the food. Eventually, the cancer re-emerged and the man 'suffered and died'.

From these stories there are two important observations: first, the killing of these animals leads to the production of negative karma that inevitably results in a punishment poetically suited to the crime. In the latter case his love of tongues leads to a death that starts with a cancer of the tongue; in the former case the man is dragged through a pineapple plantation and dies after enduring immense suffering – not only is it the same location where he tortured and killed cows, he is also forced to endure the same level of suffering. Also, second, desire plays a significant role in these affairs. This is especially clear in the latter cases where it is explicitly stated that the man has a craving for cow flesh. The point that is being communicated here is the fact that craving is the ultimate source of the bad conduct. Recall that in Chapter 3 Sanduni Akka lamented the fact that desire was an obstacle to her adopting vegetarianism. This is reflected here too where the man is dragged down by his baser desires.

A third point, more specific to this discussion of cow slaughter, is the descriptive nature of the cow's suffering and ultimate death. This is not a trivial matter because these descriptions are connected to a general feeling of sympathy towards cows that is not always shared with other animals. The details of the cow slaughter trade, and its tendency to excite annoyance and disapproval in Sinhalese Buddhists, is clear from an article in *Mavbīma*.

The article is based around an interview conducted with a cow slaughterer. In particular, the article is dealing with the practice of *halal* methods of animal slaughter and therefore takes on an anti-Islamic tone – this already indicates the way in which the cow protection movement is associated with anti-Muslim sentiment as we shall see in Chapter 7. It is clear that the purpose of the interview is to illustrate the immorality of cow slaughter in particular. The title of the article is in fact a sentimental poem. It reads:

Four legs: tied
Snouts pressed to the ground: it is done

Taking a cleaver: one strike
Necks cut straight: it is done.[31]

The author begins his story by noting that there are many different languages all over the world and that most of them are not interpretable to us. He then draws a parallel between cows and human beings by asking what language cows speak and what they would say to us.

Having gripped the audience with this sympathetic question he then proceeds to give a lively and bloody account of how cows are slaughtered. He writes, 'After that we bring the animal to the killing shed. The slaughterer should never bring the cow. Somehow, having brought the animal, the cow is laid on the ground of the meat shed. You have to do it to know it. After that the cow is put on its side and his four legs are tied together. After that the cow can't move. After that we pull his snout and put on another noose. Now, sir, you can see with your own two eyes. Like this, after getting the four legs together and tying a knot and putting the cow on its side with the snout stretched, the neck of the cow lying on the floor is stretched. Then the person who kills him comes up to the cow and pushes his nose into the ground and slits his neck from top to bottom.'[32]

After further details about the process by which the cow is slaughtered the interview ends. The author witnesses a cow being slaughtered and then provides the following tribute: 'After that I don't need to say what I saw. So that is the true story of cow slaughter that nobody wanted to talk about for a very long time. Whatever happens we all like to live – whatever language, whatever kind we speak – that's the truth. I saw the desire [to live] in the eyes of the cow that was brought to be slaughtered. I don't know what he said in his language, but despite that, if he taught us all a lesson then I remember. That's all.'[33]

As is clear from the *Mavbīma* article, and the stories in *Taksalāva*, focusing on the method by which cows are killed is an emotive method for capturing the interest of the audience. The authors of these articles write poetically and with great passion about the suffering that these animals are forced to endure. These sympathetic accounts in major newspapers lead the audience to condemn cow slaughter over and above any other type of animal slaughter. Such articles are full of Buddhist imagery and rely on Buddhist concepts. They also lean heavily on retributive notions such as karma and the possibility of a poor rebirth. The ubiquity of the cow as an object of such stories only illustrates how important the cow is in Sinhala society.

Cow protection literature

As discussed in the previous chapter, there are a number of books and pamphlets that deal with Sinhala Buddhist animal welfare. Often these books include mention of cow protectionism. Nonetheless, as general books on animal welfare they often do not focus on cows to the detriment of their general point that animals in general should be saved. Yet despite this, there are implications even in these texts that cows are owed a special level of respect amongst Sinhala Buddhists.

As with the newspaper articles there is an abundance of descriptive and visual images that illustrate the gruesome deaths these animals are subject to. Vīrakkŏḍi's *From Nonviolence to Maitreya, from Maitreya to the Buddha's Kindness* (2012) is flooded with images of cows in various stages of dismemberment. These images are often accompanied by sentimental tributes that highlight the suffering of the animal: 'Pay close attention to the methods used to slaughter these two cows. Isn't it unjust for these animals to go through such a cruel death while being nothing but innocent?'[34] These thoughts are underscored by sentimental poems that include lines such as, 'The sobbing sounds of my crying calf to be fed'.[35] The poem concludes with the observation that her milk will be consumed by a human child.[36] In short, we should pity the cow who does so much work for us.

Such poems draw heavily upon symbols and imagery of the Kiri Ammā cult. To respect the cow is to respect the deity of Kiri Ammā, who is constitutionally related to the Indian goddess Kaṃādhenu and Pattini. These poems and their affiliated images draw upon the notion that we should treat cows well because they supply us with milk just as our mother's supply us with milk. Kiri Ammā is a female goddess embodied in the cow and devotional poems such as this reinforce the necessity not to harm, but instead to cherish, the humble cow.

Such poems can also be used to reinforce the suffering that cows are forced to undergo. Such poems are intended to excite in the reader feelings of pity rather than feelings of awe and respect – which is the feeling intended to be drawn from the above devotional poem. Again, in *From Nonviolence to Maitreya* by Vīrakkŏḍi includes poems with lines such as: 'The black blood which flows when the stomach is cut open – it flows like the sea'.[37] The poem concludes by asking rhetorically whether those who have not experienced such crimes be willing to open meat shops,

In the newspaper articles there was considerable concern about the threat of an unpleasant rebirth as a result of harming cows. This concern is continued with Vīrakkŏḍi, who contrasts aiding cows with harming them: 'Is this the case that in this vicious cycle of existence we will also be reborn like these animals and would have been saved by a donation of another?'[38] This alludes to the notion that cows can be saved from slaughter by being rescued. It is not entirely uncommon for cows to be released from abattoirs by ordinary Buddhists.[39] Temples sometimes spearhead campaigns to have cows purchased from abattoirs so that they can live on counsel land.

Sometimes the reverse is the case, however. One newspaper article includes an allegation that a temple allowed a large group of cows to be taken to a Muslim abattoir.[40] Worse still, the animals had been kept at the temple for safe keeping but the temple apparently sold them on anyway. This illustrates that not all temples, and the monks who reside therein, necessarily have regard for animals let alone cows. For example, I witnessed a temple attendant beat a puppy with a stick near the Tissamahārāma Rāja Mahā Vihāra. Gombrich reports that monks sometimes swiped at harassing insects.[41] There are, therefore, divergent views about the welfare of animals. Similarly, the general moral scrupulousness of monks is extremely variable.

Concern over cow welfare is present in other animal welfare literature. For example, in Rathnakāra's *Give us Space to Live* concern over the well being of cows is evident. One of the most obvious examples of this is the cover of the book which sports a dead cow being transported on the back of a motorcycle. The book cover also shows a very famous picture in Sri Lanka of a cow seemingly bowing before, and therefore worshipping, a monk. This image appeared repeatedly throughout my fieldwork. It was shown at the *āyurvedic* clinic in Panadura (discussed in the next chapter) and was also the central image of a large poster of the Organisation for the Preservation of Life in Dehiwela. It is a standard image of the cow protection movement of Sri Lanka and seems to communicate the idea that even cows have knowledge of, and respect for, Buddhism.

Despite the prominence of the cow on the cover, cows are only mentioned in one other place in *Give us space to live*. Rathnakāra simply makes a general statement about the evils of factory farming: 'Going from place to place and selecting cows, goats, pigs and chickens, purchasing them and packing them into lorries and taking them to cattle sheds they are imprisoned without food in cages, and they go on a journey of many miles knowing that at the end they will be executed.'[42] Rathnakāra regards the slaughter of cows as being problematic but only insofar that the slaughter of all animals is problematic.

In this way, Rathnakāra is quite egalitarian in his animal welfare concerns though it does fly in the face of the general view that cows are owed special consideration and protection. It is possible, however, that Rathnakāra features cows prominently on the cover – even using the famous image of the worshipping cow – as a mechanism to draw attention to his book knowing that cows are uniquely venerated amongst the Sinhala Buddhist community.

Bhikkhu Himipāṇo is another author who is utilises and discusses cows and their welfare. In *The Question of Vegetarianism* (2011) – not to be confused with Gñanananda Thēra's 2009 book of the same name – Bhikkhu Himipāṇo actually questions the fairness of Sinhala Buddhist's favouring the cow over other animals. In the context of questioning our preoccupation with the conservation of rare animals (*durlabha satva*), Bhikkhu Himipāṇo writes, 'It's the same with many Sri Lankan people who provide unlimited love towards cows. A great many of our venerable monks take special responsibility for having cows liberated from death. They do this because of their unlimited love towards cows. Nevertheless it's true that many monks prepare and consume the flesh of other animals. Here you can see that there is no love, kindness, or compassion towards other animals apart from cows.'[43]

This comment is instructive because it shows (1) that some Sri Lankans do indeed favour cows over other animals; and (2) that there are criticisms from within some parts of the Sinhala Buddhist animal welfare movement as to the reasonableness of this. As is clear from Chapter 4, Bhikkhu Himipāno is quite right that monks habitually eat meat and this is the case regardless of whether they are sympathetic to the plight of animals – cows or otherwise.

Bhikkhu Himipāno's *The Question of Vegetarianism* does nonetheless include images relevant to the cow protection movement. At the end of the book there is a large image with the title 'Oh don't! Don't kill and eat us!'.[44] The image shows a number of different animals all pleading with the reader to spare their lives.

Even prawns and *umbalakaḍa* (cured tuna fish) are pictured in this image. A picture of a fish has a speech bubble that reads, 'We also like our lives' (*apit jīvat věnna āsayi*) while two goats say, 'We only eat vegetarian food. Why can't you?'.[45]

For our purposes here, the speech given by the two cows is especially telling. It reads, 'You feed your children from our blood which is turned into milk. Why do you kill us and cut away our udder?'[46] This speech points towards an important notion in Sri Lanka that blood is directly transformed into breast milk in the body.[47] Therefore, when a human infant drinks from her mother's breast she is indirectly ingesting her mother's blood, i.e. her source of life. Consequently, it is likewise thought that cow's milk is transmogrified cow blood. This is part of the reason why cows are considered with such high regard – because like the human mother, the cow literally sustains human life with her own blood through this process of blood to milk conversion.

We have already seen that the role that cows play as suppliers of milk is very important in Sri Lanka. In the past, milk was supplied during lunch breaks to every primary school student by the government. The importance of milk as a source of sustenance continues to be a huge issue in Sri Lanka.

The Organisation for the Preservation of Life makes a point that cows are important and should be protected in large part because they supply us with wholesome milk. In a newspaper article produced by the Organisation they write, 'Why are we suggesting the preservation of cattle? Think for a moment: If your children get to have a glass of fresh milk in the morning; If you can see your child getting healthier and stronger by consuming milk; Imagine being able to locally and freshly produce cheese and butter for a price that everyone can afford ... There is one simple way to achieve all of the above in our country which is through the prevention of cattle slaughter ... Looking at the above even you would agree that cattle are an asset to the country.'[48]

Consuming cow milk is therefore considered a social good because it improves one's health.[49] Moreover, cows supply this milk so we should be grateful to them for this gift, not kill them. This argument is clearly quite old as Gombrich mentions it during his research in the 70s.[50]

The importance of milk, and their relation to the mother (which in turn is related to the cow) is further elucidated by the *Pūjāvaliya (The Chronicle of Offerings)* which is a Buddhist Sinhala text dealing with Buddhist stories and

Milk of life 135

instructions relating to religious offerings. One passage describes in detail the feeding of Siddartha Gautama breast milk as an infant. The text describes how the different nurses all helped shape his body.[51] The Buddha's perfect physique is in part owed to his various wet nurses who attended to him.[52] It may be said that the mother's milk in fact nurtured not only the Buddha but also Buddhism as a religion. This tract therefore illustrates the utmost significance breastfeeding has from a religious perspective. Cows operate as surrogate mothers in many instances throughout Sri Lanka because, like the human mother, they also supply breast milk.

Cattle are important not only because we should feel intrinsic compassion towards them (in part because they remind us of our own mothers) they are important also for reasons of prudence: they supply us with milk. Milk is construed in Sri Lanka as the essence of life. Indeed, the cultural importance of milk also explains the enormous public reaction that arose from claims that the New Zealand owned Fonterra company was producing contaminated milk.

Fonterra operates facilities in Sri Lanka and is a major supplier of powdered milk in the country. This led to widespread protests and the Sri Lankan government was ultimately forced to intervene.[53] A Facebook group called *Anāvaraṇa (Discovery)* argues that there is an international precedent for the banning of New Zealand milk: 'Fonterra milk products have been banned in Sri Lanka. Last week countries such as China and Russia have also banned this product and prevented them from entering the market place.'[54]

At the same time, however, there is also an inherent questioning of whether it is acceptable that foreign foods be imported into the country. One of the protestor's signs mentioned previously simply states: 'Let's make our own milk powder!'.[55]

This suspicion of foreign brands is therefore in tension with the prevailing consumerist view that milk powder is more nutritious than local brands,[56] even though (1) the 'foreign' brands are produced in Sri Lanka anyway[57], and (2) this is driven mainly from a need to acquire status by purchasing luxury foreign products. So on the one hand there is a nationalist impulse to rid the nation of foreign goods, but there is also an impulse to revel in foreign goods because of the attached status.[58]

Online social media

The cow protection movement in Sri Lanka has had enormous recent success in part because it has been able to excite support amongst technologically fluent Sinhalese youth. Social media sites such as Facebook have acted as a space where young Sinhalese have been able to congregate and share their views about cow protectionism and, more specifically, their opposition to *hālal*. The details of the *hālal* abolitionist movement will be examined in more detail in Chapter 7. But it is striking how formerly outdated tropes such as the Kiri Ammā cult have met with a resurgence thanks to online media. We can also get a glimpse at the barely suppressed nationalism that underlines much of these discussions.

One major Facebook group is the International Buddhist Council of Sri Lanka, which runs numerous articles and advertisements denouncing the consumption of beef, mistreatment of cattle, and it is also a major proponent of *halal* abolitionism. One of its basic advertisements rejects the eating of cow flesh: 'The cow knows what we do not know: from cow flesh there is disease. You must read about it, tell people about it and share it with others.'[59] These objections echo earlier concerns already raised elsewhere, namely that eating animal flesh can be adverse to your health because it invites a proliferation of diseases.

Whether these concerns are grounded in reality or not is irrelevant – it is nonetheless another useful piece of propaganda for the cow protectionist movement and one that rings true for many Sinhalese who are generally quite health conscious.

Another group, the International Buddhist Council of Sri Lanka has a post depicting a live cow staring out at the reader juxtaposed with a gory photograph of another cow with its throat cut with viscera spilling out on a cement floor. The text declares: 'She gave us milk after our mother – she worked in paddy fields in order to help others harvest crops like our fathers. And in spite of all of this how can you still eat its flesh? Stop the cattle slaughter.'[60] These comments are interesting in that they draw upon the cooperative role the mother and father play together: the mother is conceived of as supplying the milk, i.e. the fluid of life, while the father cultivates and supplies the rice, i.e. the food of life.

This also conveys the importance of the rice paddy in Sri Lankan society and helps cement the social roles men and women have in society: men toil on the land while women stay at home and raise the children. The entire schema nonetheless emphasises the role of the mother, i.e. the Kiri Ammā, by arguing that without her the entire social system will collapse. Without her, one of the two basic sources of nutrition will be lost.

These ideas are clarified by the following explanation that accompanies the main image and text: 'In the past the cow was regarded as a milk mother to all. She gave her milk to motherless children and also milk to children following after their mother's breast milk. She also was the one who satisfied the nations taste buds with her milk. From the past to the present the people of Sri Lanka have been heavily dependent upon agriculture [farming] and as a result of this dependency they regard the cow as an asset to the country since most of the agricultural [farming] duties were performed using cows. Therefore the cow was a central point for survival. Cows have always been respected and treated well by our ancestors, the 'children of cows'.[61]

Indeed, online social media provides a wealth of material that illustrates the vitality and popularity of the cow protectionist movement including the prevailing importance of the Kiri Ammā cult. For example, another image prepared by the same group has a text written above several images of slaughtered animals that reads: 'Don't, don't eat the flesh of the Milk Mother'.[62] Another group called *Stop Killing Cows – Sri Lanka* (in English) is dedicated to ending cow slaughter. It also invokes the image of the Kiri Ammā: 'Cooperate to give support to the opposition of cow slaughter in Sri Lanka. Let us [do this] by protecting our milk mother.'[63] This concern over the well being of cows is sometimes expressed in terms of a religious vow not to harm cows by avoiding participating in the beef industry.

One artefact of this is a *Safe Buddhism* article that shows a small child hugging a calf. The text reads, 'I like to see you have freedom. I will never eat your flesh.'[64] The use of children as a mechanism to illustrate the wickedness of cow slaughter is a common trope in cow protectionist imagery that is intended to illustrate (1) the moral purity associated with abstinence from cow slaughter (children are viewed as morally pure and uncorrupted); and (2) to reflect the connection between the child and the mother who nurtures him (symbolised by the cow). The latter idea draws on the notion that we are all the children of cows.

Although *Stop Killing Cows* wants to prevent cow slaughter entirely, they are nonetheless realistic about their chances of this happening completely. Hence they have developed a detailed manifesto to help outline some steps that will ultimately lead to the elimination of cow slaughter in the long term.

The manifesto reads: 'It is not possible to stop cow slaughter in one day. It is not practical as well. Because of that let us propose a practical course of action: 1) The *halāl* way of slaughtering animals should be completely stopped; 2) There should be a compulsory method for minimum suffering in slaughtering; 3) The location of slaughter should be kept completely separate from the location where cows are bred; 4) There should be a limit on the number of cows killed per month; 5) There should be a complete ban on the killing of pregnant and nursing animals; 6) From the instant that you choose the animal to the moment you kill it humans should treat them humanely; 7) In regards to animal slaughter there should be a tax; 8) milk and industries relating to milk should be developed; 9) A standard should be recognized in regards to the slaughter of animals; 10) Slaughterers who cannot abide by these rules should be banned.'[65]

These examples from media illustrate the vibrancy and presence the cow protectionist movement has online. In fact, the online community seems to be a major contributing factor towards the grassroots program to improve the welfare of cows. A great deal of campaign organisation seems to occur online and online groups such as the ones mentioned above seem to help rally support behind various political movements such as Sinhala Rāvaya and Bŏdu Bala Sĕna. These organisations are also largely governed by an anti-Muslim, and anti-hālal, motivation. The intersection of cow protectionism and the *hālal* abolitionist movement, and the more insidious islamophobic elements therein, will be examined in more detail in the final chapter on animal welfare politics.

138 *Milk of life*

Cow protectionism in music

The domain of popular music contains other examples of cow protectionism. It is remarkable just how pervasive the presence of cow protectionism is. Not only is it common in newspaper articles and literature, it also finds its way into music and other popular forms of entertainment.

One popular example of cow protectionist music comes in the form of J.A. Milton Perera's *Umbǣ kiya kiyā maraṇa bayē (Say moo from fear of death)*. This song first appeared in 1965 which shows that the popularity of the cow protection movement extends at least as far back as the second half of the twentieth century – though as I have already argued from other sources it is much older than even that. The lyrics of this song depend largely on advertising the need for compassion and restraint in the treatment of cows. The song has the following chorus: 'The cow moos in fear of death. At first we humans drink her milk then we kill her and consume her flesh'.[66]

The first verse of the song laments the suffering that the Kiri Ammā is subject to and includes evocative lines such as, 'Why are humans so brutal, asks this cow? We load her up with an unbearable amount and whip her with a cane'.[67] Despite this harsh treatment the cow nonetheless feeds the entire family – a point the Organisation makes time and again. Worse, Milton tells us, even though the cow shares this bounty with us we end up slaughtering her and selling her flesh. He ends the first verse by lamenting, 'When will man ever have mercy?'.[68]

The song in fact originates from a Sinhala film called *Hatara maha niḍānaya (The four great cessations)* – a phrase that borrows heavily from the Pāli canon. An interlude in the film features the protagonist visiting a cow slaughter yard and, through song, reflecting on the unnecessary suffering cows are subjected to. Before embarking on these reflections, he doffs his hat to a large Buddha image thus rooting the entire rumination in Buddhism and the Buddhist ethic of compassion towards all living creatures.

The Kiri Ammā trope continues in other popular songs such as the famous baila musician Nihāl Nelson's song *Kiri Ammā*. This song encourages not only the better treatment of cows, but vegetarianism more generally.[69] The fact that celebrity figures such as Nelson support cow protectionism, and the better treatment of animals more generally, and the fact that he is able to create popular songs about these issues, demonstrates the success of the animal welfare movement in Sri Lanka.

Nelson can be compared to a Western musician like Morrissey, who is successful in spite of his animal welfare predilections as some who support his music may find his extreme animal rights position an embarrassment. This is not the case in Sri Lanka where successful musicians can produce extremely pointed animal welfare songs and even then these songs can be hits.

Part of the chorus to Nelson's *Kiri Ammā* reads: 'She gave her milk from her body'[70] – again this is a reference to the sacrifices made by the cow for our benefit. The chorus concludes, 'don't eat the meat of the milk mother'.[71]

Verse one is equally powerful. It includes lines such as, 'Some people sell the cow because they are greedy for money. After that, the innocent animal's destiny is resolved.'[72] Nelson concludes the verse by saying, 'people that do not eat meat from animals have contented hearts'.[73] The gods live within them (which may be an allusion to the fact that the higher deities are offered only vegetarian food).

The song also mentions the importance of the five products of the cow. As discussed earlier, this directly relates to the Hindu Tamil/Indian Hindu conception of Kāmādhenu as a supplier of these five items. This is another direct connection between the worship of Kāmādhenu in Hinduism and the veneration of cows and the Kiri Ammā deity amongst the Sinhala Buddhists.

Apart from these examples of popular music, nursery rhymes sometime also feature cows as the subjects of moral consideration. Such songs should be distinguished from nursery rhymes like *Ambalamĕ pinā waḷa kadak gĕnā* (*The salesman who carries pots by the rest spot*) because, although the song features a cow, the song does not treat the cow as a subject of moral enquiry. Instead, the cow simply runs amok and destroys the salesperson's wares. In this vein, *Ambalamĕ pinā* is akin to *Hey Diddle Diddle*, a nursery rhyme that also features a cow – both are intended to be silly rhymes that impart no moral teaching whatsoever. This is not the case with the nursery rhyme *Vahupæṭiya* (*Little Calf*):

Don't run in the hills far away
After a time your mother will look for you
Little one, if you wriggle like that
Be a good child, my fair calf, like me
Verse 1:
One day I fell down as I was running through the field
I cracked my head and the blood poured like a river
I went to the hospital and I was like a thief [i.e. she was anxious or on edge]
My fair mother cried all day and all night
I'll never make you cry again, my fair mother
Every day I will be your golden child
Verse 2:
One day I went to the forest after school
I was eating some forest fruits, I was in the hot sun, and I got lost
So in the evening I snuck into the backyard
There was my mother crying, worried and looking for me
From now on I will never hurt you, my fair mother
Repeat chorus[74]

The song is depicted as being sung by a small child to a small calf. It teaches the virtue of not straying far from the mother, and reinforces the expectation in Sinhala society that the child will be obedient and not misbehave by being overly exuberant. The child should be obedient to the mother just as the calf is obedient to the cow. This heralds back to the general Kiri Ammā trope where the mother is afforded special affection and respect because of her status as a provider. Similarly, the cow is afforded this same respect.

We have already been introduced to the importance of the Kiri Ammā cult not only through these various popular songs, but also through cow protection literature and newspaper articles. A clear argument has emerged in these materials that the better treatment of cows is fundamentally linked to feelings of sympathy that emerge from one's consideration of one's own mother. The Kiri Ammā cult therefore drives much of these sympathetic feelings towards the cow and we now turn to exploring that cult.

The Kiri Ammā cult

In his 1909 study of the indigenous people of Sri Lanka, the Væddha, Henry Parker discusses the various permutations of the Kiri Ammā cult. Parker claims that Kiri Ammā is a manifestation of the goddess Mōhinī, and that, amongst the Tamil population, the name *kiri* is derived from their word *giri* or mountain.[75] These observations, however, are all incorrect. Parker correctly identifies the name to mean 'grandmother'.

Parker regards Kiri Ammā as originating from Mōhinī rather than his other posit, namely, that she is Parvatī.[76] Although Parker notices that Kiri Ammā is associated with a 'Liquor of Immortality' and that she is involved with the 'Churning of the Ocean', he does not recognise that in both instances these matters are to do ultimately with milk. The importance of milk, and therefore the importance of the cow, finds its root in this cult. Milk, in Sinhalese society, is the substance of life itself.

As Obeyeskere has argued convincingly, the Kiri Ammā cult ultimately finds its origins in the Pattini cult. Obeysekere's critical study of Pattini in Sri Lanka illustrates the closeness that Mōhinī has to this arch mother-goddess. He writes that, 'By contrast [to the deity Mangara and the non-deity Pālanga] Pattini and Kiri Ammā are practically isomorphic: the one cult could easily have been displaced, usurped, or invaded by the other.'[77] Obeyesekere argues that Kiri Ammā simply eroded the influence of Pattini and thereafter came to dominate her cultural space. Obeysekere says that, 'I am, however, certain that Kiri Ammā will eventually go *totally* out of vogue in Sinhala culture.'[78]

On the contrary, it seems that there has been a resurgence of interest in the Kiri Ammā cult and her name is continually invoked in order to motivate the extremely popular cow protection movement. There is no indication that this has any sign of abating.

As to the nature of Kiri Ammā, Obeysekere has this to say, 'The worship of Kiri Ammā [literally, milk mother, also wet nurse or grandmother] is found all over Sri Lanka. Kiri Ammā, like Pattini, has many functions, but everywhere she is (also like Pattini) associated with infectious diseases and children's diseases and cure.'[79] When a child is sick loved ones will sometimes participate in ritual activities that glorify Kiri Ammā. The hope is that she will respond by curing the child's affliction. Obeyesekere describes the rite: 'When children are sick, generally with infectious diseases...seven lactating mothers are invited to the household of the sick child. These mothers are fed with milk rice and oil cakes. At the conclusion of this almsgiving the seven Kiri Ammā bless the sick child as they leave the house.'[80] Obeyesekere states that in 1956 these rites were widely practiced but at the time of research (the 1970s) the rituals are now 'very scarce' and I would now say that they are probably almost completely absent.

However, what these healing rites do illustrate is the importance of milk as an agent for purification. Milk gives life in the conventional sense that it nourishes and allows a child to grow, but it also has a revivifying effect – it can bring a child back from illness. It is important to also note that the relation between milk and the mother, and the cow and the mother, is reflected also in wider cultural tropes around the role of the female in Sinhala society. Traditionally, women are regarded as being best placed to care for and nurse sick children. In many respects men are largely absent in childrearing and this is also generally the case with the caring of sick children. This is considered women's work (unless the man is the doctor, but even then his role is generally diagnostic in nature and he is not directly responsible for nursing the ill).

Obeyesekere notes that this power to cure disease is itself related very explicitly to Pattini, who is a goddess who is thought to be able to cure disease. Of course, as Obeyesekere and Parker both observe, there is considerable variation in how Kiri Ammā is worshipped and what her cosmological origins are. For our purposes, it is useful simply to note that Kiri Ammā has strong affiliations with Pattini and is widely recognised throughout Sri Lanka. This is the case both for the Sinhalese, the Tamils and even the Væddas.

Kiri Ammā is associated with Pattini but it is impossible not to also note the relationship between Kiri Ammā and Kamādhenu. This connection was made clear in my fieldwork when we encountered the Organisation for the Preservation of Life. One of their marketing strategies was to supply a bumper sticker that prominently featured an image of Śiva, Parvātī and Kamādhenu. The bumper sticker reads in verse:

> The country of mine wakes up to the five products of the cow
> The cow has always been the local's treasure
> The empty and cruel people who kill her and consume her meat
> Is like consuming the flesh of the mother who gave you birth
> Let's all refrain from eating beef [81]

The sticker clearly connects these three deities – and notably Kamādhenu – with cow protectionist activities. Moreover, it links these deities with the importance of the mother and consequently Kiri Ammā.

In India Kamādhenu is worshipped as the endlessly lactating cow. Parmeshwaranand writes that, 'She is the first mother of cattle. She is a goddess with marvellous powers and attainments who Purāṇs declare that all the cattle in the world today are descended from Kamādhenu.'[82] Just as with Parker's account of Kiri Ammā, Kamādhenu is said to be associated with a great sea of milk.[83] It seems extremely likely that there is a co-relationship between Kamādhenu, Pattini and Kiri Ammā. As Obeyesekere states in specific regard to Pattini, these three deities are likely isomorphic with one another.

The Kiri Ammā cult is clearly significant and underpins the entire cow protectionist edifice. We can see that the Kiri Ammā cult is grounded in the notion of healing and sustenance. Kiri Ammā, and therefore all mothers, protect, heal, and nurture their children.

Yet this seemingly compassionate impulse of cow protectionism strangely manifests itself in ugly and divisive ways. This specific transformation of the nurturing into the destructive is indicative of a wider peculiarity within the animal protection movement: although it is a movement that is ostensibly concerned with celebrating and cherishing life through the Buddhist notions of compassion and kindheartedness, it nonetheless is turned towards violent ends. This is clear from the case of the *halāl* abolitionist movement.

Conclusion

The cow protection movement in Sinhala Sri Lanka is a wide-ranging and multifaceted movement that has considerable influence over many Buddhist Sinhalese. Its presence is felt in a vast range of cultural areas: from the literary field of books and pamphlets to the popular arena of music and film. What underpins much of this is the existence of the Kiri Ammā cult and, in this fashion, the cow protection movement has a quasi religious element to it. This helps explain the peculiar fascination that Sinhala Buddhist have with the cow over other animals: the cow has reached a quasi deified status while other animals have not. Therefore, when Sinhala Buddhists see a cow, they not only see a beast that supplies them with milk and dairy, they also see a creature that exemplifies the religious symbol of Kiri Ammā.

This symbol also connects directly to the sacredness of one's own mother since Kiri Ammā discourses frequently associate the cow with the maternal instinct of the mother. Milk is an important food in Sinhala culture as it is associated with breast milk. Cow milk is viewed as an alternative or a supplement to a mother's milk and helps develop growing children long after they have stopped drinking their mother's own milk. Along with rice, milk is the most important foodstuff in Sinhala society and is practically regarded as being of national significance. This will be discussed in the next chapter. Ultimately, the cow is at the heart of this idea that milk sustains the entire nation.

Finally, the cow represents the apex of innocence amongst the animal kingdom. The idea that the cow is harmless and innocent is frequently made note of by cow protectionist authors. The fundamental docility of the cow is thought to be evidence of this. In this way, kind actions towards the cow are an ideal way to demonstrate one's Buddhist credentials. Cows are innocent creatures that serve Sinhala society and therefore are more deserving than anyone of kind deeds. The vivid descriptions of cow killing serves as a way to draw an emotive response from a reader when they consider the unjust character of any action that leads to such a harmless animal's brutal death.

Cow protectionism, of course, has also had an effect on national politics with the emergence of the *hālal* abolitionist movement. Radical Sinhalese political groups use the cow protectionist agenda to target Muslim businesses and even individual Muslims. The extent and effects of this Sinhalese nationalism will be examined in the final chapter.

Notes

1 The full text of the billboard reads as follows: *sōbā dahama ōbaṭa dunnu. me suratal duhuṇa balala. minisun vana api kōhōmada. me osvala rasa balannĕ. gava mas kaemĕn valakimu.*
2 *ĕpā ĕpā mas kannaṭa kiri ammāge…2600 srī sambudṭhatva jayantiya samaramu. gavamas kaemĕn valakimu. saṃviṭhānaye panivuḍayaki …* [picture inset]: *gava sampatha rakimu ape mava vage.*
3 *mav kiri māsa hayayi. eḷakiri divi ætiturā.*
4 Jha, 17.
5 Crooke, 277.
6 Gabriella Eichinger Ferro-Luzzi, 394.
7 Fuller, 74.
8 Jha, 38.
9 Sayers, 312.
10 Swami Parmeshwaranand, 733.
11 Ibid., 734.
12 Bonnefoy and Donniger, 99.
13 Burma is a similar case to Sri Lanka. It is a Theravāda nation of considerable pedigree and it too has a thriving cow protectionist movement. Like Sri Lanka, this cow protectionist movement is deeply associated with anti-Muslim rhetoric. The great Buddhist monk Ledi Sayadaw was involved in cow protectionist activities (Braun, 34–38). At the present time the modern formulation of this movement has received international press because of their ongoing conflict with the Muslim community in Sri Lanka.
14 Gough, 230.
15 Ibid.
16 Jones and Ryan, 330.
17 In Chapter 1 it was pointed out that early Portuguese and other European colonists were associated with meat and alcohol. Here we find a reverse of this immoral diet in the form of the celebrated rice and milk formula. The Sinhala diet is based on a pure (moral) dyad while the foreign diet is associated with an impure (immoral) dyad.
18 Bastin, 46, 67, 69, 119, 196.
19 Ibid., 168–169.
20 Peiris, 150.
21 Knox, xvii.
22 Percival, 220.

23 Bond, 1992: 118.
24 *dǽḍi mānsha lōliyaku vū ohu thalagŏyin, itthǣvun, hāvun, mīminnan vǣni kuḍā sathun vĕḍi tabā marā kǣ atara masvalaṭa ohu dǣkvū gijukama kŏtaramda yat vandaran, vavulan vǣni sathunda ohuge āhāraya udĕsā biliviya.*
25 *mŏhuge pradānatama pāpakara kriyāva vūse harak marā mas kirīmayi.*
26 *mŏhugĕ visheśatvaya vuye ohu harakā mǣrīma sandahā ohuṭama āveṇika vū kramavedayak bhāvita kaḷa heyini. gĕna ena lada harakāge gĕla kambayaka mǣda sādana lada puḍuvaka sira karana atara kambaye kŏndĕka gasdĕkka bandinu laĕbe. … gĕla siravana bava dǣnīmat samaga harakā dǣngalīmaṭa paṭan gannā atara ema avasthāva eḷambĕtva dābarege mulika baḷa pitat vĕyi. asaraṇa harakā kambaya dĕpasaṭa adimin paĕna yāmaṭa dangalana atara eviṭa vaḍa vaḍāt maḷapuḍavaṭa uge gĕla hiravĕyi. mĕma maḷapuḍuva dābare visin sakas karanuye e ākārayaṭaya. mĕlĕsa gĕla hiravana harakā bŏhō velā dangalamin dǣḍi vedanā vindimin miyagiya harakāge siruta pasudā udase ohu visin mas karaganu lǣbe.*
27 *ek manuṣyaku harak mǣrīme nirata viya. ohu itā priyakaḷe harakungĕ diva kǣmaṭaya. harakun mǣrǣ viṭa unge divaval ǣda kapā gĕnavīt āhārayaṭa gǣnīma ohuge sirita viya. birinda lavā ē diva kŏṭas luṇu ǣmbal damā pisavā ganiyi.*
28 *harakungĕ kaṭa vivarṭa kara bĕlla ḷanga kaṇudĕkak nŏǣlanĕ se bǣnda, siyum pihiyakin ohu, gavayāge diva kapāganne itā siyum lĕsaṭaya. harakāṭavat mĕ siduvanne kumakdǣyi sitāgat nŏhǣki taramaṭa ohuge ata ǣti pihiya kaḍisaraya.*
29 *divĕ amāruvaṭa bĕt bivvat ohu harakunge divaval kǣma natara kaḷe nǣta. 'onna oya vǣḍe ata arinava,' kiyā anya hitavat gava ghātakayaku kīvat harak dive rasaya vinda ohuṭa eya atahǣriya nŏhǣki viya.*
30 *mĕ kālayeḍī divapuru bibili nǣvaka pǣtira giyeya. ārogyashālāveḍī eya piḷikāvak bava tīraṇaya kĕriṇi. diva kapannaṭa vaidyavaru sitā gatha.*
31 *kakul hatara gǣṭa – gahalā / hŏmba bimaṭa tada – karalā / mannĕ aran eka – pārama / bĕlla kǣpuva hira – karalā.*
32 *(hari, hari, itin…) īta passe api gihin satā aragĕna ĕnavā marana oḍuvaṭa. kavadāvat marana kĕnā aragĕna ĕnne nǣ satāva. kŏhŏma hari satā aragĕna ǣvit mas oḍuvĕdi bima pĕraḷanavā. eka itin karalama dǣnaganna ōne. ĕtakŏṭa harakā pǣtta vǣṭuṇāma uge kakul hataraṭa dānavā gǣṭayak. ĕtakŏṭa harakaṭa hĕlavĕnna bǣ. īṭa passĕ ūge hŏmba ǣdalā dānavā tava tŏṇḍuvak. ǣn balanna puluvanne mahattayāṭa ǣs dĕkĕnma. mĕhema kakul hatara ĕkaṭa karalā gǣṭayak dālā harakava pǣtta pĕraḷalā hŏmba ǣdalā bima inna satāge bĕlla ǣdilā tiyĕnne. ĕtakŏṭa īṭa passe marana kĕnā pihiya aragĕna hŏmba bimaṭa tadakaralā bĕlle ihaḷa indalā vatema ĕka pāra kapanna ōne.*
33 *īṭa passĕ dǣkka de gǣna kiyanna ōne nǣne. kalāpa navayak kavuruvat kavadāvat katā nŏkarapu harak masvala ǣthuḷe katandare ohŏmayi. mŏnavā vuṇat api kavurut jīvat vĕnnayi kǣmǣti. mŏna bhāshāva, mŏna jātiya katā kaḷat ĕka tamyi ǣtta. maṃ ḍǣkka maranna aran āva harakage ǣs dĕkĕt tibuṇe ē āsāva. ū uge bhāṣhāvĕn mŏnavā kicchada kiyalā maṃ danne nǣ. ē vuṇṭa ū api hǣmōṭama pāḍamak kiyalā dī lā giyā kiyalanam maṭa matakayi.*
34 *mĕma harakun dĕdĕnā marana hǣti hōdin nirīkṣhaṇaya karanna. mĕvan ruduru maraṇavalaṭa varadak nǣtiva gŏduruvīma kĕtaram asādharaṇada? (28–29).*
35 *ikibina haṇḍan magĕ kiri daruvagĕ.*
36 Vīrakkŏḍi, 29.
37 *bŏṭuva kapana viṭa ena kalu le* (Ibid., 67).
38 *ruduru maṃchakayĕn pudgala dhana parityāgayĕn berāgat gavayina 88 dĕnāgĕn dĕdĕnĕk, balanna asaraṇa satvayin dĕdĕnā pān rāttal kihipayak anubhava karana sǣti. mĕ ruduru saṃsāraye apat mĕvat sathunva ipida anantavat kappavā gannaṭa ǣti neda?* (76).
39 A practice maintained in other Buddhist cultures too. Duncan Williams discusses the release of animals in Japan in his article *Animal Liberation, Death, and the State: Rites to Release Animals in Medieval Japan* (150).

40 'Moo is a sound that can be produced from fear of death. How can human beings go and take my children?' (*umbæ kiya kiyā mara biyĕ haṇḍa tǣduvo kohidǣyi hĕna giye vinisuni vagĕ daruvo*) in *Mavbima* (20 October 2013, 15).
41 Gombrich, 1991: 306.
42 *thænin thænaṭa gŏs gavayan, eluvan, ūran, kukuḷan torā berā gĕna, milaṭa gĕna, lŏrivala gāl karagĕna, kuḍuvala hirakaragĕna nirāhāra va sæthæpum gaṇṇāvak yana gamana keḷavara porakaya bava ovuhu daniti*. (14).
43 *ĕsema apa shrī laṃkāveda bauddha janatāvagĕn bŏhomayak gavayāṭa asīmitava ādaraya dakvati. apage bhikṣun vahanselā bŏhomayakda gavasin maraṇayĕn mudavā gannaṭa visheṣayĕn mulikatvayak gena kaṭayutu karati. e ovun gavayinṭa asīmitava ādaraya karana nisāya. ĕhĕt ǣtǣem bŏho bhikṣun vĕnat satva māṃsha hŏndākārava vaḷandati gavayin hǣerĕnnaṭa an satvayinaṭa ovunge hadavat tula ādarayak maitriyak karuṇāvak nŏmǣti ova mĕyin pĕnī yayi*. (31).
44 *ane epā! ane epā! apava marā kanna epā* (Ibid., 231).
45 *api kanne nirmāṃsha āhāra pamaṇayi. ǣyi obalāṭa bǣri?*
46 *ape le kirikaralā neda ŏbe daruvanṭa pŏvanne. ǣyi apa marā apage kiri burulla kapā damanne* (231).
47 Dennis McGilvray makes this point in his *Crucible of Conflict: Tamil and Muslim Society on the East Coast of Sri Lanka* (113). McGilvray's comment concerns the view of Tamil Sri Lankans, but this these views on blood and milk are the same with Sinhala Buddhists.
48 *gava sampata rukagannaṭa apa yŏjanā karanne aǣyi? sitanna: obaṭa raṭe daruvanṭa udeṭa nævum eḷakiri ṭikak bŏnnaṭa læbĕnavānam; nævum kiri bimĕn obe raṭe daruvan nirŏgī vĕnavā obaṭama dakinnaṭa læbĕnavānam; kiri āshrita niṣpādana vana chīs, baṭar ādiya aḍu milaṭa me raṭema nævum vidihaṭa kæmaṭa bahulava læbĕnavānam...me siyalu de raṭathula vǣḍi mahansiyak nætiva karaganna kramayak niyĕnavā. sri lankā thula gava ghāthanaya natara kirīma vī sandahā ekama visandamayi....gavayā raṭaṭa sampatak bavaṭa obat anumata karanu aæta.*
49 A traditional doctor that was interviewed, Mrs De Souza, pointed out that the medicinal effect of cow's milk was that it was cooling and therefore was useful in treating ailments stemming from overheating. This is all consistent with basic principles of ayurvedic medicine where one of the goals is to 'balance' the heating and cooling of the body. The importance of milk is also illustrated in the book *Food and Nutrition* by Sedī Pranāndu where it is recommended as a food supplement for pregnant women alongside eggs and sprats (*hālmæsso*) (11).
50 1991: 305.
51 *Pūjāvaliya*, 146–147.
52 Doctrinally, the Buddha is viewed as having a completely flawless body. It is constantly described as being dazzling and marvellous. In fact, his body is so perfect that followers have gained enlightenment simply by gazing at him. For details on the Buddha's body see Powers (2009).
53 Protestor signs featured slogans such as: 'Let's make our own milk powder' (*ape kiri piti apima hadāgamu*) and 'Stop advertising poisonous yogurt!' (*viṣa yogaṭ dænvim vahā tahanam karanu*).
54 *fŏnterā kiri nishpādana – lankāvet tahanam. pasugiya satiye chīnaya hā rusiyāvada mema navasīlanta nishpādana eraṭaval vala tahanam kara tibĕ. vĕḷada pŏḷaṭa nikut kirima athiṭuvayi.*
55 *ape kiri piti apima hadāgamu.*
56 Kemper, 7.
57 Ibid., 155.
58 An associate of one informant, for example, imported – at enormous cost – a number of large foreign appliances from overseas for their kitchen on the basis that they were better quality than local variants. The reality is that these items were imported as a matter of status.

59 *harak danna api nŏdanna; harak mase tiyĕnā lĕḍa; oba anivāryĕnma kiyavanna, an ayaṭada kiyanna, mitaran atare share [in English] karanna.*
60 *ammāgĕn pasu kiri dun ammā bat dĕnnaṭa kumbure vĕhĕsunu appacchi. marā kannaṭa hækida? gava ghātanaya navatama.*
61 *atītaye nam sinhalayinṭa gavayā kiri ammā viya. ammā næti daruvanṭa upan dā siṭa kiri dun, ammā æti daruvanṭa ammāgĕn pasu kiri dun kiri ammā vīya. pasgorasayĕn ape pinavu kiri ammā vīya. edā siṭa adu turuma gŏvinænin yæpĕna lānkika samājayaṭa edā nam gavayin sampatak vīya. ovunṭa jīvat vĕnnaṭa gavayā shaktiyak vīya. maḍaṭa bæsa sī sāna viṭa, kamate oḍeta viṭa, 'ambaruvo' lĕsin ape pæruntatgĕn sælakum læbū gavayo, 'gava duruvo' vĕmin sinhalayitgen sælakum læbūta.*
62 *epā epā mas kannaṭa kiri ammāgĕ.*
63 *lankave gava ghāthanayaṭa erehiwa sahayŏgaya laba denna. ape kiri ammā api wisinma raka ganimu.*
64 *mama kæmati oyā nidahase innavā dakinna mama kavadāvat oyāge mas kanne næ.*
65 *gava ghātanaya eka davasin nævætviya nŏhækiya. eya preyagika da næta. Ēnisā api ē vĕnivaṭa prāyŏgikava kala hæki dĕyak yŏjanā karannĕmu. 1. halāl væni amānuṣika ghātana karma hakulā gata yutuyi. 2. kṣaṇik, vĕdanāva avama vana karma anivāryaya kaḷayutuyi; 3. satun maraṇa sthānaya, gāl kara tabana sthānayĕn sampūrṇayĕn vĕn kaḷa yutuyi; 4. satun maraṇa pramāṇey māsika sīmāvak tibiya yutuyi; 5. gæbiṇi saha kiridĕna satun mærīma sapurā tahanam kala yutuyi; 6. satā tŏrāgannā mŏhŏte siṭa maraṇa mŏhŏta dakvā mānuṣikava sælakiya yututi; 7. sattava ghātanāgāra sandahā amatara baddak pænaviya yutuyi; 8. kiri saha ē āshrita karmānta diyuṇu kaḷayutuyi; 9. sattva ghātanāgāra sandahā pramitiyak hadunvā diya yutuyi; 10. mē ṭika karannaṭa bæri mas maruvan tahanam kara gĕdara yæviya yutuyi.*
66 *umbæ kiya kiyā maraṇa bayē // kiri ṭika muladhi bŏyi passē marā kayi.*
67 *minisā daruṇu æyi mē eḷadĕna asayi / bæri bara palavalā kĕchiṭĕn tala talā.*
68 *vadādo minisāge tirisan gati duralanne / minisā daruṇu æyi mē eḷadĕna asayi / bæri bara palavalā kĕchiṭĕn tala talā / ræ dāval ude vindu vindu dahavade / niraye duka dukī daru pavalama rakī / antimē mē hŏnā mas kara vikuṇnā / kaḍayaṭa pavaranā minisāmayi tirisanā / kavadādo minisāge anukampā æti vane // daruvaṭa mava nætī dĕvaruva kiridĕtī / gŏma tika pŏhŏra vē gŏḍamaḍa saru kĕre / mæræṇat nŏnævatī hamaṭada bæṭa dĕnī //.*
69 Baila music has not always had positive associations, however, and it has sometimes been regarded as an example of a colonial/Western corruption that displaces traditional Sinhala folk music (Kemper, 86).
70 *kiri dunnĕ daruvanṭayi sirurĕn ægē.*
71 *epā epā mas kannaṭa kiri ammāgĕ.*
72 *mudal tanhāvĕn samaharu gavayā vikuṇanne / ahiṃsaka satakugĕ iraṇama inpasu visadĕnne.*
73 *mēvan satakugĕ mas nŏkana ayaṭa sēta sælasĕnne.*
74 *duwan epā dura kandē lande baḍabvætiyē / vilāpa di, soyayi numbē ammā / pæṭiyo, danga nokaran, oya vāgē / hŏnda ḷamiyak vĕyan / magē sudu vahupæṭiyŏ, mang vagē //watila mang davasakdā / duvaddī ovaṭa mædde / pæḷilā oluva magē / lē gæluvā gagak vage / gihilla ispirītāle / mang hiṭiye hŏrak vagē / sudu ammayi nonida mulu ræ / ikibidamin hæḍuvē // aāyĕt, kavadāvat, næ aḍavannē sudu ammā / hæmadāmat, mang innam / vī ammāgĕma rangpæṭiyā // kælē gihin davasakdā / mang ærīlā iskŏlē / dang himbuṭu kaka gini awwe / maga æræhā pænimŏra landē / eddi mang hændævē / hŏrā vagē piḷikannē / siṭiyē æ valipannē / vilāpa di haḍamannē // tarahin mĕt / maṭa bætnat / ādarvanē magē ammā / min passē / kavadāvat / næ rīdavannē sudu ammā. (repeats chorus).*
75 Henry Parker, 1909: 135.
76 Ibid., 136.
77 Gananath Obeyesekere, 1984: 294.
78 Ibid.

79 Ibid.
80 Ibid.
81 *mas gorasin pubudana raṭa dæya – māge / vas thuva gava mavayi kavadat hĕḷa – yāge / his minisun marā mas katanam – aǣge / mas kanavā væniya bihikaḷa – ammāge.*
82 Swami Parmeshawaranand, 733.
83 Ibid., 734.

6 Meat aversions
Vegetarianism, health food and medicine in Sinhala society

Panadura is a large town south of Colombo. A secondary road near the Panadura shopping area takes one past a monastery overshadowed by a large *stūpa*. Soon after, one turns down a narrow and steep road that passes through a bushy rural area. A nearby river cuts through this scenic locale. It is at the end of this road that the eye clinic run by the Fernandos is located.

The clinic is called *Gangula Veda Medura (River Medical House)*. As one drives down the road one is struck by the unexpected sight of a multitude of patients wandering to and from the clinic. The number of patients immediately causes one to realise how popular this clinic is. But what is most alarming are the *āyurvedic* masks that each patient wears. The masks, which act more like compresses designed to deliver topical medicine directly onto the skin surrounding the eye, are composed of a complex of *āyurvedic* medicines. These medicines are a unique invention of Ishara Fernando, the patriarch of the family practice. In addition to those people leaving and entering the clinic, there are also a large number of people seated in an open air waiting area just inside the clinic complex.

The reason for the popularity of the clinic soon becomes apparent. Not only is the clinic free, it is also a place of great reputation. The Fernandos run a practice based on a commitment to community well-being and non-violence. Unlike many other traditional doctors in Sri Lanka, the Fernandos only utilise plant products in the composition of their medicines. The Fernandos display a rare concern for animal welfare. This concern over animals was also manifested in his encouragement of vegetarianism.

The medical centre, and the Fernandos themselves, are well known and well respected. Ishara Fernando is known simply as the *æs vēda mahaṭiya* or 'the eye doctor.' Several mounted newspaper articles have been proudly hung outside his office facing the waiting area.

One article written for the magazine *Sirikata* (i.e. Lakśmi the goddess of wealth)[1] has the title, 'Treatment through the nervous system of the body instead of treatment through the eyes – a message from the doctor of the River Medicine House'.[2] A second article from an English newspaper reads, 'Assistance sought for ingenious medical practitioner using ancient formulae offering free eye medication.'

Other articles attest to Fernando's Buddhist credentials. One article states: 'A place where they treat patients and also feed them – the River Medicine House',[3] while a second reads, 'Giving sight to the blind is a meritorious cause'.[4] Both articles have Buddhist implications. The first because it is associated with the act of giving (*dāne*) which, as we have seen, is a fundamental feature of Thēravāda Buddhist ethics. The second article is more explicitly Buddhist in its use of the term *pinkamak*, which refers to an act of merit. Doing meritorious deeds is central to Buddhist ethics. This article states that the action in question is an act of gift giving. Such deeds in turn produce good karma and therefore a good rebirth.

These articles highlight the role of giving in Ishara Fernando's practice. His religious commitment to such acts was made clear in our interview. Fernando stated that he offered his services for free and always provides a free meal for his patients. He is proud that he is providing a social service to the community. In addition, he utilises uncommon medical treatments based upon a radical system that deviates not only from Western medical norms, but also the norms of his rival traditional medical doctors. Unlike many other doctors he recommended universal vegetarianism.

He said: 'I don't recommend my patients any fish and meats. We are vegan. My partner doesn't even eat cake because it has eggs in it. And as you know we provide free lunch for our patients and we never cook any meats or fish. It's completely vegetarian.'

This deviation from medical convention illustrates how the Fernandos are similar to some of the monks that we examined in Chapter 4. Ven. Kosgoda, for example, the monk who ran the Organisation for the Preservation of Life, was virtually a monastic renegade in that he rejected the meat consumption practices of his fellow brethren.

The Fernandos, as we shall see, are similarly unusual in that they do not believe that the use of meat products in the preparation of traditional medicine is either medically or ethically warranted. This viewpoint was not the convention followed by the other doctors that were interviewed. Again, it is notable that entrepreneurial individuals such as Ishara Fernando and Ven. Kosgoda often develop good reputations not only because their methods are perceived to be effective and correct – medicine in the case of Ishara Fernando, politics and interpretation of Dharma in the case of Ven. Kosgoda – but also simply because they are charismatic leaders who have developed a following based around their strong personalities.

Body shape and medical risk

Health foods and healthy eating are also topics of great interest for many Sri Lankans. Indeed, the ideal body type traditionally sought after by female Sinhala Sri Lankans is in part governed by inferences about food consumption. In the West, highly athletic (but not muscled) female bodies are considered ideal. In the Sinhala community, however, this would not necessarily be considered attractive, except, of course, amongst the more wealthy elite who have been exposed to Western cultural norms.[5]

For most Sinhalese women, the ideal body type is a thin waist that ends with a few gentle rolls of fat near the hips. It is important that the body itself not be overly fat, but a body completely without fat (in contrast to the Western ideal) is not considered feminine. This is critically related to the issue of food: a well-fed (but not fat) woman is traditionally viewed as one who not only knows how to supply quality food, but is also one that has food readily available. Although the above analysis also applies to men, as in the West, there is some evidence that Sri Lankan women prefer men with a well-muscled physique.[6] Overall, however, there are greater allowances made for a larger body shape.

Gender norms around body types also tell us something about attitudes towards food and healthy eating. In Sri Lanka, healthy eating is not necessarily concerned with fat-free foods eaten in moderation so as to reduce the total number of calories. On the contrary, healthy eating is concerned with being well fed. As I have already argued, food is a central part of Sinhala society and eating is a critical social lubricant. It operates in much the same way as alcohol is used in many Western countries – it is an item of consumption that is shared in a social group. It helps create an easy environment in which hearty conversation can be had. Food brings people together. It can also tear people apart, however, and I heard a number of stories concerning food being poisoned. Fear over food being poisoned by one's enemies is not uncommon.

This love of food, however, is not without its risks. Diabetes and obesity are on the increase in Sri Lanka and this has been attributed by some to poor nutritional decisions.

Pushpa Wijeysinghe notes that obesity was an issue for 20.3% of men and 36.5% of women in the western provinces (i.e. the more urbanised part of Sri Lanka).[7] Wijeysinghe attributes this increase in rates of obesity to not only greater access to Western fast foods but also a general lack of physical activity.[8] Other studies have also indicated that Sri Lanka has a relatively high rate of diabetes which is also attributed to inadequacies in the average diet.[9]

Wijeysinghe's claim about the introduction of Western fast foods as being a causal factor, however, are questionable and I will argue in the following that such claims might be an example of an anti-Western – and, more generally, an anti-foreign – narrative about food that is present in health food literature. For one thing, I think it is clear that despite the increase in Western fast food restaurants in urban centres like Colombo, few Sri Lankans would regularly eat this food. Western fast food restaurants are perceived as places to visit on special occasions, usually with a family accompanied by young children, and it is not considered a place to go for a quick meal. Besides, Western fast food restaurants are far too expensive for the average consumer and are, in any case, appealing only to the wealthy elites who are influenced by Western trends. For most Sri Lankans, a cheap meal in Sri Lanka would consist of pastries bought from a baker or small bowl-shaped pancakes called āppa (hoppers).

Still, Wijeysinghe is correct that an increase in the availability of refined and processed foods do play a role. One study claimed that in 1995 20% of cancers were attributed to inadequate fruit and vegetable consumption.[10] Similarly, another study from 2004 observed that a majority of schoolchildren in a large study of Colombo schools received an unsatisfactory number of servings of fruits per week.[11]

Another consideration here is the presence of an over-abundance of food amongst wealthier segments of the urbanised population and a commensurate lack of portion control in the consumption of that food. A research article in *Diabetic Medicine* also shows that there is a high prevalence of diabetes in Sri Lanka especially in urban population centres like Colombo.[12] The authors blame this largely on obesity and physical inactivity.

Regarding physical inactivity: strenuous physical activity is generally considered an exclusively male pastime and even then it should be avoided since it is in turn associated with labouring and therefore is considered low class (and low caste). One study shows that there has been a decrease in physical exercise by young children in Sri Lanka, which the study attributes to greater academic competition, and therefore a greater need to attend extra classes, as well as greater availability of processed foods and a more sedentary lifestyle.[13] The hot and humid climate can make physical activity unappealing for the urban middle class and urban elite. The practical and cultural norms surrounding physical activity, not to mention norms surrounding food consumption, therefore contribute to the prevailing problems of obesity and diabetes in Sri Lanka.

This is a problem, however, of the (largely urban) rich elite. It is a problem of excess. There is also massive poverty in Sri Lanka and, as suggested by Wijeysinhe, malnourishment and anaemia are therefore an ongoing issue.[14] The relationship between wealth and weight is also illustrated by the Wickramasinghe study: private school children were typically heavier than public school students.[15] Note, however, that this problem only confirms the social perception that full bodiness is associated with wealth while thinness is associated with poverty. As we discovered in previous chapters, social perception is an enormous and overriding issue for many Sri Lankans. It is so important that it denies even what is known to be morally ideal. It may well also be the case that it similarly negates what is known to be healthy. Keeping up appearances – literally in this case – is an urgent issue for many Sinhalese Sri Lankans.

History of healthy eating

Contrary to this glorification of food common in Sinhala society, what we find in the Pāli canonical literature is an attitude that is quite opposed to gluttony and over-eating. Examining the Pāli literature, the religious texts upon which much of Sinhala Buddhist ideals are based, is a lesson in showing how far social practices tend to fall from religious and moral ideals. It is also instructive in illustrating another subtle way that lay expectations differ from monastic ones.

The Buddhist canonical literature is clear that food should be eaten only in moderation and that it should only be regarded as an instrumental good for the betterment of Buddhist practice. This view naturally contrasts with the celebration of food that is so evident in every day Sinhala Buddhist society.

On the other hand, it should not be thought that the Buddha encouraged his followers to avoid food either. He did not recommend a starvation diet. In fact, before his enlightenment – when the Buddha was merely Siddhartha Gautama, a bodhisattva striving for Nirvana – Siddhartha experimented with various unusual ascetic dietary practices. These practices were considered by the wandering ascetics of ancient India to be critical for the goal of realising enlightenment. For example, one dietary practice that Siddhartha undertook was a series of diets that comprised only kola fruit, beans or rice. But the Buddha later reported that these dietary experiment were useless and that from them he, 'did not attain any superhuman states, and distinction in knowledge and vision worthy of the noble ones.'[16]

An even more strenuous example of these ascetic practices of dietary restriction involved the abstention from all food at all. In an extraordinary passage the Buddha describes how, 'because of eating so little my skin adhered to my backbone; thus if I touched my belly skin I encountered my backbone and if I touched my backbone I encountered my belly skin.'[17]

These ascetic practices were clearly unsatisfactory. The Buddha concluded from these experiments that drastic and extreme dietary practices are not only useless, they are positively obstructive to the goal of enlightenment. What was needed was a robust and healthy diet, but one that did not involve overeating. Hence the Buddha also struck a balance by insisting that his disciples not eat after midday, except in the evening to take medicine. These restrictions have been discussed previously in considering their practical and real application amongst modern Sinhala Buddhist monks. But the philosophical point is clear here: diet should be controlled, but it should not be reduced drastically. Others have argued, as we have seen in Chapters 2 and 4, that this attitude already negates vegetarianism from a doctrinal standpoint. To make matters worse, the Buddha himself was not a vegetarian.

Overall, the goal here is instead moderation and mindful control over consumption of food. Food should be treated as a necessary fuel for the task of meditative contemplation. It is a way of sustaining future endeavours on the Buddhist path. On this matter, the Buddha says, 'Reflecting wisely, he uses almsfood neither for amusement nor for intoxication nor for the sake of physical beauty and attractiveness, but only for the endurance and continuance of this body, for ending discomfort, and for assisting the holy life, considering: 'Thus I shall terminate old feelings without arousing new feelings and I shall be healthy and blameless and shall live in comfort.'[18] Elsewhere he says, 'He [the monk] should have an empty stomach, taking food with little desire, without covetousness.'[19]

Notice that these remarks are primarily directed at monks. As we saw in Chapter 3, lay people sometimes make the task of moderation in diet difficult because they insist on lavishing monks with large amounts of gourmet food. Monastic regulations help here and monks are not permitted to eat food after lunch.

No real instructions, however, are provided for lay people as to what constitutes a proper diet for them. This lack of direction for lay people is not altogether unusual as the Pāli canonical literature seems to primarily directed towards those devoted to the path for enlightenment, namely other monks. In fact the so-called householder lifestyle is entirely repudiated by the Buddha. The worldly existence of the laity is just too rife with desires.

Of course, the overall implication is that lay people – if they are to be good Buddhists – should also not overindulge. However, it is certainly not mandatory and the requirements laid out in the Pāli literature are directed very specifically at monks and nuns. As we saw in Chapter 3, such implications are taken seriously only by the pious. Those who restrict their diet appeared to be more overtly religious. Meat eaters, for example, were overall much less concerned about the consumption of food and viewed Buddhism as being generally permissive about food consumption. Voluntary dietary restrictions are perceived as a clerical matter. Monks were expected to avoid gluttonous behaviour and maintain an appropriate attitude of moderation towards eating. This illustrates another break between clerical and lay expectation.

Nonetheless, attempts have been made to communicate the Buddha's recommendation for a moderate diet. Take, for example, the book *Four Foods of Life* (*jīvitayē āhāra varga sathara*) by Pūjaya Gñānapōnika Himi (2008). Gñāṇapōnika's book is largely concerned with the elucidation of several Pāli *sūtras* in Sinhalese that help instruct followers on what constitutes healthy food. Another book is even more explicit on this subject. It has the title *A Compilation on the Preservation of Good Health in the Tripitaka* (*tripitakāgata sauḵhya sangrakshaṇa viḍi*) (2007) and directly translates into Sinhala extracts from the Pāli canon on the subject of health foods and healthy living.

As Gombrich and Obeyesekere have noted, Sinhala translations of Pāli texts are very rare.[20] Generally, most lay people only have access to Sinhala translations of particular texts, such as certain *Jātaka* tales, and there are in fact no reliable and easily accessible Sinhala translations of the Pāli texts. The only full Sinhala translation of the *Tripiṭaka* is the Buddha Jayanti translation. As Gombrich and Obeyesekere notes, however, the translation is obtuse at best and very difficult to read.[21] It is not meant for the average Buddhist. Hence, these translations of particular passages serve a specific purpose: shaping and changing the laity's perspective on food. It is an attempt to modify consumption habits in the same manner that the vegetarian literature previously discussed is an attempt to modify consumption habits.

These texts therefore aim to modify lay behaviour. It is assumed that monks are already virtuosos in this area. It is important to observe, however, that although the food practices recommended by the Buddha are expected to be upheld by the clergy it does not follow that these monks are necessarily very good at upholding these expectations. Nor is it the case that laity are very good at supporting the monastic aversion to gluttony. As I discussed in Chapter 3, lay people are expert at divining what sort of foods monks prefer and go out of their way to provide it. Food and the consumption of food is therefore a vexed issue not only for the laity, but equally so for the clergy.

Traditional medicine

The above discussion particularly illustrates the tension between conventional lay attitudes towards food versus the attitude towards food recommended by the Buddha himself. This is an issue about healthy eating and lifestyle. Lay people are also interested in consuming another edible item: medicine. Most Sinhala Buddhists, and indeed most Sri Lankans in general, routinely use traditional medicine to alleviate at least some of their everyday maladies. Traditional medicine is also utilised for the treatment of more advanced afflictions. This is not to say that Western medicine is not also sought out, and many view Western medicine and traditional medicine as complementary.

Western medicine, however, is not always sought out as a first port of call and some regard Western medicine with a certain degree of suspicion. Nawanga and his wife, for example, suspected that doctors trained in Western medicine were charlatans out to make money and that they might very well make things worse.[22] This is why, when Nawanga developed cataracts, he went to see Ishara Fernando and his son for treatment.[23]

Western medicine is nonetheless still widely utilised. For example, despite his concerns Nawanga ultimately had his cataracts corrected through surgery. Western medicine and traditional medicine are both used, but they are not the only options available: magic and exorcism are also considered potential ways to relieve illnesses. Hexes, magic and bad karma are all causes of illness. Illnesses can also occur as a consequence of social and personal issues: delaying marriage is sometimes thought to lead to infertility. Excessive preoccupation with sexual fantasies can also result in gonadal disorders. In all cases, the problem can be diagnosed through a skilled practitioner because these problems are all expressed through a lack of balance in the humors.

Attitudes towards Western medicine may also be influenced by historical factors. During the colonial period there was opposition to the notion that traditional medicine and western medicine were complimentary.[24] One colonial official attached traditional medicine saying: 'Surgery is in an extremely rude state. Knowledge of pharmacy is equally limited. Their physiology is of the most fanciful kind.'[25] It is possible that some modern Sri Lankans view being treated by traditional doctors as a patriotic duty in light if these patronising historical attitudes.

Whatever the cause may be, traditional medicine continues to be very popular in Sri Lanka. The structure of traditional medicine is multifaceted. The sociological and medical structures of traditional medicine in Sri Lanka have been studied at length by scholars such as Obeyesekere (1976), Liyanaratne (1999) and Arseculeratne (2002). I direct the reader to those studies for further details. One important point, however, is that there has long been a connection between traditional medicine and Buddhism and, historically, monks often acted as doctors as well as priests.[26]

In brief, traditional medicine in Sri Lanka is made up of the ubiquitous *āyurvedic* and *siddha* medicine, which is of Indian origin.[27] In addition, there is an indigenous Sri Lankan tradition known as *desiya chikitsa* ('local therapeutics' or 'local medicine').[28] Regardless, this is all comes under the label of *āyurveda* in the Sri Lankan context.[29]

Āyurvedic medicine is based around the concept of the three humors and illness stems from a lack of balance in the humors and their related vital fluids.[30] Excessive 'heating' and 'cooling' leads these humors to become disrupted and this results in illness. For example, a common worry is the bare head getting rained on. This leads to cooling which causes an excess of phlegm.[31] Sickness follows from this. Diet plays an enormous role in the development of illness because some foods are classified as 'heating' and others 'cooling'. Thus, without proper attention it is easy to fall into sickness through a failure to have a diet that balances heating foods with cooling foods.[32] Milk has a restorative effect because it is considered a prime cooling food.[33] This merely cements the virtue of consuming milk.

In Chapter 1 it was pointed out that meat consumption is sometimes associated with the demonic. Demonology is, in fact, a branch of *āyurvedic* medicine.[34] A demon's natural interest in meat eating can therefore be explained in terms of traditional medicine: demons, being very angry, crave meat and flesh foods because of its 'heating' properties. Meat is a food that heats the body.[35] This, of course, only aggravates their condition of anger. Perhaps one of the reasons Kataragama is offered certain vegetarian foods is because it reduces his exposure to heating foods. There is therefore an attempt to civilise Kataragama and bring him into line with his more level-headed co-deities. On the other hand, canny *dāyaka* may give him meat as a way to 'heat' him, increase his anger, and thus increase the effectiveness of their prayers.

These various types of medicine so described are generally taught to traditional practitioners in medical colleges and other institutions. There is also a process of accreditation and practitioners are supposed to hold a licence. For some doctors traditional medicine is a family tradition. Three of the four doctors we interviewed stated that their work was inter-generational. These doctors are also very experienced. Between the four of them there is over 120 years worth of medical experience.

All four specialised in different areas. As mentioned, Ishara Fernando and his son specialised in eyes (though Mr Fernando stressed that they also treated paralysis, arthritis and head injuries). Mr Gunadasa, however, treated bone breaks, dislocations and abnormalities of the limbs. His work was a combination of osteopathy and physiotherapy. Mrs De Souza and Mr Abayaratne (who were related) were more general in their work. They both seemed to treat a wide range of illnesses and diseases. They might therefore be compared to general practitioners as we know them in the West.

Meat as a form of treatment

Three of the four clinics regularly used animal products in the preparation of their medicines. The Fernandos were the exception in this regard and their views will be examined in some detail in the following.

In general, the doctors saw no moral or ethical obstacle in utilising flesh. In fact, the view was that for many treatments to be effective meat was positively necessary. Take for example Mrs De Souza. Mrs De Souza is a middle-aged doctor with 22 years' experience. She operates her own clinic because, as she says, working in a public hospital is less than ideal since they lack the necessary resources. Her clinic is located on a busy main road in central Colombo and she does not seem to be short of clients.

Mrs De Souza routinely uses meat in her medical preparations. She explains that for illnesses of the nervous system, 'there are medicines we make using mutton…we also use the liver of the goat to make some medicines. We use medicine made from eggs for illnesses involving the eye.' She adds that, 'There are instances where we use goat liver to make medicine when treating children suffering from iron deficiency anaemia.'

She went onto explain the process by which some of these medicines are produced, 'We pretty much use skin, meat, and liver and most of the goat. And we boil it down and use the extracts of it to make different types of medicine. I know it sounds unethical and harsh to kill a goat and use its parts for medicine but then again if it means healing patients I think it's worth it.' Tigers and spiders remains are used for the treatment of eyes. Elephant skin is necessary in order to counter skin diseases such as vitiligo (a condition where the skin is discoloured in patches all over the body).

Mrs De Souza accepted the necessity of using meat for medicine and was not particularly fazed by the question of animal conservation. For example, when asked about the use of rare animals, especially tigers, in the preparation of medicine she said, 'Yes, it is hard to find but if it comes to a situation where we need such meat we will have to get our hands on it by any way possible.' There are some limits to this disregard for conservation, however: 'There are instances where we have to use the skin of an elephant as an ingredient. This can only be obtained from an elephant which is already dead due to natural causes. We cannot and will not kill an elephant just for this reason. It is also illegal to transport elephant skin. If it comes to a point where we have to, we need to get permission from the relevant authorities.'

It is possible that this reluctance to use elephant could be because the elephant is an animal of special importance in Sinhala society. Laws concerning the killing of elephants in Sri Lanka are highly restrictive and the killing of wild elephants carries serious penalties. The tiger, on the other hand, has no special meaning in Sinhala culture.

Regardless, Mrs De Souza ranks animal welfare as being less important than human welfare. This was so even in instances, perhaps, where the human ailment is relatively minor. The doctor's duty to aid the patient is a sacred and urgent matter that overrides concerns about the animal's welfare. Even Sri Lankan law is sometimes no barrier to curing the patient's ailments. 'Having no access [to the animal materials] is not an excuse. If it's needed [then] as doctors we have to provide the patient with the necessary medicine.'

Meanwhile, Mr Gunadasa was more conscious of the issue of animal welfare. He more explicitly combined his private Buddhist beliefs with his professional practice. He says, 'As Buddhists we consider all animals to be living beings with feelings just like humans. And we believe that all animals have feelings such as pain. So as humans, being more evolved and intelligent, [we] should understand this fact and respect all animals.' Mr Gunadasa's clinic is located just outside of Kandy. He maintains an excellent reputation as a healer of broken bones. We were present during two consultations – one was a young girl, the other an older man. Both had arm injuries. The girl's arm was in a sling and was recently fractured. The older man's forearm was in its final stages of recovery. It was interesting to see how forceful and vigorous Mr Gunadasa was in his treatment of the injuries. For example, the girl's arm was removed from the sling and an *āyurvedic* solution was liberally rubbed over the affected area. The girl was clearly in considerable discomfort during this procedure. The same basic principle applied with the older man: a solution was applied and rubbed onto the injured arm. All the solutions used in these procedures would have inevitably included some form of meat extract that, Mr Gunadasa explained, was derived from boiling down animal remains and extracting the oils. Therefore, regardless of Mr Gunadasa's Buddhist concern for animal welfare, he still maintained that meat was a critical ingredient in the preparation of *āyurvedic* medicines.

Like Mrs De Souza, he observed that a whole range of medical treatments practically demanded animal components. He noted, for example, that 'when treating someone with internal swelling…we would make a soup out of a certain snail…' and, 'in cases of snake bite we sometimes use cow urine as an ingredient in the medicine to treat the bites' and more alarmingly, 'we even have instances where we use the urine of children under the age of 12 years as a medicine to control the spread of poison in the body.'

He was absolutely clear, however, that oils obtained from processing meats – especially mutton – were critical ingredients in the preparations that he produced. It was apparent, in fact, that utilising meat in his medicines had never really been an issue for him and he explicitly stated that he had never had any patients question him about such matters. He accepted that, in such an event, he would attempt to find alternatives for their treatment.

Like the other two doctors, Mr Abayaratne was similarly insistent that meat was an important part of medical preparations. It was suggested by Mrs De Souza that we interview Mr Abayaratne as they are related. Their entire family is in fact deeply invested in the *āyurvedic* trade. Like the others,

Mr Abayaratne had been practising traditional medicine for 26 years, He had little time for meat free medical alternatives: '*Āyurvedic* medicine points out various nutritional facts of various animals. They're categorized as animals that live on the ground, water and air. [*Āyurvedic* medicine] specifically points out which animal meat is beneficial for which type of illness. ... So it clearly stated in the practice of *āyurvedic* medicine to utilize various types of animals.'

It is clear from the views of these doctors that meat is a vital part of traditional medicine and that its absence would severely hamper their ability to provide adequate treatment for their patients.

The virtues of vegetarianism

The above cases likely represent the vast majority of traditional medical practitioners in Sri Lanka. For these doctors, meat is an integral part of the treatment process. Not everyone agrees with this view however. Certain medical entrepreneurs have opposed this traditional treatment method and have adopted a meat-free approach. This is the case, for example, with the Fernandos. Ishara Fernando is a proud vegetarian and regards his meat-free approach as a point of difference between himself and other doctors.

Ishara says that, 'I agree that fish and meats have the proteins and vitamins we need. But we find the same proteins and vitamins in local leaves such as *gotu kola* (centella leaves), kunkun and bitter gourd. In my opinion, if a patient wants a speedy recovery we recommend that they stay clear of foods that increase the heat of the body and [adopt] a vegetarian diet.'

Ishara also has an interesting interpretation of *āyurveda* medicine that differs from the more traditional approach adopted by practitioners such as Mr Abayaratne: '*Āyurvedic* medicine was born from soil. And *āyurveda* and Buddhism always go hand-in-hand. Therefore, *āyurvedic* medicine is all about herbs and we try and stay away from meats and fish as much as possible.' Ishara repeatedly links vegetarianism to Buddhism. His comment that *āyurvedic* medicine being 'of the soil' also echoes a discourse that will become important later, namely the idea that the Sinhala people are the 'sons of the soil.' This harks back to the idea that what comes from the soil is natural and pure. It draws upon the virtues of being a farmer – one who tills the soil and feeds the nation. *Āyurvedic* medicine is therefore implicitly connected with the idea that this is a national medicine and stands apart from foreign influences.

According to Ishara's view, Buddhism encourages vegetarianism. Ishara believes that a commitment for vegetarianism also entails a commitment to meat free medicine. Indeed, Ishara takes nonviolence very seriously: 'I was always told from a small age not to harm animals or humans and was taught to practice good deeds and live according to the teachings of the Buddha. ... As I grew up I started to understand that animals are living beings too. They feel pain like us. I mean, would you like it if someone injured you? The same applied for animals. It's the teachings that lead to a greater understanding of why no beings should be harmed.'

Buddhism permeates many aspects of his medical practice. Not only does it influence his decision to only prepare meat-free medicines it also influences his consultation practices. 'Before I see my first patient I worship my parents then I worship Lord Buddha. It's the same with my son: he worships my parents and me and then he worships Lord Buddha as well. This practice has been handed down from previous generations like the *āyurvedic* medicine that we practice.'

Apart from the moral necessity of meat-free medicines as a way to reduce cruelty towards animals, Ishara believes that vegetarianism in general has significant direct health benefits. He illustrates the power of vegetables to cure illness through the following story: 'Once a farmer's bull was heading down a slope while eating grass. And it is said that the bull fell down the slope into some creepers. The bull's legs were broken and couldn't move. The only source of food the bull had were the creepers he fell into. The bull kept eating the leaves off this creeper. Within a certain period of time his legs were completely healed and he could walk again. This creeper was named as *gonike* which means 'bull consumed.' This shows how leaves alone possess a great power to heal.'

Ishara's attitude towards those who used meat in their medical preparations was somewhat permissive. Because of his respect for ancestors and generational wisdom Ishara would not condemn alternative (conventional) medical practices. He said that the truth or falsity of a particular course of action in traditional medicine, 'depends on what has been handed down from your ancestors.' His views on vegetarian medicine is sanctioned by the fact that his ancestors allowed it. This subjective attitude towards truth, and this unwillingness to criticise others, is consistent with the attitudes of many of our – generally lay – informants who routinely said that whether vegetarianism was right or not is a matter of personal judgment. This attitude may be an example of an unwillingness to criticise others publically and not necessarily a genuine adoption of relativist principles. Maintaining a good outward appearance is important in Sri Lanka as it is in many other countries, especially in Asia. Nonetheless, Ishara did say, 'that being said, if you kill animals for the sole purpose of making medicine questions should be raised.'

This is not to say that the other doctors were completely against vegetarianism as a general diet. Mr Abayaratne, for example, maintained that sometimes vegetarianism had health benefits. But even then he claimed that Sri Lankan vegetarians typically were unhealthy because, unlike vegetarians in India, they did not consume enough milk to make up for the short fall in protein from the meat. Note that this position echoes a view found in Chapter 5 on cow protectionism. Milk is regarded as particularly important within the Sinhala community. Mr Abayaratne also refused to eat beef presumably for ethical reasons relating to the importance of the cow. Again, such matters were investigated more fully in Chapter 5. In any case, Mr Abayaratne praised Hindus for conducting their vegetarianism correctly by supplementing their diet with milk from animals. The implication of all this, of course, is that consuming animal products is indispensible for healthy living. It is interesting to contrast this view with other pro-vegetarian Sinhala writers who view Sri Lankan produce as being uniquely supportive of vegetarianism. For them, Sri Lankan vegetables are exceptional in their nutritional properties.

Despite his suspicion of Sri Lankan vegetarians Mr Abayaratne also celebrates the unique health-giving properties of Sri Lankan food. Although Mr Abayaratne's prefers Indian style vegetarianism, he still thought that typical Sri Lankan food was the healthiest option of all. This is because Sri Lanka has an abundance of fruit and vegetables, not to mention an excess of fish. This diet of vegetables, fruit and fish – prepared in a range of agreeable ways using a variety of methods – is, for this doctor, the most ideal diet of all. As we shall see in examining health food literature this view is found elsewhere too and represents an unusual convergence of diet and nationalism.

Mrs De Souza was somewhat ambivalent about vegetarianism. Although Mr Abayaratne said that, in principle, he would prescribe vegetarianism, Mrs De Souza did not explicitly admit this. Rather she said that it entirely, 'depends on the situation.' Overlooking meat and fish is problematic because, 'meat and fish do have large quantities of proteins and necessary nutrients in them' but 'at the same time [they] can be unbeneficial to the treatment process.' In particular red meats are 'heating' foods and therefore can lead to certain medical ailments. Mutton and fish are generally helpful, however, and 'boost the immune system.' She did not comment on the prospective virtues of vegetarianism. It was apparent that she was sceptical.

In contrast to this, Mr Gunadasa thought that vegetarianism had the benefit of making people more 'calm.' Presumably this was because vegetarianism can have a cooling effect when it replaces meat, which is heating and therefore can increase emotions of anger. There was no evidence at all, however, that he himself was a vegetarian or that he suggested his patients be vegetarian – but this may have been due to the restrictions of his speciality.

Only the Fernandos were completely committed to the notion that vegetarianism is mandated by Buddhism. Ishara hoped that others would avoid eating meat but, as with many lay informants, he believed it was just a subjective matter: 'it's a personal choice.'

Mr Gunadasa, the bone doctor, was sympathetic to vegetarianism from a religious point of view but he thought it was unrealistic from a universal point of view: 'although as Buddhists we are not supposed to harm animals, due to various lifestyles sometimes it is inevitable that animals will get harmed.' Mrs De Souza doubted vegetarianism as a moral necessity more explicitly. She said, 'Just because you are a vegetarian doesn't mean that you're not committing any sin.' Regardless, she didn't believe that Buddhism required vegetarianism, and neither did Mr Abayaratne. He says: 'Buddhism does not say not to eat meat. It only says not to kill animals.' As we have seen previously, such comments are perfectly in keeping with a traditional interpretation of the Pāli canon. Others choose to interpret the canonical sources in a more liberal fashion, however.

Vegetarianism in health literature

There is a wealth of literature in Sri Lanka available that promotes vegetarianism as an ideal dietary lifestyle. In this literature, the reasons given for why vegetarianism should be adopted is generally similar to reasons already encountered amongst the informants and vegetarian/animal ethics literature: (1) ethics, i.e. concern over animal welfare that is usually motivated by a Buddhist sense of compassion; and (2), prudence, i.e. the view that vegetarianism is a healthy lifestyle and that it sometimes can even prevent the development of illness altogether. Since we have previously considered health literature and animal ethics, this chapter has been primarily concerned with the issue of prudence and the advantages vegetarianism has for improving health.

It should be remembered that pro-vegetarian materials discussed previously are exceptional and that most conventional nutritional guides recommend – or at least assume – the consumption of some meat or fish. Sedī Pranāndu's *Food and Nutrition (āhāra hā pōṣaṇaya)* (2012) is a good example of this.[36] In a section concerned with pregnant women it is recommended that the mother maintain good calcium levels by consuming, 'milk, eggs and sprats'.[37] In order to counteract the risk of neurological impairment in the developing child Pranāndu also recommend that the mother consume a whole range of foods including, 'yellow coloured foods, fruit, green leaves, meat, liver, brown rice.'[38] Of course, vegetables and fruits are important for raising inadequate levels of, for example, vitamin A. For this, 'additional green coloured vegetables and leaves should be taken'.[39]

But meats and fish are essential for breast-feeding women just as they are for pregnant women. Pranāndu suggests that, to maintain an appropriate protein intake, 'meat, fish, winged beans, various sorts of seeds, dry fish, and eggs'[40] can be consumed. In general, however, she does advise readers to reduce the amount of meat they consume in order to reduce their cholesterol.[41] She also encourages the increased consumption of fruit and vegetables on the basis that it helps improve one's health and well-being. For example, she states that fruits and vegetables provide vitamin A and D and that this helps reduce osteoporosis and osteoarthritis. It also 'affects the gonadal hormones'.[42]

It should be stressed that Pranāndu is not an advocate of vegetarianism and she provides no instruction for the general adoption of this diet. Like many nutritionists in the west, Pranāndu simply advises that people consume a sizeable amount of vegetables and fruits and that they cut back on their meat intake. This is all motivated from the view that such a diet has health advantages. One would be hard pressed to distinguish such a book from similar Western nutritional guidebooks.

Pranāndu, who has a background in nutritional science, takes a sober and scientific look at nutrition. *Food and Nutrition*, of course, is written with a Sri Lankan audience in mind and therefore discusses the virtues and vices of various foods widely eaten in Sri Lanka, including popular fruits and vegetables such as jackfruit (*kos*) and ripe jackfruit (*děl*).[43] The purpose of *Food and Nutrition*, and nutritional books like it, is not to consider animal ethics as such, but rather to provide advice on how to improve one's health through better eating practices. Abandoning meat is not *necessarily* considered advantageous to one's health. *Food and Nutrition* is therefore an interesting case study in what the average Sinhala language nutritional book might look like.

But even in cases such as these there are deviations. Take, for example, the *Health and Physical Education Teaching Guide and Manual: Grade 8 (saukyya hā shārrikaadyāpanaya guru mārgōpadesha sangrahaya: 8 vana sreniya)*. This is an educational syllabus issued by the Sri Lanka Ministry of Education. Interestingly, although there is no explicit condemnation of meat eating in the document, there is an attempt to make students aware of some of the harms that might befall animals as a consequence of meat eating. Under the heading 'production [of food]' the syllabus states that the instructor should educate students on 'the amount of harm to animals' food production produces'.[44] Likewise, under 'storage' the instructor is asked to look at the ways animals are harmed in the ways they are kept (presumably prior to their slaughter).[45]

These requirements are quite startling when you compare this to Western health syllabi where such instructions are often absent. It is clear from even these documents that there is a culture, at even a basic educational level, that some awareness of animal suffering is crucial. Of course, it is impossible to know the extent to which these instructions are actually carried out by individual teachers, though, as we have seen previously, there is some understanding of these issues amongst the laity.

The Grade 9 Syllabus (similar title) goes into greater detail about nutritional matters and advises that a good diet should consist of the following items:

1 brown rice
2 red millet (ragi flour) and a range of appropriate flours, roti, string hopper and *pittu* made out of red millet[46]
3 all types of vegetables and leaves
4 dry seeds (mung, kidney beans, soya, lentils, chickpeas)
5 all types of fruit (apart from avocado)
6 egg whites
7 fresh fish or tinned fish which is prepared with no additional oil
8 fat-free milk.[47]

It then adds 'regarding adult food there are three views: 1) minimize the intake of foods derive from animals; 2) maximise foods based on plants; and 3) only get food for strengthening the body, not food that is overly heavy (reduce the quantities of excessive salt, oil and chili).'[48]

In the initial list we find a whole range of foods that are considered suitable for general consumption. Fish is considered a basic item on this list. In the two additions, however, it is recommended that 'animal food' should be reduced. Whether this includes fish is unclear. Plant-based foods should, on the other hand, be increased. Meat is therefore treated with a certain level of caution.

As I argued in Chapter 1, there are various socio-cultural, historical and religious forces at play here that influence this cautionary attitude. For example, red meat is not only associated with European invaders, and therefore tainted, it is also associated with violent exorcism practices. Red meat is violent in an occult way and therefore should be avoided. In the above it was also observed that according to the *āyurvedic* tradition meat has a heating effect on the body and should be reduced in order to prevent illness.

Regardless, these lists show that meat consumption – and especially fish – is still assumed even in the school curriculum. Meat is not to be abolished, merely reduced. Vegetarianism, meanwhile, is not recommended at all. These facts are so even though students in Grade 8 are asked to think about the way their consumption of food may affect or even harm animals.

The above discussion includes examples of documents used to educate people about health foods. We will now focus on the more unusual cases, namely those books and documents that exclusively encourage vegetarianism and universally repudiate meat for being unhealthy.

Nationalism and food practices

One of the more important documents that advocates for vegetarianism from a primarily prudential/health perspective is *Buddhism and Health, Health and Food* (*buddāgama hā saukyya saukyya hā āhāra*) (2004) by Madihē Paññāsīha Mahā Nāyaka Māhimipāṇan Vahansē. At the same time, this document and others like it (such as other government issued documents we will look at presently) are also case studies in how food ethics and nationalism intersect. This nationalist background is important and operates as a context for any discussion of what constitutes a proper and healthy dish in Sri Lanka.

In general, nationalist propaganda seems to infect even the most obscure subject matter. It seems to be a basic feature of Sri Lankan marketing. Take, for example, an anti-mosquito product called Madura. The blurb on the reverse of the packet says, 'Our ambition is to prevent our fellow countrymen from using foreign poisons and to build up a healthy and prestigious society for the future, using the natural resources in our own mother land.' This product suggests a distrust of Western remedies and this might include Western medical preventatives (such as DEET). As we saw above, there is a view that Western products are potentially hazardous. There is also a view here that Sri Lankan society should be self-sustaining and independent. Relying on foreign products is not only potentially unsafe, it is also humiliating. Such statements echoes comments made by groups discussed in Chapter 5 who protested against the presence of foreign milk producers in Sri Lanka. They insisted that Sri Lanka produce its own milk. Again, the fear of poison was a significant factor in such arguments.

164   *Meat aversions*

This patriotic concern over the degradation of Sri Lankan society is clear in the health literature too. Ven. Māhimipāṇan laments the deleterious state of the contemporary Sri Lankan diet. In particular, he regrets the apparent absence of healthy rice. He describes this rice as *nividu sahal* which means 'brown rice.' Ven. Māhimipāṇan contrasts this type of rice with the more popular rice in Sri Lanka, *sudhu sahal* or white rice. The prevalence of *sudhu sahal*, he says, is because, 'at one time we had plenty of healthy rice varieties such as brown rice and red rice. But now these varieties are fast disappearing from the marketplace. At present people are just focused on filling their stomachs and not focused on creating a healthy generation of people.'[49]

Ven. Māhimipāṇan continues to complain about the prevalence of processed foods in Sri Lanka. 'Sri Lanka is ruled by three types of food which are despised in the Western world and treated as a menace to society. These are white rice, white bread and white sugar.'[50] For Ven. Māhimipāṇan these processed foods are not native foods – in comparison to brown and red rice. In the above passage Ven. Māhimipāṇan recruits the West as an ally in condemning processed food. Yet the processed food eaten in Sri Lanka is even worse than the processed food overseas: 'The bread that we receive is 60 percent less nutritious than the white bread that western people receive.'[51]

This concern over processed foods is a basic concern, not only of Sinhala writers, but also of health professionals the world over. In Sri Lanka these concerns do take on a unique patriotic quality as we shall see presently.

To begin with, it is worth recalling – as discussed in Chapter 1 – that processed foods are used in offerings to *prētas* or hungry ghosts. Traditionally the processed foods are conventional Sri Lankan 'short eats' such as *kaum* or *kokas*. These items are fried and therefore considered unhealthy. The point, of course, is that these unhealthy foods are sometimes associated with fallen occult beings, just as meat is associated with demonic forces.

Having discussed the prevalence of unhealthy food in Sri Lanka, Ven. Māhimipāṇan thereafter criticises the Sri Lankan government for failing to intervene in these matters. He notes the first Prime Minister of Singapore, Lee Kuan Yew, was advised by trusted analysts to avoid the introduction of these unhealthy foods. Ven. Māhimipāṇan states that, 'Like this, these individuals were able to say that if you go and feed people then illness will be frequent and so the body's health will suffer. Like this, if stomachs are filled then the energy in the body diminishes.'[52] The Prime Minister's point was that excessive eating leads to lethargy and diminished health. For Ven. Māhimipāṇan over-eating is associated with unhealthy foreign food practices.

Ven. Māhimipāṇan is critical of food consumption practices in foreign countries. Take for example the following passage: 'Western countries have less vegetable varieties when compared to the rest of the world. Because if this we see an abundance of products derived from animals.'[53] Meat eating is prevalent in the West due to a lack of alternative food options. He adds that, because there is a lack of fibrous vegetables – for example coconut fibre (*kohu*) – there is a high rate of gastric problems because there is nothing to cleanse the gut with. Ven. Māhimipāṇan is comparing the situation in Western nations with Sri Lanka, where people commonly consume coconut and other fibrous vegetables and fruits. Because of a lack of such plants Ven. Māhimipāṇan states that, 'in order to prevent indigestion and promote normal bowel motions one must drink a special beverage at night to have a normal motion in the morning the following day.'[54] In other words, Westerners are virtually required to consume laxatives due to their improper diet.

For Ven. Māhimipāṇan the West is rife with common health problems in part because they lack foods common in Sri Lanka. This celebration of Sri Lankan food, and the commensurate denouncement of foreign foods, further supports my earlier statement that there is even a proto-nationalistic element evident in the health and food literature.

An incredible passage in Ven. Māhimipāṇan highlights this anti-foreign, and pro-Sinhala Buddhist, discourse. He writes, '50 percent of the Sri Lankan population are living in misery. In addition to this another 30 percent also live in misery. The remaining 20 percent are very well off. They [the 20 percent] are 80 percent non-Sinhala, non-Buddhist. But do not be jealous or hate these people. These people are often very sick. You can find this out for yourself if you visit one of the leading private hospitals in Colombo and see the patients there.'[55] This unspecified 20% who are not Sinhala or Buddhist are consuming foods that lead to ill health. There is an implication that these foods are not of native origin. This is to be compared with native Sinhala foods that are inherently healthy. Consequently, Sinhala people should not be envious of their richer corrupted rivals because they will be crippled with illness while the good Sinhala people will remain unscathed thanks to the indigenous foods they consume.

Other foreign food practices have also intruded on Sinhala cooking. For example, Ven. Māhimipāṇan writes that the 'tempering' of curries (i.e. the application of a fried oil mix in the final stages of cooking) should be completely stopped due to ill health effects and that the word for tempering is not even Sinhala and is, in fact, a Christian word. His reason for why tempering is bad is that it results in smoke inhalation.

This intersection of nationalism and food is evidenced even in the government's own educational materials on health. These materials are used to teach school children.

The first line of a pamphlet titled *Having a Culture of Healthy Food (saukyavat āhāra sanskrutiyak karā)* reads, 'Even before Sri Lankans made claims to a brilliant cultural heritage they had a local ideology about food.'[56] The use of the term 'local ideology' (*dēshīya chinthanaya*) here is noteworthy as this is a term widely used in nationalist discourses to denote a way of thinking, with its concomitant particular lifestyle, which is uniquely Sinhalese.

The text notes that, 'the world is amazed' by ancient Sri Lankan engineering in the form of their great reservoirs and water works. But this great (Sinhalese) civilisation with its glorious food culture has fallen on hard times, and though the West is not explicitly mentioned here, modern life is certainly to blame:

'Due to the recent economic changes in the country there has been a major change in local food patterns. It is reported that the consumption of ready-made food parcels are on the rise. This is causing various health issues amongst individuals. According to a report released by the Health Ministry it is stated that a majority of people consume about 50 or 60 calories less than the recommended daily intake. Due to the fast paced lifestyle, and the lack of knowledge about cooking and storing food, these reasons are causing major health issues.'[57]

Passages like this reinforce the distinction between an 'original' Sinhala food culture and lament its loss as a result of modern changes. For Ven. Māhimipāṇan the fault lies with the corrupting influence of the West while the educational document above simply blames modern life. Furthermore, the fact that there is chronic malnutrition in Sri Lanka due to poverty and a lack of food is not addressed by this document.

It is evident from this document that there is a romanticism of ancient Sinhala culture where food practices were considered healthier and society flourished in an authentic way. This romanticism also extends to the way food is gathered. In some sectors of Sinhala society there is a tendency to mythologise the paddy worker who, it is believed, reflects an ancient work ethic that reflects true Sinhala society.[58] The mantra that the true Sinhalese are the 'sons of the soil' is part of this romanticisation of agrarian society.[59] According to this view, originally Sinhalese had to work hard for their food. The mass manufacture of food is therefore anathema to all of this. Under this view the commodification of food in modern society is to be lamented.

This is apparent in the above educational document where, in the modern world, ready-made food parcels are becoming increasingly popular. People no longer have to work hard to make food. As a consequence of that, they have forgotten the ethos of Sinhala food preparation and are unable to recover its health benefits. This is also clear in Ven. Māhimipāṇan's comments about the suffering of ordinary Sinhalese versus non-Sinhala people who have access to processed foods: even though Sinhalese suffer because they toil and work hard – perhaps in the fields – they are fed well, while non-Sinhalese eat unhealthy food that lands them in hospital.

Another more subtle example of this romanticism is perhaps embodied by the Sarvōdaya movement which focuses on the rejuvenation of rural agrarian practices and, more importantly, village independence or *gram swaraj*.[60] This movement is based on the Gandhian principle of *swaraj* or self-rule, which is itself governed by anti-colonial principles and a celebration of a nation's ability to be able to sustain itself without foreign help or interference.[61] This doctrine has been adopted in Sri Lanka through the Sarvōdaya movement and this desire for prideful independence is another facet in the complicated nationalist sensibilities of modern Lanka.

As George Bond points out, the founder of Sarvōdaya, A.T. Ariyaratne, in part locates the genesis of the Sarvōdaya movement in Buddhist canonical myths such as the *Mahāvaṃsa*.[62] In modern Sri Lanka, the innovation of the

Mahāvaṃsa automatically conjures up the spectre of nationalism, Buddhism and Sinhalese independence.[63] The role that the mythic texts play in shaping nationalism in Sri Lanka will be discussed in Chapter 7.

The desire for the nation to work its own land and to feed itself from that land is part of this and these government educational documents, and Ven. Māhimipāṇan writings, are examples of how this aspiration is manifested and disseminated in the written literature.

For the good of one's health

We have already seen that the Fernandos view vegetarianism as a preferred dietary alternative to meat eating because it not only improves one's overall health, but also because meat-free preparations can even prevent or cure specific diseases. Even one of the medical informants who advocated for non-vegetarian medicines accepted that vegetarian diets might be helpful in some instances. It was also abundantly clear from the interviews with lay and monastic informants that prudential considerations were a considerable factor in decisions to adopt a vegetarian diet. Health benefits have therefore been a prevailing theme throughout this study. In the above discussion of nationalism and food it is quite apparent that individuals such as Ven. Māhimipāṇan are concerned about healthy eating, but what is less apparent is the fact that he explicitly endorses vegetarianism. He champions vegetarianism for a range of reasons, chief amongst them being its health benefits.

There are, of course more superficial attractions: 'In Sri Lanka there is a growing clamour and desire for vegetarian food. For instance, an increasing number of people seem to be patronising vegetarian restaurants in Colombo more than non-vegetarian ones. Also when you go past a shop that sells flesh food you smell dried fish and flesh being fried. When you go past a shop that sells vegetarian food there is a pleasant aroma. There is a difference from the sweat that is produced by the human body between a vegetarian and non-vegetarian.'[64] These arguments about smell hark back to arguments found in the Mahāyāna *Laṅkāvatāra Sūtra*. The *Laṅkāvatāra Sūtra* argues against meat eating on the basis that meat eaters purportedly smell bad.[65] But Ven. Māhimipāṇan is concerned with more than just these superficialities, there are also significant health disadvantages to consuming meat: 'Even though it is true that flesh food is tasty it produces an abundance of illnesses. You have heart disease and an untimely death. With vegetarian food you have a healthy, long life [that is] full of fortune.'[66]

Ven. Māhimipāṇan is not the only one who accuses meat of producing illness and death. It is a common trope in the pro-vegetarian literature. For example, Ratnakāra, in *Give us space to live* (2009), also advises readers to adopt vegetarianism for health reasons, stating that, 'Let us be completely aware that our bodies receive poison out of meat and flesh and we are preyed upon by various diseases.' He links meat and fish directly to cancer and other health problems. 'We consume various forms of meat knowing what adverse

168 *Meat aversions*

effects it will have on our health. The root causes of cancer and intestinal problems have now been found in foods such as meat, fish and eggs.'[67] He adds that contaminated meat can lead to diseases of the brain that, in turn, drives people insane. Meat contamination and fear of poisoning is a factor that helps support the vegetarian movement.

These concerns are made worse by the fact that additives are used in the preparation and preservation of foods. Ratnakāra writes that, 'Already, with fish and eggs, numerous chemical substances are used and now this is a frequent occurrence.'[68] Another risk with meat is that it is easily contaminated: 'Poisonous substances [such as] bacteria begin to quickly grow.'[69] Meanwhile, vegetables do not pose the same risk of rotting as meat does and are therefore safer to consume.[70]

Ratnakāra concludes that, 'These various things mean that if people consume perishable meat and fish then there will not be a good outlook [it's inauspicious]. ... Your subsistence on this meat and fish will result in your entire body being permeated with poison. Today by eating that poisonous meat, you can receive a terrible death.'[71] Ratnakāra is concerned about the contamination of meats both through the introduction of chemicals and through the presence of disease.

Ratnakāra is not the only pro-vegetarian author concerned with the contamination of meat and the effect it has on an individual's health. The Vegetarian Society of Sri Lanka is similarly concerned. As we saw in Chapter 2, the Vegetarian Society notes that vegetarianism is good because it improves the safety of society and the environment. It adds that the processes involved in meat production emit chemicals that pollute the environment. Chemicals also find their way into meat products that we consume.[72]

Like Ratnakāra and the Vegetarian Society of Sri Lanka Ven. Māhimipāṇan is very concerned about food contamination, in particular contamination caused by industrial chemicals.[73] It should also be recalled from Chapter 5 that an entire campaign against the foreign milk company Fonterra was based around a fear that milk had become contaminated by supposed poisons.

For authors such as Ven. Māhimipāṇan the issue of contamination is more directly related to his anti-modernity thesis. Industrial chemicals contaminate everything: not just meat, but also vegetables and grains. For him, it is critical to go back to reliable traditions that allow for the cultivation of safe and wholesome foods free of impurities and harmful substances introduced by modern (non-Sinhala) civilisation.

In fact, Ven. Māhimipāṇan not only argues in favour of vegetarianism, he especially favours vegetarian food of Sinhala origin. Under the subtitle 'when you go and take Sinhala food routinely' he writes, 'Sinhala vegetables are also tasty. They are nutritious. Not just *kohila* and cucumbers alone but also a great number of other vegetables that have a fibrous nature. From that food the stomach and the large intestine are cleaned. Also once or twice a month one should have the extract of the core of the stem of a banana tree. From this food the stomach and large intestines are swabbed and like that cleaned.

This ideal arrangement of food is not very well known. People are not told. Schools teach [children] to break eggs for making cakes and pudding. The correct method for the preparation of milk gravy is not taught.'[74] If Sinhala food is prepared in a particular way, using particular vegetables available in Sri Lanka, then there are enormous health benefits. But these techniques are not taught in school, i.e. they are being lost due to foreign interference exemplified through the fact that students are instructed to make cakes.

Again, Ven. Māhimipāṇan cannot help but note the deficiencies in Western diets: 'There are few varieties of fruit in Western countries. In foreign countries they have to get tinned fruit and thick-skinned Cavendish bananas. [But] in Sri Lanka there are a lot of varieties of fruit.'[75] Ven. Māhimipāṇan then lists the wide variety of fruit available in Sri Lanka. He also includes a number of tables that include a range of Sinhala vegetables and fruits. These tables detail the abundant vitamins, minerals and proteins they possess.

Ven. Māhimipāṇan goes on to add that eating a large amount of fruit is important for health: 'Fruit is very necessary for the improvement of people's bodies. If small children do not receive a certain amount of dairy foods and fruit they become malnourished. Big children suffer from moderate nutrition. At this time the price of milk powder and the price of fruit has gone up somewhat so poor parents, and parents in the middle class, are unable to give the necessary amount of milk, food and fruits.'[76] This outcome is disastrous for the following reason: 'As a result it is thought that children between 5 and 14 years old, to the amount of 33 thousand [people], are suffering from malnutrition. And 18 thousand small children are showing signs of malnutrition.'[77]

As we saw previously, empirical medical evidence indicates that school children do receive inadequate amounts of fruits and this does lead to a number of nutritional problems later in life, so Ven. Māhimipāṇan's concern here is not without warrant.

Lack of proper nutrition in the form of fruit, milk and vegetables (it is notable that dairy is considered vital here) has a catastrophic effect on children's developmental progress. But it is also interesting to see what this means for nations that struggle to access important foods such as fruit – they will be condemned to inferior fruits and a lack of variety. In any case, it is clear that Ven. Māhimipāṇan has no regard for the quality of processed foods that are implicitly and explicitly of foreign invention. He is also critical of Sri Lankan culture for failing to feed their children adequately when there is such an abundance of food available. He blames this squarely on politics.

It is also clear from authors such as Ven. Māhimipāṇan that meat and fish are poisonous and unhealthy while good vegetarian food (i.e. Sinhala vegetarian food) is the ideal type of food to nurture the body and mind with. Meat eating is entirely rejected.

The Vegetarian Society of Sri Lanka is similarly critical of meat eating and regards it as fundamentally unhealthy. In Chapter 2 we saw that the Vegetarian Society regards vegetarianism as being good because it is healthy for the body as well as for the mind. The document in question goes onto say that, the benefits of receiving vegetarian food include: 'The recommended level of cholesterol is maintained; the risk of cancer of the large intestine, heart disease and high blood pressure are all reduced; excess bile is minimised (gastritis); mental stress is minimised; obesity is kept to a minimum; indigestion is minimised.'[78]

In another place in the same pamphlet the Society adds that meat eating leads to 'deficiency in the movement of semen' (*æṭa dirā yǣma*) while vegetarian food causes semen to have 'energy/power' (*shaktimat*). Vegetarianism even improves one's sexual vitality.

The document continues to advocate the health and cosmetic benefits of vegetarianism by noting that meat eaters are overweight while vegetarians have a slender build (*sihin sirurak ætikarayi*). The Vegetarian Society of Sri Lanka, as is the case with other pro-vegetarian authors examined here, regards vegetarianism as an obvious way to improve one's physical and mental health. Unlike Ven. Māhimipāṇan, however, there is no obvious attempt to politicise healthy eating or view meat eating as a corruption of Sinhala food traditions.

Conclusion

Vegetarian food is considered to have numerous health advantages by various Sinhala health entrepreneurs. It is important to note that these individuals are unusual cases. For example, animal products – including processed animal flesh – is fundamental to traditional medicine. Those who use meat free medicines are very much in the minority. Individuals like Ishara Fernando of the *Waterfall Medical Centre* are outliers. Similarly, health food documents – including official documents produced by the government for the purpose of educating the youth – are generally indifferent to vegetarianism as a recommended diet, though they do encourage healthy eating through the liberal consumption of fruits, fish and vegetables and the minimisation of meats, especially red meat. Health is obviously a motive in reducing meat intake here.

Another important aspect of health food discourses is the presence of nationalist commentary. This has been especially clear in cases like Ven. Māhimipāṇan, who views non-Sinhala food and practices as a corrupting influence that harms people's health. Again, the non-Sinhala, non-Buddhist Other emerges as a potential threat even in the seemingly innocuous arena of health food literature. At the same time, this Other is pitied due to the lack of nutritional food that is available in their respective countries. These foreign influences, however, are associated with mass manufacturing and industrialisation (and its chemical contaminants) and as such are contrasted with the supposed pristine Sri Lankan environment and its traditional cultivation practices.

Writers like Ratnakāra, however, are less nationalistic in their pro-vegetarian food discourses. For him, he discusses health in a more politically sanitary fashion. The consumption of meat leads to health problems, especially cancer. But it should be born in mind that operating in the background of any anti-meat discourse are implicit assumptions about the apparent evilness of meat

Meat aversions 171

and its association with colonising forces – be they British, Portuguese or Dutch (and more recently American, Australasian and Muslim). These historical influences are clear from the investigation in the first chapter. In this way, politics and nationalism are inescapable even in this domain.

Notes

1. This magazine is aimed specifically at a fashion-orientated female demographic who have a disposable income (i.e. they have enough money to actually spend on luxury items such as magazines).
2. *æs valaṭa běhět nŏdamā snāyu harahā pratikāra: gangulē věda gědara æs věda mahatā.*
3. *lěḍaṭa běhět dī kanna bŏnanat děna: gangulē 'æs věda gědara.*
4. *æs děkak pādana eka nivam dakina pinkamak.*
5. This is supported by some analytic evidence. One study compared Western and Asian families (including Sri Lankan) and found that, 'white subjects preferred a thinner ideal shape compared with the Asian subjects' but it adds that, 'the ethnic group was not related to present body shape or either measure of body dissatisfaction' (Ogden and Eldar, 313). This means that, although the Asians studied tended to be more indifferent to thinness than the Western cohort, this did not mean they were happy with *their own* body shape. It should also be noted that the Sri Lankan sample was very small and the study does not mention the specific ethnicity (they could be Sinhalese, Tamil or Moor and the study does not tell us which).
6. Dixson *et al.*, 36.
7. Wijesinghe, 809.
8. Ibid.
9. Popkin, 43.
10. Popkin, 43.
11. Wickramasinghe, V.P., 117.
12. Katulanda *et al.*, 1068.
13. Wickramasinghe, 114, 117.
14. On under-nutrition also see Popkin, 44.
15. Wickramasinghe, 116.
16. MN 12.52, 176.
17. MN 26.28–30, 339–340.
18. MN 2.14, 94; and also MN 39.9, 364; MN 53.9, 462.
19. S 707, 88.
20. Gombrich and Obeyeskere, 447.
21. Ibid., 448.
22. However, the concept of *āyurvedic* medicine has been used as a pedagogical tool to explain the virtues of Western medicine (Sachs, 345).
23. It is notable that the Fernandos reflect the moral views already held by Nawanga. It will be recalled from an earlier chapter that Nawanga is an avowed vegetarian and that he believes vegetarianism to be a necessary part of good Buddhist practice. The Fernandos, as we shall see, maintain similar views and prescribe a special type of traditional medicine that is meat free.
24. Arseculeratne, 5.
25. Ibid., 5.
26. Liyanaratne, 4–17.
27. Arseculeratne, 4; also Liyanaratne, 3.
28. Arseculeratne, 4.

172 Meat aversions

29 Liyanaratne, 3.
30 Obeyesekere, 1976: 201.
31 Sachs, 339.
32 Obeyesekere, 1976: 203.
33 Ibid.
34 Ibid., 204.
35 Ibid., 208.
36 Note that the name Pranāndu is the Sinhalised version of the Portuguese name Fernando which is an extremely common name amongst Sinhalese Sri Lankans. Not all choose to revert to a Sinhala rendition, however.
37 *kiri, bittara hā hālmæssan kælsiyam bahula āhāra vargaya* (Pranāndu, 11).
38 Ibid.
39 *koḷa pæhæti eḷavalu, palā varga væḍipura gata yutuya* (Ibid.).
40 *mas, mālu, dambala, æṭa varga, karavala, bittara* (Ibid., 14).
41 Ibid., 23.
42 *lingika hōmōna da mēyaṭa balapāyi* (Ibid., 25).
43 Ibid., 35.
44 *Health and Physical Education Teaching Guide and Manual: Grade 8*, 121.
45 Ibid.
46 *Piṭṭu* is local dish usually eaten for breakfast. It is cylindrical in shape and made from flour and coconut milk.
47 *1. nivuḍu hāl bat; 2. kurakkan piṭi hæki karam mishra kaḷa piṭṭu, rŏṭī, indi āppa; 3. piyalu vargayē elavalu hā palā kŏḷa; 4. viyali æṭa varga (mung, kavipi, sōyā, parippu, kaḍḍala); 5. siyalu vargayē paḷaturu varga (kaha ali gæṭa pēra hæra); 6. bittara sudu madaya; 7. alut mālu (hŏ amutuvĕn tĕl musu nŏkaḷa ṭin mālu); 8. mēda rahita kiri* (Grade 9 Syllabus Teaching Guide, 132).
48 *emĕnma væḍihiti āhāra piḷibanda muladharma tunaki. 1. hæki taram satthva āhāra aḍu karanna. 2. shāka āhāra sulabava ganna; 3. kavara ākārayayakin gaththada sharīra bara væḍi nŏvana taramaṭa pamaṇak āhāra ganna (amatara luṇu, tĕl, miris bhāvitaya hækiṭāk aḍu karanna)* (ibid., 133).
49 *sahal – mē raṭehi tubuṇe nivuḍu ahita sahal ya. dæn eya kramayĕn næti kæra gĕna yanavā. mē kala bŏhŏ āhāra visheṣañayanaṭa vuvamanā karanne væḍivana janagahanaye baḍaval puravannaṭa vinā nīrōga manuṣaya paramparāvak æti karannaṭa no vē.* (Buddhism and Health, 15).
50 *baṭahira ugat lōkayā samājaye saturan hæṭiyaṭa salakana āhāra tunak srī lankāvē rajakam karayi. enam sudu bat, sudu pān, sudu sīni.* (ibid., 15).
51 *baṭahira janatāvaṭa læbĕnāva sudu pānvalaṭa vaḍā apaṭa læbĕna pānvala pōṣaya shakti pratishataya siyayaṭa hæṭakin aḍu ya* (ibid).
52 *oya vidiyaṭa baḍaval puravannaṭa giyŏt rogīn bahula vī saukya anshayĕn mē pamaṇa pāḍu sudu vĕnavā yayi eyin kĕnaku kiyannaṭa piḷivana. oya vidiyaṭa baḍaval pirĕvvŏt kāya shaktiya hīna vĕnavā* (ibid).
53 *baṭahira raṭavala ætte eḷavalu varga sulhu gaṇanēki. ehēyin mānsāhātaya bahula vi ya.* (ibid., 17).
54 *eyin mala baḍḍaya væḍi ya. bŏhŏ dĕnāṭa ude baḍa shuddha vīmaṭa pēra dina ru baḍḍa shuddā vana yam kiyivak bŏhnnaṭa vuvamanā ya* (ibid).
55 *srī lankāvē janagahanayĕn siyayaṭa panahak vāsaya karanne itā dukse ya. tavat siyayaṭa tihak itā dukse ya. itiri siyayaṭa vissa itā suvase ya. ovun gĕn siyayaṭa asūvak asinhala abouddayŏ ya. īrsyā no kaḷa yutu ya. leḍa bahula vĕnavā. kŏḷamba pradhana pēḷē paudghalika rōhalvala innā lĕḍun gæna sōyā balanna* (13).
56 *vishiṣṭa sanskrutiyakaṭa himikam kiyana pærahi srī lankikayan satu āhāra piḷibanda dēshīya chinthanayak viya* (103).
57 *pasugiya kālaya tuḷa æti vū ārthika gaman mangehi vĕnaskam nisā dēshīya āhāra raṭāvē vĕnaskam sudu vĕmin pavatī. Dinĕn dina kṣaṅika āhāra mĕn ma, piḷḷiyĕla karana lada āhāra pārsal paribhōjanaya væḍi vĕmin pavatina bavaṭa vārtā vē. enisā*

ma pōṣaṇaya sambandha vividha gæṭalu pæna nægī æta. saukhya amātyangshayē samīkṣaṇa vārtā anuva shī laṅkāvē bŏhō dĕnĕku dinapatā avashya pamaṇaṭa vaḍā kælari 50–60k pamaṅa aḍuvĕn labā gannā bava vārtā vē. samāja sachalatāva nisā æti vū avivēkī bava mĕn ma pōṣaṇa mūladharmavalaṭa anukula va hā ñānvita va āhāra tōrā gænīma, piḷiyĕla kirīma āhāra kal tabā gænīma væni karuṇu piḷibanda aḍu avabōdhaya nisā bŏhō pōṣaṇa gæṭalu æti vana bava vidhēṣaña matayaki (103).

58 This is also reflected in Sinhala literary texts such as the *Janavaṃsa* which romanticises the paddy farmer as a virtuous person in Sri Lankan society.
59 This is perhaps part of the reason that political parties like the Jathikā Vimukthi Pĕramuṅa (JVP) flourish in rural areas of Sri Lanka. The JVP is a Marxist–Leninist party that focuses on the virtues of the working people. Inevitably, this involves the celebration of agricultural workers who make up much of the Sri Lankan labour sector (rice cultivation, rubber, coconut and other agricultural products are some of Sri Lanka's major exports).
60 Bond, 2004, 45.
61 Ibid., 27.
62 Ibid., 46.
63 It should be noted that Ariyaratne did not necessarily see things in this way and that Sarvōdaya was meant to encompass all religions and nationalities. Sarvōdaya programs were even instituted in Tamil areas under Tamil Tiger control, for example, and Tamils have held prominent positions in the Sarvōdaya movement (Bond, 2004, 30). Furthermore, Ariyaratne conceived of Sarvōdaya as a non-violent peaceful movement and was supposed to counteract the violence that had sprung up during the 80s. My point here is that, while this may have been Ariyaratne's intention, in the minds of many these noble goals can become corrupted and co-opted into traditional nationalist narratives.
64 *srī laṅkāvē da nirmānsabhōjanaya ruchi karana pirisa vædi vemin pavatī. eyaṭa hŏnda ma sādhakaya nam kōḷamba nagarayē mānsāhāra rĕsṭōranṭvalaṭa yana pirisaṭa vaḍā nirmāsāhāra rĕsṭōranṭvalaṭa yana pirisa vædi bava pĕnīmayi. mānsāhāra hōṭal ḷabhin yana viṭa mas karavala badin ganda tadin ma dænĕnavā. nirmānsāhāra hōṭal ḷabin yana viṭa dænĕnnĕ ekatarā pramāṇayaka suvandak ya. manuṣya sharī rayĕn piṭavana dahaḍiyĕhi da ē vĕnasa æta* (29).
65 'Mahāmati, there is generally an offensive odour to a corpse, which goes against nature; therefore, let the Bodhisattva refrain from eating meat. Mahāmati, when flesh is burned, whether it be that of a dead man or of some other living creature, there is no distinction in the odour. When flesh of either kind is burned, the odour emitted is equally noxious. Therefore, Mahāmati, let the Bodhisattva, who is ever desirous of purity in his discipline, wholly refrain from eating meat' (D.T. Suzuki, 214).
66 *mānsabhōjanaya ætæmunaṭa rasa vuvat rōga bahula karayi. krudaya rōga hā akāla maraṇa vædi karayi. nirmānsabhōjanaya nīrōgakama hā digāsiri vædi karayi* (29).
67 *dana dana ma apē siruraṭa mas mānsa samaṅga viṣa kavā gannā api nŏyĕkut rōgavalaṭa gŏduru vannĕmu. piḷkā rōgaya, baḍavælē gaṭa gannā rōga min vishēṣa tænak ganī. sattvayan tuḷa, matsyayan tuḷa, pakṣīn tuḷa, bittara tuḷa, piḷikā rōga lakṣaṇa tibēha bavaṭa dæn sōyā gĕna tibē* (16).
68 *māḷu, bittara kal tabā gænīma sandahā vividha rasāyanika duvya pāvchivi kirīma da dun bahula va sidu vē. ... viṣa duvya, bæktīriyā kṣaṅikava vardhanaya vannaṭa paṭan ganī. eḷavalu mĕtaram ikmanin kuṅu vīmakaṭa lak nŏvē* (17).
69 Ibid.
70 Ibid.
71 *mĕse nan ayurin narakvana mas, māḷu anubhavaya manuṣyakamaṭa nam kisi set nŏgæḷape. mē mas māḷu tamāgē sharīra gata vīmĕn mulu sirura ma vasa viṣaṭa gŏduru vē. ada mas budinnā ē vasa visin ma bhayānaka maraṇayak karā gĕna yanu labayi* (ibid.).

174 *Meat aversions*

72 Vegetarian Society of Sri Lanka, Pamphlet 1.
73 *Buddāgama hā saukaya, saukaya hā āhāra (Buddhism and Health, Health and Food)*, 2004: 31.
74 *sinhala elavalu rasavat ya. pōṣyadayaka ya. kŏhila hā væṭakŏluvala pamaṇak nŏ va an bŏhŏ elavaluvala da kŏhu gatiya æta. eyin āhāra bŏkka hā maha baḍavæl pirisudu vĕnavā. ĕ atara masakaṭa varak dĕkak kĕhĕl baḍa usā āhārayaṭa gannavā. eyin āhāra bŏkka hā maha bæḍavæl pisa dæmmāk mĕn pirisudu vĕnavā. mĕ utum āhāra piḷivĕḷa bŏhŏ dĕnā danne næta. kiyā dennet næta. pæsalvala uganavannet bittara kaḍā damā kek hadana hæṭit puḍin hadana hæṭit ya. kiri hodda taram deyak hadana hæṭi vat uganvanne næta* (ibid., 18).
75 *baṭahira raṭavala palaturu varga svalpayak æta. piṭaraṭavalin gĕnvā gat ṭin palaturu lĕlla gaṇakam ānamālu kĕsĕl ætha. srī lankāvĕhi palaturu varga bŏhŏmayi* (ibid., 19).
76 *palaturu manuṣya sharīra vardhanayaṭa itā avashya yi. kuḍā lamayinaṭa kiri āhārat palaturut pramāṇavat va nŏlæbuṇot ovun mandabuddhikayan vĕnavā. taramaka lamayin manda pōṣaṇayĕn pĕḷĕnnan vĕnavā. mĕkala kiripiṭi mila hā palaturu mila da næga tibĕna pramāṇaya anuva duppat mavupiyanaṭa pamaṇak nŏ va madhyama pantiyĕ mavupiyanaṭa da vuvamanā pamaṇaṭa kiri āhāra hā palaturu āhāra dadīmaṭa piḷivankamak næta* (ibid., 21).
77 *ehi aniṭa vipākaya vashayĕn vayasa 5 siṭa 14 dakvā lamayin tistun dahasak pamaṇa mandabudhika væ siṭinavā. pŏduvĕ lamayin daha aṭa lakṣayak pamaṇa mandapōṣaṇayĕn pĕḷĕnavā* (ibid).
78 *nirmānsāhārikayakuṭa læbĕna pratilābha: 1. yōgaya kŏlĕsṭarōl maṭṭamak pavatvāgĕna yāma; 2. maga baḍavælē piḷikā, hruda rōga saha adhirudira pīḍanaya ætivimĕ; 3. amil pittaya (gasṭrayitis) avama vĕ; 4. avama mānasika ātatiyak ætivĕ; 5. tarabāruva avama karagata hækivĕ; 6. malabaddaya avama karayi* (Vegetarian Society of Sri Lanka, Pamphlet 1).

7 Food politics

Ethnic conflict and halāl abolitionism in Sri Lanka

'We are not asking the Muslim people to stop eating beef,' says Akimīmana Dayāratana, 'we are just asking them to stop cattle slaughter.'[1] Dayāratana is the President of Sinhala Rāvaya, a nationalist Buddhist organisation that seeks to protect and nurture the Buddhist dharma in Sri Lanka. One of its key objectives is to outlaw *halāl* foods in Sri Lanka.

There is marked hostility towards Muslims in Sri Lanka and this hostility has only increased since the end of the civil war. In Sri Lanka, food consumption practices are a flash issue that can lead to great conflict and animosity. An alarming number of Sinhala Buddhists who maintain nationalistic sentiments have banded together to oppose Islam. Their view is that Islamic *hālal* practices are immoral and un-Buddhist and, furthermore, represent a threat to the purity of Buddhism on the island.

The above quote from Dayāratana comes from an interview with the newspaper *Divayina*. These remarks highlight the attitude organisations like Sinhala Rāvaya have towards the Muslim minority in Sri Lanka. The subtle distinction Dayāratana wants to draw between Muslim beef consumption and the ending of cow slaughter is of course incoherent. This distinction is a weak attempt to try and mollify any criticism that Sinhala Rāvaya, and other nationalist organisations, are targeting the Muslim community specifically. But subsequent comments in the same interview further betray the fact that this issue about beef consumption and cattle slaughter is as much about ethnic politics as it is about the Buddhist ideal of compassion.

Dayāratana continues, 'See whether pigs can be killed in the Middle East. They can't. In 13 states of India cow slaughter is banned. Similarly, in Bhutan cow slaughter is completely banned. So if in our country 93% do not eat cow flesh, why is the ending of cow slaughter so troublesome?'[2] These remarks reflect a long-standing perception amongst many Sinhala Buddhists that the opinions and aspirations of the majority should override the opinions and aspirations of the minority. According to this view, the needs of minority groups are not relevant and they are consequently not considered true members of the Sri Lankan community. These domestic minority groups are regarded as amounting to little more than foreigners who have no legitimate right to reside in Sri Lanka. It is not considered especially significant that these minority groups have lived in Sri Lanka for sometimes thousands of years.

This entanglement of animal welfare with xenophobia and islamophobia is a peculiar development in modern Sri Lankan politics. On the face of it, one would imagine that animal welfare organisations would tend to be progressive organisations that are more likely to promote tolerance and mutual respect. In particular, one might be inclined to make this assumption when one considers the fact that the Buddha preached a doctrine of loving kindness towards all beings. This apparent tolerance in Buddhism is supposed to hold regardless of religion or creed – recall the case of Puṇṇa from Chapter 2, who was willing to accept the callous violence of non-believers and even sacrifice himself if the situation demanded it. Buddhism therefore seems to discourage hostility and enmity.

But as it turns out, many Sinhala Buddhist animal activists are heavily invested in anti-Muslim activities. These activities are often not just benign criticisms of *hālal* practices, however they also include incitements that lead to marginalisation and even violence against Muslims. This violence has even led to injury and death in some cases. This tension between the avowed non-violent premises of the Buddhist animal welfare movement, and their actual intolerance and persecution of the Muslim minority, therefore requires some unpacking and analysis.

Before we move on to a more detailed examination of this situation, a few preliminary matters should be considered. Although this tension is surprising, it is not entirely unexpected. First, this is not the only example of purportedly 'progressive' political institutions harbouring xenophobic and racist sentiments. Consider, for example, the case of the Western Palestinian rights movement. This movement is generally populated by progressively minded liberals who believe that Palestine deserves to be recognised as a state and that Israel should adopt a more tolerant attitude towards its much-harried neighbour. While many in the Palestinian rights movement engage in their criticism of Israel in a fair and sober manner, some members of this movement also display a bigoted and anti-Semitic attitude towards Jews. This is similar to the situation in Sri Lanka where xenophobia towards Muslims is present in the seemingly politically progressive animal welfare movement.

A second point is that there is already a history of ethnic politics infecting nearly every aspect of Sinhala philosophic and political opinion, regardless of how innocuous the subject matter seems to be. We have already seen this situation play out in the health foods literature. Recall that some of the health literature was critical of non-Sinhala foods (usually construed as Western) whilst at the same time celebrated the virtues of Sinhala cuisine.

Finally, Sri Lanka has a long history of exclusionary politics that has led to the vilification of non-Sinhala communities. The origins of nationalist politics will be addressed briefly in the following.

Nationalism in Sri Lanka

The origins of Sinhala nationalism in Sri Lanka is a complicated affair and much has been written on this subject, so only a very schematic outline can be attempted here.

The origins of Sinhala nationalism can be found in mythic chronicles such as the *Mahāvaṃsa* (fourth century) and *Cūlavaṃsa* (sixth century). The *Mahāvaṃsa* maintains that the island of Lanka was thick with demonic forces that were ultimately expelled by the Buddha himself on his first visit to Sri Lanka.[3] The *Mahāvaṃsa* describes how subsequent Sinhala kings defeated Tamil polities on the island through force of arms. These Sinhala heroes are described as proud Buddhists who united the island under the banner of the Buddha's teaching.

According to these myths, and despite Sri Lanka's originally fractured and corrupted state, it is said that the island of Sri Lanka is destined to ultimately unite under a single Buddhist polity. According to the *Mahāvaṃsa* this is a prophecy made by the Buddha himself. In this way, political unity has sanction from the most authoritative figure in all of Buddhadom. The unification of the island under this Buddhist polity involves the banishment of evil forces through the power of Buddhism, through violence, or a combination of both. It is easy to see how these myths contribute towards contemporary exclusionary politics in which minority groups – such as Tamils and Muslims – are considered to have no rightful place in Sri Lankan history or society.[4]

During the Buddhist revivalist period these ideas heavily influenced efforts to expel European colonists and bring about a sense of unity amongst Buddhists throughout the island.[5] These mythic texts were used to create a narrative that celebrated the supposed 'native' Sinhala Buddhist people and contrasted them with European missionaries who were spreading a false doctrine of Christianity. Christianity was viewed as a foreign force that threatened to supplant Buddhism. If this were to happen then the prophecies found in the *Mahāvaṃsa* and other similar texts would be compromised. This would be doctrinally unacceptable. The Buddhist revivalist period was therefore critical in the modern formation of Buddhist nationalism and the exclusionary politics apparent today.

This tendency to identify the island of Sri Lanka with Buddhism and, in turn, the Sinhala people continued after independence was realised. The Sinhala Only Act of 1956 is a watershed moment in the development of modern Sinhala nationalism on the island and is a prime example of exclusionary politics aimed at marginalising minority groups.[6] The law was originally intended to remove colonial legislation that enshrined English as the official language of the country. But conflict immediately arose when Tamil representatives insisted that the Tamil language be made an official language along with Sinhala. A number of Sinhala politicians saw this situation as an opportunity to gather support from a voter base already steeped in pre-independence racial politics. The net result was the Sinhala Only Act, a piece of legislation that effectively ostracised Tamil speakers and this included many Muslims.

This, and further legislation that limited educational opportunities for non-Sinhala speakers, seriously undermined Tamil and Muslim communities in Sri Lanka and made life exceptionally difficult. These political decisions were rooted in a prior view, expressed in the mythic texts mentioned before, that the state of Sri Lanka is a Buddhist nation that belongs to the Sinhala people. Therefore, under that view, it is right that the national language be Sinhala and that other minorities be barred from participating in significant national decisions. These other communities, and their traditions, customs and languages, were perceived as being simply accidental cultural accretions that should be grudgingly tolerated by the Sinhala majority. Although these minorities are to be tolerated, they must also be carefully watched lest they try and displace the rightful owners of the island.

The Tamil separatist movement began to develop throughout the twentieth century and reached a point of radical departure after the 1983 riots. The Tamil separatist movement, although originally a product of Sinhala racism and exclusionary politics, was perceived as a realisation of these fears. Moreover, it was the realisation of a threat already mentioned in the mythic texts. Like the great Sinhala heroes of those ancient texts, the role of the modern state is to destroy such menacing forces and reassert Sinhala dominance over the island. Roshan Wijeyeratne describes this view as a dynamic in which the fractured whole of the island must be repeatedly repaired so that a Buddhist unity can once again be realised.[7]

The end of the civil war represents an apparent recovery of the ideal polity promised in the *Mahāvaṃsa* and the successful defeat of yet another Tamil threat. But this nationalist ideal does not mean that every threat has been conquered and there is a constant fear that this unity will again be disrupted. In the following we will see that one discourse that has since emerged is an anti-Muslim narrative that tells us that it is now Islam that is a threat to the prosperity of Buddhism on the island.

The narrative of displacement is a strong theme in this discourse and there is a constant fear that Sinhala Buddhists are at risk of being removed from their rightful homeland. This fear of displacement is evident in the following discussion of Buddhist–Muslim relations.

A brief history of Muslim–Sinhala conflict

Lorna Dewaraja maintains that Muslims have lived peacefully in Sri Lanka for at least 1,000 years. For her, this peace ended with the anti-Muslim riots in 1915. Her view is that Muslims have, for a long time, been well integrated into Sinhala society but in recent times Muslims have become increasingly radicalised and therefore have sought to separate themselves from the wider Sri Lankan community.[8] So despite Dewaraja's progressive communitarian outlook there is still a tendency to view the Muslim minority as being at fault.

The possibility that Muslims have become more insulated as a response to external pressure from nationalist forces is not fully considered by Dewaraja.

Dewaraja's romantic view of Sinhala–Muslim relations prior to 1915 is also questionable. It is true that there is little evidence of outright conflict between Muslims and Sinhalese prior to 1915. It is also true that Muslims and Sinhalese were allied at various occasions. For example, during the medieval period Muslim officials acted as brokers between rival Sri Lankan polities.[9] But there is also evidence that, at least during the pre-independence period, when Sinhala nationalism was in its infancy, anti-Muslim sentiment was present. Take for example Aṇagarika Dharmapāla, a crucial figure in the Buddhist revivalist period already discussed at length in Chapter 1.

In his autobiographical writings, Dharmapāla singles out Muslim invaders as being responsible for the downfall of Buddhism in India.[10] Contrary to such claims, there is evidence that Buddhism was already in a state of decline in India at the time of these invasions though these conquests ultimately helped accelerate the decline.[11]

Yet this attitude that Islam is a force of displacement is a signature of modern Sinhala Buddhist nationalists who blame Muslims for defeating Buddhism in countries as diverse as Afghanistan and Indonesia. This view is a fundamental part of the displacement narrative that will be discussed in detail presently. Such views position Islam as a natural enemy of Buddhism and Buddhist teaching – including the Buddhist attitude towards animal welfare.

In these early writings, Dharmapāla also argues that Muslims were a threat to the prosperity of Sinhala traders and businessmen. Sangharakshita (himself a nationalist) writes that Dharmapāla, 'inveighed against the Sinhala people not only for surrendering their religious and cultural individuality to the Christians but also for giving up their economic independence to the Hambayas, a class of immigrant Indian Muslim traders who had practically monopolised the retail business of the coast and the interior.'[12] The view that Muslim traders were marginalising Sinhalese retailers is a perspective that has led to anti-Muslim hostility and the destruction of Muslim property.

Such attitudes culminated in the 1915 riots. Some scholars have suggested that these riots in part stemmed from economic rivalry (though Kunnangara maintains that it was only one factor in the formation of this conflict).[13] Meanwhile De Silva has argued that perceived religious differences were a convenient way to justify settling scores against Muslim business rivals.[14] The 1915 riots were certainly a watershed moment in Muslim–Sinhala history that brought to an end whatever harmony Muslims and Sinhalese had previously maintained. The riots began as a result of a disagreement between Muslims and Buddhists in Gampola concerning the passing of an annual Buddhist procession (*perahæra*) through the town. It was claimed that it would disturb the newly developed and extended mosque that was now abutting the traditional path of the procession.[15] The matter was not adequately settled and, in addition to other confounding conflicts arising from the development of mosques elsewhere on the island, violence broke out. This violence quickly spread beyond Gampola to locations all over the island.[16] Numerous Muslims were killed and the Colonial Government was forced to intervene.

Anagarika Dharmapāla's response to this conflict is telling. He writes in a letter to the Secretary of State for the Colonies in June of 1915, 'What the German is to the Britisher that the Muhammedan is to the Sinhalese. He is an alien to the Sinhalese by religion, race and language. He traces his origin to Arabia, whilst the Sinhalese traces his origin to India and to Aryan sources.'[17] Here, Dharmapāla draws a comparison between the British conflict with Germany – with whom they were at war with at the time the letter was composed – and the Sinhalese's relationship with the Muslim community. The Sinhalese are at war with Muslims.

But for Dharmapāla this conflict between the Muslim and Sinhala community is unavoidable and predetermined. He writes: 'The British officials may shoot, hang, quarter, imprison or do anything to the Sinhalese but there will always be bad blood between the Moors and the Sinhalese. The peaceful Sinhalese have at last shown that they can no longer bear the insults of the alien. The whole nation in one day have risen against the Moor people. The causes are economic and spiritual.'[18] Muslims are aliens. They have insulted the Sinhalese people. The conflict will remain forever. Recall that Dharmapāla remains a major figure for proud Sinhalese and die-hard nationalists alike and his image is sometimes found hung on people's walls. His views on Muslims will of course colour how some Sinhalese view Muslims even today.

The stereotype that Muslims are unwanted interlopers that have monopolised a native economy is reminiscent of the notorious stereotype of Jews. This stereotype has historically pervaded Europe, and in fact the entire world, and is based on the mistaken view that the Jewish people are vagabonds who occupy non-Jewish spaces to exploit local labour and use their intrinsic financial skills to further their own economic interests. Evidence of this racist stereotype is present to some extent in reference to Muslim Sri Lankans. Muslims are stereotypically perceived as wealthy and cunning. They are sometimes thought of as people who use underhanded tricks to exploit others for financial gain. As with the case of Jews in Europe, Muslim businesses have been targets of violence.

Incredibly, Dharmapāla himself compares Muslims to the Jews directly revealing, not only his own anti-Muslim prejudices, but also a shocking level of anti-Semitism. He writes in the aforementioned letter: 'The Muhammedans, an alien people, who in the early part of the 19th century were common traders, by Shylockian methods became prosperous like the Jews.'[19] He concludes his elaborate conspiracy by writing, 'The alien South Indian Muhammedan comes to Ceylon, sees the neglected illiterate villager, without any experience in trade, without any knowledge of any kind of technical industry and isolated from the whole of Asia on account of his language, religion and race, and the result is the Muhammedan thrives and the son of the soil goes to the wall.'[20]

These comments indicate the kind of support and antecedent conditions that fuelled the violence in 1915 and also cast light on the type of violence that we see even today in Sri Lanka.

Violence against Muslim businesses has continued in recent times. In 1915 the genesis of these riots was a perceived privileging of Muslim interests against majority Sinhala religious and business activities. This continues in modern times. Recent protests in Sri Lanka have targeted Muslim businesses and places of worship. One of the earliest incidents in this string of attacks on Muslim property was an attack in 2013 on a large Muslim owned garment business in Pepiliyana, Colombo.[21] However, attacks on Muslim religious institutions started well before that. In Dambulla in 2012, a Muslim mosque was forced to close down by the Government.[22]

Some of the most violent anti-Muslim clashes occurred in June 2014 near Aluthgama in the Kalatura district. The violence began after allegations that a monk had been attacked by Muslims. Rallies held by the nationalist group Bŏdu Bala Sēnā soon turned into riots. Muslim businesses were attacked and destroyed by armed mobs. Three men protecting a mosque were shot dead by gunmen.[23] Non-Muslims were also injured by these mobs. In response to these riots further violence and reprisal attacks spread throughout the island. In June 2014, a clothing shop called 'Nolimit' was destroyed in a fire-bomb incident.[24]

These are just a sample of incidents where conflict has arisen between the Muslim and the Sinhala community. Usually Muslims bear the brunt of the violence and sometimes others are also caught up in the aftermath.

As argued by De Silva, eliminating business rivals is probably one factor in these assaults on Muslim businesses. But religious sentiment is certainly another cause of this violence. For example, in the last few years a number of Muslim owned butcheries have been attacked by Buddhist protestors. In one case a vehicle used to transport beef was destroyed. Attempts have also been made by Buddhists to undermine trade in beef by purchasing tenders for Muslim butcheries. One article reads, for example, 'Monks look at getting tender for Talgasvala meat shop'.[25] By holding the tender these activists are able to prevent the operation of the business.

Whether violent or non-violent these activities have the same basic intention, an intention made clear in the interview with Dayāratana – the forcible prevention of cattle slaughter by Muslim traders.

On the face of it, such actions may be thought to stem from a high-minded concern for animals. As we saw in Chapter 5, many Sinhala Buddhists regard cows as being in unique need of protection. Yet it is important to also recall that most Sinhala Buddhists are avid meat eaters who somewhat arbitrarily avoid the consumption of beef. Therefore, their moral credentials are, at best, dubious and it is impossible to overlook the fact that xenophobia plays a fundamental role in these violent transactions. Xenaphobia and islamophobia are unfortunately extremely well evidenced in connection to animal welfare activities. In such conditions whipping up violence only requires the

182 *Food politics*

intervention of a few skilled orators who know what the appropriate triggers are for violence.

Buddhist nationalist groups

Key players in recent developments in Sinhala nationalism are the introduction of two political organisations: Bŏdu Bala Sēnā (Buddhist Strength Army) and Sinhala Rāvaya (Voice of the Sinhala People).

Bŏdu Bala Sēnā is frequently translated as 'Buddhist Strength Force' in international media. This translation, however, is slightly misleading. The translation of *sēnā* as 'force' has the effect of sanitising the meaning of this word. The term *sēnā* is more militaristic in its implications.[26] The correct translation for this term is therefore 'army.' Not only is Bŏdu Bala Sēnā organised in the manner of a military force, it has the aggressive disposition of a military too. It seems to me that the tendency to merely translate *sēnā* as 'force' is almost an apologetic attempt to civilise what is otherwise quite a brutal organisation that even the Rajapaksa Government are beginning to respond to.

Bŏdu Bala Sēnā is a splinter group of the Buddhist political party Jātika Hĕḷa Urumaya (National Heritage Party). As a parliamentary entity, Jātika Hĕḷa Urumaya favours Sinhala Buddhist culture and its purpose is to represent Buddhist culture in the face of what it believes to be encroaching non-Buddhist, non-Sinhala forces.[27] The founders of Bŏdu Bala Sēnā, Kirama Wimalajŏthi Himi and Galagŏda Gñanasāra Himi, believed that Jātika Hĕḷa Urumaya was not sufficiently radical enough and was not effective in engaging their perceived political enemies. In general, the promotion of peace by monks involved in politics has been an exception rather than a rule.[28]

Wimalajŏthi and Gñanasāra had grown disillusioned with conventional politics. These monks may be regarded as non-traditionalist and their engagement in politics itself stems from Buddhist revivalist period and its associated Protestant Buddhism discussed in Chapter 4. A traditionalist perspective typically demands that monks not engage in politics at all. This ideal of separation of temple and state is almost certainly false, historically. The clergy have always been close to the various courts that held power throughout Sri Lankan history. But in such cases monks were generally advisers and the direct involvement of monks in politics is somewhat unprecedented. In addition, organisations like Bŏdu Bala Sēnā not only engage in politics they also completely overturn the traditional idea that monks must be completely passive. For Bŏdu Bala Sēnā even violence is justified so long as it is done in defence of Buddhism.

In accordance with the mythic principles already encountered earlier, Wimalajŏthi and Gñanasāra believe that Sinhala Buddhism needed to react against encroaching foreign forces that seek to corrupt Sri Lanka. Hence, they believed it necessary to found a grassroots movement to fight back against elements that they believed were seeking to dislodge Buddhist and Sinhala culture from the island of Sri Lanka, hence the origins of Bŏdu Bala Sēnā.

These motives are clear from the Bŏdu Bala Sēnā mission statement which can be found on their website. There are twelve objectives: '(1). A Buddhist society; (2) To produce a fearless monastic heritage; (3) To have a reformed and modernised monastic heritage; (4) To develop a regional Buddhist monastic headquarters; (5) To develop a female monastic order; (6) To do Buddhist work and establish the development of Buddhist temples; (7) To do Dharma publicity and the building of Sri Lanka's reputation; (8) The development of a reputation of cooperation and networking for Buddhists; (9) The establishing of funding for Buddhists; (10). The protection and building of Buddhist businesses/entrepreneurships; (11) To guard Buddhist archaeological sites; (12) To step up, protect and face the challenges against Buddhism.'[29]

A number of the items on this list can be construed as 'progressive' in comparison to traditional monastic values. Most obviously, the statement aims for a 'modernised' monastic culture. Again, this desire for modernisation harks back to the so-called Protestant Buddhist impulse.

Perhaps the more surprising case of this desire for modernisation is the aspiration to develop a female monastic order. This has objective has been generally resisted by the traditional clergy for some years. Wimalajōthi and Gñanasāra can therefore be separated from other members of the *sangha* in that they do have some desire to reform old systems and beliefs. However, their conservative and xenophobic agenda is already implied by some of the other items on this list including the desire to protect Buddhist businesses. As we have seen above, this is sometimes a code for the targeting of non-Buddhist enterprises that are viewed as threats to Sinhala Buddhist businesses.

Likewise, the statement that they must, 'guard Buddhist archaeological sites' is similarly a gesture towards the idea that non-Buddhist venues – such as mosques – are interfering with Buddhist religious venues. The events in 1915 that triggered the anti-Muslim riots were, it can be recalled, concerned precisely with the abutting of a mosque onto a traditional Buddhist processional route. Such spatial conflicts continue now. For example, conflict arose in Kuragala when Bŏdu Bala Sēnā objected to the building of a mosque near a Buddhist site. Their view was that Buddhist rock caves in the area were being destroyed by Muslims. These claims are rooted in the notion that Muslims, and other unwanted ethnic and religious minorities, are displacing Buddhists from their rightful place.

Since, in accordance with the mythic prophecies, nationalist groups like Bŏdu Bala Sēnā view the entire island of Sri Lanka as the rightful space of Sinhala Buddhists there is, in fact, nowhere for any Muslim structure to be built or any Muslim activity to take place.

This concern over the way Muslims occupy Buddhist space is made clear in a range of ways. One social media article, no doubt inspired by Bŏdu Bala Sēnā, presents a piece that originally appeared in the *Lankadīpa's Taksalāva*. The title of the piece is 'The Eastern Small Arabia: In an area of six kilometres there are 47 mosques'.[30] Likewise, another social media graphic, this time produced by the International Buddhist Council of Sri Lanka, blares, 'A

Mosque in the sacred city of Mayiyangana. Another Buddhist Sacred city at risk.'[31] Mayiyangana is one of the sacred locations in Sri Lanka supposedly visited by the Buddha when he appeared in Sri Lanka. Therefore, the presence of a Muslim structure here is a threat to the sanctity of that location and also alludes to the nationalist fear that Sri Lanka will be swamped by Muslim culture that will displace native Buddhism, just like in Afghanistan and Indonesia.

As described above, Sinhala Rāvaya is directed by Akimīmana Dayāratana. Sinhala Rāvaya maintains similar objectives to Bŏdu Bala Sēnā. They are a nationalist Buddhist organisation and, like Bŏdu Bala Sēnā, they believe that Buddhism needs to be protected against outside threats. Their mission statement reads as follows: 'Let it never happen that the Sinhala and Buddhist nation be swept from the Earth because of foreign and domestic plots. We have seen many situations with similar results of such plots. The reason for that is there are a lot of organisations and governments arising that do not have an aim to protect Buddhists and Sinhalese. Our presence exists for this, to recognise it, to suppress and control the development of similar challenges. In this moment it is urgently felt necessary, regarding this, that there be a Sinhala Buddhist national association. We are the spearhead organisation for that noble aspiration.'

Both Bŏdu Bala Sēnā and Sinhala Rāvaya are preoccupied with a nationalist agenda that celebrates Buddhism and Sinhala culture and demonises foreigners and other perceived interlopers. Bŏdu Bala Sēnā's official website has nationalist music playing in the background the subject of which is concerned with 'our country' and how it must be protected from harm. In fact, the term 'protection' (*ārakśāva*) is a term commonly heard in almost any political discourse. Sinhala Rāvaya utilises similar nationalistic lyrics to excite patriotism in their followers. On their official webpage, for example, there is the following poem by the famous poet Mahinda Himi:

> My country, my nation, and my village
> My true tradition and national heritage
> All of this is kept free and independent by my effort
> Everyone should consider this their duty too[32]

This poem was written during the Buddhist revivalist period as a call to arms against the British colonial government. It acted as a rallying cry that encouraged ordinary Sri Lankans to remember that Sri Lanka was their home and nation and did not belong to the British Empire. Its present use continues to evoke memories of oppression and hardship, only it is now applied to a small and voiceless minority. In the case of Sinhala Rāvaya this minority is quite explicitly the Muslim minority. Indeed, the page where the poem appears is predominately concerned with attacking the Muslim community. Such propaganda has enlivened support for these organisations and the outcome can often be ugly. Members of Sinhala Rāvaya have been involved in attacks on Muslim enterprises and individuals. Like Bŏdu Bala Sēnā, they are aggressively anti-Muslim and are engaged in efforts to prevent the spread of non-Buddhist activities and institutions.

Hālal abolitionism in Sri Lanka

The main source of this islamophobia comes from the cow protection and *halāl* abolitionism movements. Both Bŏdu Bala Sēnā and Sinhala Rāvaya are engaged in activities to try and prevent the slaughter of cattle and the production of *halāl* food. One way of distinguishing between the cow protection movement and the *halāl* abolitionism movement is that the *halāl* abolitionism can be defined as a *type* of cow protectionism. After all, an individual might support the better protection of cows but not necessarily be against the practice of *halāl*. Cow protectionism, in principle, is not intrinsically xenophobic, while *halāl* abolitionism typically is. *Hālal* abolitionism is a distinctly anti-Muslim species of the cow protection movement. In practice, however, this distinction is not well drawn and many Sinhala Buddhist cow protectionists are also *halāl* abolitionists.

The meaning of *hālal* is fairly benign. In Arabic *hālal* simply means 'permissible' and is usually contrasted with the term *harām* which means 'impermissible.'[33] In Islamic law, for example, the consumption of blood is considered strictly *harām*, as is the consumption of meat not slaughtered in the correct manner. As with other Abrahamic religions, pork is interpreted to have come from a cloven hoofed animal and is therefore also considered *harām*. Hālal foods are simply foods that avoid such sanctions through the implementation of correct ritual procedures.

Correct ritual slaughter is similarly straightforward. The animal must be killed by a person of good moral standing; the person must be a devout follower of Islam; the animal must be slaughtered according to a particular ritual procedure that ends with the animal's throat being cut so the blood can drain away (since blood is completely *harām*). This last point is what draws the bulk of the ire from Sinhala Buddhist *halāl* abolitionists.

As discussed at length in Chapter 5, many Sinhala Buddhists are against the notion of consuming cow flesh for a range of socio-cultural and religious reasons. Such objections, in conjunction with prevailing xenophobic sentiments rooted in historical political forces, have led to the burgeoning *halāl* abolitionism movement. The extremeness of this movement runs the gamut from mild to very severe. There have been frequent public protests against the practice. One Sinhala Rāvaya organised march from Kandy to Colombo carried a banner that read, 'The start of a motivating journey. Don't kill cattle'.[34] The march was to urge the Government to ban cattle slaughter. Other campaigns are more insidious and more directed in their targeting of Muslim religious practices.

Anti-halāl literature often targets the apex Islamic religious body, All Ceylon Jamiyyathul Ulamā. Bŏdu Bala Sēnā ran a lengthy campaign to try and prevent All Ceylon Jamiyyathul Ulamā from issuing halāl certification. It was successful and Ceylon Jamiyyathul Ulamā ultimately stopped issuing *halāl* certification in 2013. The process was taken over by another body instead.

During the period leading up to this decision All Ceylon Jamiyyathul Ulamā was subject to considerable criticism. Take for example this statement from a Sinhala nationalist social media group ominously called The Sword *(kaduva)*. The statement is placed alongside a racist caricature of an Arab man that was originally produced by Charlie Hebdo, a French satirical magazine. The text reads: 'Ulamā has deceived the entire nation. Ulamā will go through the ear of the government [i.e. this is a Sinhala idiom that means they will pass through undetected]. Instead of making *halāl* illegal *halāl* will be sold under a different name.'[35] The fact that Sinhalese – assumed to be Buddhist – are pitted against the Muslim community is a common trope with these organisations.

Another lengthy polemic produced by Jātika Hěla Urumaya targeting All Ceylon Jamiyyathul Ulamā is indicative of this. It is titled *Halāl: truth or untruth?* (*halāl – ætta hā nætta*). One of its chief objections is that Muslims are not fully committed to *halāl* and that they practice it in an arbitrary fashion. It reads in part, 'Muslims do not donate blood. Nonetheless, if they are ill they will accept blood from another person. The *halāl* way is not to take Western medicine...But in Sri Lankan hospitals most Western medicine is used by Muslims. In that place there is no *halāl* way. Likewise, in Middle Eastern nations, higher society knows how to live in those countries without being prohibited from alcohol, women and pork [that is, despite the fact that these things are not allowed in Islam].'[36] This is used as evidence that All Ceylon Jamiyyathul Ulamā is not a credible organisation in Sri Lanka.

A social media group called Bokka similarly prosecutes the view that Muslims are insincere in their religious activities. The graphic has the title: 'The truth about *halal*.' It reads, 'Our Muslim brothers and sisters talk about the fact that you eat a quantity of *halāl* food. We will accept the right thing, but if it were necessary to give blood to Muslim people would they receive *halāl* blood?'[37] The graphic is positing the notion that Muslims reject blood only when it suits them, but if they were in need of a blood transfusion they would not hesitate to ignore these restrictions.

Halāl: truth or untruth? also presents the view that Muslims in the wider Sri Lankan community are responsible for ethnic divisions through their food practices while Sinhala Buddhists are more concerned with unity of the wider community. It reads as follows: 'From the beginning of time Sinhala Buddhist people have acknowledged he importance of acts of compassion and kindness. Buddhist food culture is unique and is shared amongst other factions in society. Following from that, on Sinhala new years Sinhala Buddhist people give *kaum* and *kokis* are distributed amongst neighbouring Hindu, Christian and Islamic people. On Vesak and during the Esala ceremony food is distributed from the Buddhist refectories. For the festival of Hajji, Muslims also give food such as buriyani, jaggery pudding and dates to their neighbours. This is said to develop friendship and harmony in Muslim communities. However, as a whole, *halāl* promotes distrust and separation in society.'[38]

This passage is significant in a number of ways. First, it contrasts the behaviour of Sinhala Buddhists with Muslims regarding the former favourably whilst being critical of the latter. Buddhists share food and faultlessly create a sense of community. Muslims attempts to build bridges within the wider community but this is ultimately undone by their preoccupation with *halāl*. *Halāl* food breaks this sense of communitarian multi-culturalism. However well intentioned a Muslim may be, his religion leads him into error, unlike their Sinhala neighbours. This discourse harks back to the mythic idea that the Sri Lankan nation should be unified under a Sinhala Buddhist polity. Foreign interlopers only fracture the community, as is the case – so they say – with the Muslim community.

Second, this comparative exercise illustrates how ethnic politics intersects the domain of dietary practices. We have already seen examples of this in the previous chapter on health foods.

It was earlier mentioned that for many Sinhala nationalists Muslims are depicted as being frugal and greedy merchants who exploit others for financial gain. This was compared to the anti-Semitic ethnic stereotype of the greedy Jew. Such Muslim stereotypes are used in *halāl* abolitionist propaganda. For example, social media group The Sword posted a graphic also targeting All Ceylon Jamiyyathul Ulamā. As with the accusation that this group will 'go through the Government's ear' this time the group is described as 'cunning' (*kapatikama*) and 'deceptive' (*kēratika*). The article maintains that Jamiyyathul Ulamā will have *halāl* food fed to the Sinhalese without their consent unless action is taken to stop Jamiyyathul Ulamā being able to issue certification.

Muslims are often characterised as using their perceived wealth as a mechanism to apply pressure to political bodies in order to further cement their supposed economic monopoly. Consider the following from Sinhala Buddhist. Next to the image of a group of monks receiving a plaque from Mahinda Rajapaksa there is text that reads, 'The President is taking steps to pass a law that bans cow slaughter completely throughout the nation. However, Muslims who are engaged in the trade of cow slaughter are spending a large amount of money in order to get the backing of different nations to prevent him from passing such a law.'[39]

To further cement the power of this piece the accompanying commentarial text mentions the Kiri Ammā deity and says that, 'To all milk mothers (cows) we Sinhala Buddhists are ready to pay back the debt that is owed for the milk that we have drunk until now.'[40] In other words, the contrast here is between the Buddhist Sinhalese who appreciate the graciousness of the mother cow and extend towards her good will and beneficence while Muslims are depicted as disrespectful of the Kiri Ammā deity and slaughter her icons on a daily basis. All the while they profit from these immoral activities financially. The

188 *Food politics*

text is also an obvious threat. The Sinhalese are willing to pay some price (what price is unclear) in order to defend the rights of cows. In the context of the violence meted out against Muslims by Sinhala nationalists the threat is especially sinister.

Not only are these Muslim businesses problematic because they displace Sinhala Buddhist enterprises and profit from the slaughter of animals, they are also problematic because they purportedly fund terrorist activities in Sri Lanka and overseas. Coming out of a civil war in which Sinhala civilians were the target of terrorist attacks references to terrorism are especially effective at evoking a highly emotive response from the typical Sinhalese reader. Hence graphics by The Sword that say, 'The major controls of the Colombo port belong to Muslims and they are actively involved in funding Muslim Jihadists.'[41]

Such observations about the perceived purpose of Muslim businesses, and the associated conspiracies that they have their hand in major commercial operations around the island, is important in order to get a sense of some of the wider prejudices associated with the *halāl* abolitionist movement. The movement not only draws upon outrage over Islamic cow slaughter practices, it also draws upon the implicit fear associated with extremist Islamic groups and the widespread assumption that all Muslim activities inevitably lead back to global terrorism. Such Islamophobic beliefs are common the world over. But even the seemingly innocuous animal welfare movement of Sri Lanka is not immune from contamination by these fears.

It is a characteristic of Islamophobia that ordinary Muslims are assumed to be caught up in international terrorism or are at least implicitly responsible for doing nothing to condemn it. The supposed existence of such conspiracies in Sri Lanka is evidence of these prejudices.

The upshot of this rhetoric is a general call for a boycott of Muslim restaurants. The group Sinhala Buddhist provides a good example of this. One of their graphics reads, 'Eat water and rice instead of eating *halāl*! I will never go to any Muslim shop no matter what! Even if I die I will not sell my country and religion!'[42] It was earlier stated that patriotic Sinhalese should make an undisclosed sacrifice in order to stop the alleged Muslim menace. Here, the sacrifice is of a culinary sort. Instead of frequenting Muslim owed businesses – the assumption being that Muslim food shops are spreading out of control – the patriotic Sinhalese should eat nothing but rice and water. In other words, a poor person's meal.

Not all anti-halāl material is explicitly xenophobic, however. Xenophobia is most evident in the case of online social media. Animal welfare literature, on the other hand, is less severe in its approach to the issue.

Observe, for example, the measured attitude Virakŏḍi's takes in *From Nonviolence to Maitreya*: 'What we have heard, according to the Muslim religion, is that it is said that if you want to slit the throat of an animal one must do so while standing on a piece of metal which has been heated to the point it is glowing. This act alone shows compassion towards animals. The prophet Mohammad has said that if you kill an animal for food, that animal should not be tied and made to fall over, nor be seen by another animal. The weapon should not be shown to the animal being killed. Afterwards, one must remove all footwear and stand on a hot iron bar and then cut the animal.'[43] This is a remarkable passage in the context of the xenophobia of other Sinhala Buddhist writers.

Here, Virakŏḍi argues that Islam is actually quite against animal cruelty because its ritual stipulations make it extremely difficult. The implication, it seems to me, is that Muslims are not correctly following their own religion because they make the killing of cattle much easier than their own religion allows. He does not condemn Islam. Instead he praises Islam and is indirectly critical of its followers. Part of his argument here is to suggest that the Prophet Mohammed wanted the animal to be killed as painlessly as possible. The implication, then, is that Virakŏḍi considers this evidence that the painful methods associated with *halāl* slaughter are un-Islamic.

This general argument that Muslims are not following their own religion correctly is clear from the title of his chapter: 'Correctly worshipping your religion' (*tamangē āgamavat hariyaṭa adahanna*). In comparison to others critical of *halāl* Virakŏḍi might be viewed here as remarkably pluralistic.

Again, this more measured approach is evidenced later in his book where he recognises that Muslim practices are just one amongst many different ways animals are killed and that there is a certain kind of arbitrariness to our preference surrounding meat eating:

> In Korea dog meat is considered extremely delicious, it is not a difficult food to eat. For Catholic people pork is a very precious food. Their God created them as human's food. Nevertheless for Muslim people that is a type of poison. For the Hindu religion cows are worshipped as a god. Cow flesh is extremely abhorrent. It is like human flesh for us. Nevertheless, for Muslims and Christians, cows flesh is the best to eat. In China and Thailand snakes, frogs and many worms are considered a cuisine. In those countries just as there are chicken farms there are snake farms. For those meat eaters in our country these sorts of meats are disliked. Chicken, goat and so on are the most popular dishes.[44]

Virakŏḍi's point here is that the Sinhala objection to cow flesh is just as arbitrary as other cultures' rejection of various flesh foods.

'These are all points of view. Sit and think about who is truly wrong in their eating. Be impartial and observe the meat eaters. Can you see that these people are wrong?'[45] Virakŏḍi more tolerant attitude towards Muslim eating habits are now much clearer: people in glass houses should not throw stones. The only moral perspective here is a position of total vegetarianism in which all types of meat eating is rejected and one should not be partial in one's rejection as the *halāl* abolitionists have been.

Most cow protectionists are not as tolerant as Virakŏḍi, however, and most organisations resort to marginalisation, and even violence, in order to communicate their point.

Fears over Muslim food contamination

The *halāl* abolitionist movement is concerned specifically with the boycotting and targeting of Muslim businesses associated with the cow slaughter industry. The reason for this is fundamentally religious and nationalistic. It is perceived as an attack on the icon of the cow which is itself connected to the holy deity of Kiri Ammā. But there are other ways in which Muslims are the subject of fear and suspicion because of their connection to food. The main example of this is the fear that Muslim vendors are intentionally contaminating food with the objective of poisoning Sinhalese Buddhists.

As an introduction to this conspiracy theory consider the following post on Sinhala Buddhist that warns, 'Be careful of secretly hidden things in the *vaḍē* and *pæṭis* that Muslim people sell.'[46] *Vaḍē* is a South Indian savoury snack primarily made from a batter of dhal and gram flour which is then shallow fried. *Pæṭis* are fried pastries that contain a range of fillings, usually fish. These foods are popular for practically all Sri Lankans regardless of ethnicity or religion and consequently vendors of almost any background prepare these foods.

The following story that appeared in the Sinhala Buddhist Facebook feed concerns a Muslim business selling these foods. It involves a byzantine conspiracy to poison ordinary Sinhalese, in particular pregnant Sinhala women. The supposedly true story is told by an avowed Sinhala Buddhist who discusses an experience he had on a bus between a Muslim couple and another Muslim snack seller. In Sri Lanka, snack sellers will briefly board buses at stops to sell food items to hungry passengers.

He writes, 'The female Muslim was pregnant and after a short time a *vaḍē* seller climbed on to the bus. A Muslim seller. As the man was selling the *vaḍē* the woman wanted to eat some. She told her husband. The Muslim man called to the *vaḍē* vendor to come over to the couple. He came over and they spoke in their own language [presumably Tamil?]. The vendor told the couple not to eat the *vaḍē*. I saw the vendor get off the bus and he went over to a Sinhala restaurant and bought the lady some *vaḍē*.'[47]

The author then asks, 'Why is that? Isn't that suspicious?' (*æyi e? sæka hitēnnē nædda?*). He adds, 'You must have seen the Muslim vendors in every city who go from place to place selling small foods like *vaḍē* and *pæṭis* from small carts. These Muslim vendors cross the paths of our school children…go near the schools…you look carefully…from those places Sinhala women get small foods…for their school kids. You must have read in the past about how in both these things [the *vaḍē* and *pæṭis*] chemical compounds are mixed to torment our nation, haven't you? It was proven by that small story I just told wasn't it? Muslim people do not give that food to their children, expectant mothers and young girls. So why would you annihilate future generations from craving a small pastry? Don't buy *pæṭis*, *vaḍē* and *muruku* from these Muslim vendors. If you are hungry buy a packet of biscuits and eat it. From these small transactions these vendors are part of a Muslim conspiracy in our country. Don't get caught in this conspiracy.'[48]

I have reproduced this story in full to give a sense of the perverted logic of the Sinhala nationalist movement. It is clear that (1) the conspiracy theory (and it is explicitly referred to as a conspiracy using the word *kumattraṇa*) provided here is virtually absent of any evidence whatsoever except for a very thin inference about the assumed motives of the man in dissuading a customer from buying the *vaḍē*; (2) the persuasiveness depends entirely on the readers accepting the viability of this inference. Of course, this inference, however weak it may appear to be, must be somewhat persuasive since the post has over 7500 'likes' on its Facebook page; (3) the story is another example of Sinhala nationalists arguing for a boycott of Muslim food enterprises in favour of Sinhala owned businesses. The reasoning in this case, however, is not to do with animal killing but fears about a poisoning operation that targets Sinhalese.

Because of the opacity of this poisoning conspiracy, some inference is needed to unpack its meaning. The view of the author of the conspiracy seems to be that Sinhala women in particular are being targeted by a Muslim conspiracy. Furthermore, there is an implication that the conspiracy is to do with children – older school age children but also unborn children because the author is concerned about pregnant women. Note the author is clear that Muslim women are made not to eat this food. Likewise, there is a fear that a generation of Sinhalese will be destroyed.

This needs to be put in context to the fear that Sinhalese are being displaced from their own land. Operating in the background is rhetoric that Muslims want to take over the island altogether. This is already clear from our earlier discussion of how there are fears that Muslim places of worship are replacing Buddhist sites. It appears that this poisoning conspiracy is rooted in the idea that this poisoned food will somehow wipe out one or more generations of Sinhalese while leaving the Muslim population able to take over. As a side note, it is quite striking to observe just how unsubstantiated and wildly speculative this conspiracy is. But for our purposes, it is important to observe how food is used as a device to propagate such fears.

Food is used to stir up nationalistic sentiment in at least two ways. First, by appealing to feelings connected with religious sentiment. This is clear in the case of the *halāl* foods conflict which is principally about the threat this practice has to the holy figure of the cow in Sinhala mythos. Second, we have cases such as the *vaḍē* conspiracy where there is a fear about the health of the Sinhala people. But in both instances nationalist groups prey upon an underlying fear that Sinhala Buddhist culture and society will be disrupted, displaced and perhaps even expelled altogether by outside forces. Ultimately, this fear originates in the proto-nationalist movement that targeted British colonial forces that occupied Sri Lanka for hundreds of years.

Suicidal ideation and cow protectionism

Bowatte Indaratane Himi is a name frequently invoked by Sinhala Buddhist nationalists and those involved in the *halāl* abolitionist movement. He is an example of just how extreme the *halāl* abolitionist movement is and how seriously its members are in executing their objectives.

Indaratane Himi was a monk who committed suicide by self-immolation outside the Srī Daḷada Maligāva in Kandy in May 2013. In a letter written on monastic stationary he stated that his death was in protest to cattle slaughter as well as what he believed was the practice of unethical conversions from Buddhism. The letter that he left behind read: 'Let us stop the slaughter of cows in this island of Buddhism.[49] Let us remove terrorism. Let parliament accept the bill that opposes being turned to religion by force. Let the union of multi-national, multi-religious, pan-religions that destroy the Buddha's teaching disappear. Let us construct a suitable constitution for a Buddhist nation.'[50]

His death resulted in much controversy amongst the Sinhala Buddhist community. Some labelled him an extremist who had acted in a way that contravened the Buddha's directive not to take life. Others supported his actions and viewed him as a martyr who died to protect the basic virtues of Buddhism. Even Indaratane Himi's remains were subject to dispute as nationalist groups demanded that his remains be handed over so that his last rites could be performed in Colombo. Shortly after his death, there was a spate of failed suicide attempts by other nationalist monks. Indaratane Himi has since been enshrined as a hero in the nationalist movement for his strident support of cow protectionism.

Suicide as a protest against cow slaughter may seem extreme, but it should also be remembered that we have already encountered other extreme actions undertaken by nationalist groups on behalf of cows. Onerous protest marches have been organised that take participants all the way from Kandy to Colombo. Rioting and violence against Muslim owned businesses is a signature of the *halāl* abolitionist/cow protectionist movement. Some of this violence has led to injury and death. In the West, such actions would most commonly be associated with movements of human significance such as the Civil Rights movement, but in Sri Lanka there is an extraordinary situation where these actions are undertaken on behalf of animal rights – albeit the rights of one animal.

As we saw in Chapter 5, cows are highly valued within Sinhala Buddhist society, so these extreme actions in their defence are as much a religious matter as it is an animal rights matter. Despite the fact that cow veneration probably has its origins in large part from Hindu influences, Sinhala Buddhists have adopted the Kiri Ammā cult as their own and, consequently, the Muslim practice of cow slaughter is viewed not only as a violation of a sacred religious icon, it is also viewed as tarnishing a vital part of Sinhala culture. Given the heady culture of nationalist sentiment that is so pervasive in the Sinhala Buddhist community it is not entirely surprising that such extreme actions are occasioned.

Indaratne's suicide, however, is unique in terms of his personal sacrifice. Even taking into account the perceived significance of cow slaughter, what would drive someone to commit suicide in this way? There are a number of unique factors in Sri Lanka that can explain this. His zeal for cow protectionism is only one causal factor here.

First, it should be recognised that South Asia has a long history of figures engaging in acts of self-sacrifice for the purpose of achieving a particular religious goal. Perhaps one of the most famous (in the West in any case) examples of this is Mohandas Gandhi who routinely participated in fasts in order to either protest Colonial government actions, or to try and force his own followers to cease engaging in acts that he disagreed with (such as the communal riots).[51] Gandhi is a well known figure in Sri Lanka and his political activities are influential amongst Sinhala nationalists as he is viewed as a South Asian figure who successfully threw off the shackles of the British Empire. His methods for fighting against political institutions are therefore emulated in various ways, though his non-violence actions are not always widely adopted. Gandhi, of course, did not engage in self-immolation but his willingness to use his body as a vehicle for political change is clearly an influential force within South Asian civil disobedience.

Second, suicide was also used frequently as a way of creating political pressure during the war as suicide bombers targeted civilians and government agents. Consequently, suicide, as a way of advancing one's political agenda, is a normal practice in Sri Lanka.

A third factor in Indaratne's suicide is the Buddhist justification for self-sacrifice. The Pāli canon makes occasional reference to monks who had committed suicide by using 'the knife.' In each of these cases there is a strong implication that the Buddha endorsed their suicide. There has been considerable literature written on this complicated subject.[52] But there are a few relevant points to consider here in assessing Indaratne's suicide.

To begin with, the Pāli canon makes it clear that all the individuals who committed suicide had already reached a state of arahatship and were therefore not going to be reborn again in a future life. In other words, all their previous karma had been voided and so the fuel for their continued existence had been destroyed. Second, all these individuals committed suicide only because they were terminally ill and were in tremendous pain (an enlightened being can be enlightened and also be in considerable physical pain – as we know in the case of the Buddha – and the two are not mutually exclusive).

As far as I know, these are the only conditions where the Buddha allowed for suicide thus making suicide a genuinely difficult action to justify in Thēravāda Buddhism. Indaratane Himi's actions are therefore doctrinally questionable as he (1) was not enlightened – and, indeed, in Sri Lanka it is commonly thought that no one can become enlightened in the current era because we are simply too distant from Gautama Buddha and the practice of his Dharma is therefore too corrupted; and (2) he wasn't terminally ill. Besides, the reason that the arahants in the Pāli canon were able to do such an act of violence at all is because they were freed from the possibility that such violence would produce bad karma. That is why Puṇṇa – who we discussed in the opening of Chapter 2 – refused to act in self-defence against the villagers: it was an act of violence that would have produced bad karma for himself. Suicide, outside the domain of an arahant, is out of the question because it is an act of violence that will lead to a bad rebirth.

But that is a strict reading of the Thēravāda literature. In Mahāyāna Buddhism self-sacrifice as an act of devotion is not uncommon and in fact self-immolation is an alarmingly frequent amongst Mahāyāna protest communities. The case of Tibet is the most obvious here, as numerous Tibetan Buddhists have self-immolated as a protest against the Chinese Government's occupation of Tibet. In China such actions are also not doctrinally out of the question and the *Lotus Sūtra* discusses the virtues of sacrificing one's limbs as an act of devotion for the Buddha.[53]

It is thought that these actions are justified only if it is done as a demonstration of one's faith. In this way one can escape the karmic consequences and in fact be rewarded. The fact that Indaratane Himi conducted his suicide outside the Daḷadā Māḷigāva is noteworthy as it implies that there is the possibility that he regarded his actions as an act of human sacrifice for the Tooth relic which is the most significant icon of the Buddha in Sri Lanka. Such an act is consistent with the deified nature of the tooth relic and certainly has Mahāyāna undertones.

A final motivating factor in this case is the general preponderance of suicide in Sri Lanka in general. Sri Lanka has one of the highest rates of suicide per capita in the world. As Tom Widger has argued, there are a myriad of reasons for why this is the case.[54] Widger argues that suicide has become an available and plausible response to general social stresses. Suicide is a typical response to fracturing in kinship relationships.[55] My own experience has been that suicide is treated as a taboo subject even though it is relatively common. An extended family member of one of my informants likely committed suicide but the informant merely referred to him as dying in a traffic accident. In general, it is not acceptable to reveal the possibility of mental illness in Sinhala society. In any case, as Widger's work illustrates there are a range of social pressures that can lead to suicidal ideation in Sri Lankan society.

What this means is that Indaratane Himi's suicide is complicated by a range of historical, religious and socio-cultural factors. It is not enough just to regard him as a religious zealot. But at the same time, his stated reasons for his actions cannot be disregarded.

The letter further cements the fact that cow protectionism is deeply connected to issues of nationalism. The first request is, of course, that cow slaughter be banned. But there is also reference to 'forced conversions,' which is also a concern of Bŏdu Bala Sēnā. The reference in the letter is to a bill put forward in parliament by Jātika Hĕḷa Urumaya that requires that forced conversions be outlawed. What a 'forced conversion' actually is remains unclear, but it is apparent that the purpose of the bill is to prevent the spread of non-Buddhist religions. It is part of an attempt to undercut the multicultural character of Sri Lanka and ensure that Sinhala Buddhist culture remains dominant. Again, the fear here relates directly back to the notion that Sinhala Buddhist culture is being displaced by outside cultural forces. This fear over displacement is transparent in Indaratane Himi's letter which notes that these multicultural forces are threatening to destroy Buddhist culture.

Indaratane Himi is therefore a crucial figure in the animal welfare movement of Sri Lanka. It is quite clear that he was a zealous individual who would stop at nothing to advance the nationalist agenda of the cow protectionist movement. At the same time, his death is not entirely explainable only in terms of this zeal. As we have already seen many times throughout this book, there are always complicating factors that influence the development of animal welfare initiatives and these factors are not always exclusively determined by religious interests.

Conclusion

The rise of anti-Muslim rhetoric and violence in Sri Lanka coincides neatly with the close of the civil war. Although there has been a history of violence against Muslims in Sri Lanka since at least 1915, and certainly some degree of hostility towards them even before that, the recent spate of attacks against Muslims has accelerated markedly since 2009.

One plausible explanation for increase in violence is the unsatisfactory way the civil war was drawn to a close. The civil war did not end in an amiable way and it seems that one of the conclusions that was drawn from the struggle was that conflicts with minorities can be solved through recourse to violence. In other words, the end of the civil war proved to nationalists that the pacifist agenda of the anti-war faction of the country's political elites was wrong and ineffective. So there may well be a perception that the problems between the Muslim and Sinhala Buddhist community can be addressed through similar avenues.

As with the case of the Tamil separatists there is a view that Muslims are encroaching on Sinhala Buddhist territory. The chief difference here is that Muslims, as with the racist Jewish stereotype, are regarded as having a cunning character and so their methods of taking over Sinhala Buddhist territory is regarded as equally devious. Sinhala Buddhist nationalists therefore maintain an irrational fear that Muslims will take over the country and displace Buddhist traditions. This displacement takes place not only through the actual purchase and development of land for Muslim businesses and places of worship, but also through the erosion of Buddhist culture such as the continuation of Muslim religious practices like *halāl*. Incredible theories are even created with the notion that Muslims are conspiring to poison Sinhalese women. The association between Muslims and terrorism only helps stoke these fears.

All of this is possible in part because of Sri Lanka's specific historical and cultural context. Prevailing nationalist narratives that originate from mythic stories and legends encourage this agenda of exclusion. These stories have led to a fear that Sinhala Buddhists will be expelled from Sri Lanka despite the promise that Sri Lanka is a nation meant solely for them.

196 Food politics

In the midst of these burgeoning fears step nationalist groups like Bŏdu Bala Sēnā and Sinhala Rāvaya. These groups tap into Sinhala Buddhist hostility and exploit it in order to drive their own political agenda. Meanwhile, Sinhala Buddhist concerns over animal welfare – especially the cow protectionist movement – are co-opted as a vehicle to expedite this agenda.

The role of Protestant Buddhism is also significant here. As discussed in Chapter 4, Protestant Buddhism is a tendency that allows for modernisation and so-called 'improvements.' It is this impulse that allows for Buddhist movements that overturn conventional Buddhist behaviour including monastic pacifism. This is why organisations like Bŏdu Bala Sēnā are able to engage in heated politics and even violence. It is a reformed view of what Buddhism is allowed to do. It is a view that allows Buddhism to be reactive.

The *halāl* abolitionist movement represents the dark side of this seemingly innocuous movement to better the lives of cows and other animals in Sri Lanka. As with the previous chapter on health foods it is incredible to observe how nationalism can so easily contaminate even the most well-intentioned institution. The violence associated with the *halāl* abolitionist movement and its affiliated nationalist organisations also highlights a peculiar tension within this Buddhist paradigm. On the one hand we have paragon examples of tolerance and benevolence such as Puṇṇa and the Buddha himself; but on the other hand we have purportedly Buddhist organisations such as Bŏdu Bala Sēnā and Sinhala Rāvaya that want to defend Buddhism through force. This strange tension between violence and non-violence will be explored in my closing chapter.

Notes

1. *api muslim janatāvaṭa gavamas kana eka navatvanna kiyalā kiyannē nǣhǣ. api illannē gava ghātanaya navatvanna kiyalā vitarayi* (Divayin: Sunday Edition, February 23, 2014).
2. *balanna mǣdapěradiga raṭavalvala ūran maranna puluvan da kiyalā. bǣhǣ. Indiyāvē prānta 13k gava ghātanaya tahanam karalā. bhutānaya vǣni raṭavalat gava ghātanaya sampūrṇayěnma tahanam. itin apē raṭē 93%k gavamas kannē nǣtinam gava ghātanaya natara karanna bǣri ǣyi* (ibid.).
3. The intersection of the demonic and state politics is discussed by Kapferer in his analysis of violence in Sri Lanka (2011: 54). Also see Wijeyeratne (2014: 130–140, 150–152).
4. These points have been discussed in detail by a number of scholars. See, for example, Obeyesekere (2003, 200); Bartholomeusz (2002: 21–25); Tambiah (1992: 130); DeVotta (2004: 26).
5. Bond, 1992: 55–56.
6. DeVotta (2004: 42–72); Kapferer (2011: 92); Tambiah (1992: 48).
7. Wijeyeratne, 129, 133–139.
8. Dewaraja, 2.
9. McGilvry and Raheem, 90.
10. Return to Righteousness, ibid., 573–574.
11. Kanai Lal Hazra, 573–574.
12. Maha Sthavira Sangharakshita, 1980.
13. Jayawardana, 224; Kannangara, 132–133.

14 De Silva, 225.
15 Kannangara, ibid., 133.
16 Ibid., 135.
17 Return to Righteousness, ibid., 541.
18 Ibid., 541.
19 Ibid., 540.
20 Ibid.
21 Pepiliyana Fashion Bug attacked, *The Colombo Gazette*, 28 March 2013. See also The Fashion Bug case: a turning point for Muslim rights in Sri Lanka, *Groundviews*, 9 March 2013.
22 Sri Lanka government orders removal of Dambulla mosque, BBC online, 22 April 2012.
23 Sri Lanka Muslims Killed in Aluthgama clashes with Buddhists, BBC Online, 16 June 2014.
24 Nolimit building destroyed by fire, Rs. 300 m damage, *The Sunday Times*, 22 June 2014.
25 *Talgasvala maskaḍa ṭĕṇḍaraya pujāta himiyō balā ganiti.*
26 The term can be traced to the word *sĕnaga*, which means 'multitude or army' (Geiger, 185).
27 Deegalle, 2004: 19.
28 Ibid., 4.
29 *1. bauddha samājauak; 2. abhīta adīna bhīkśu parasurak; 3. bhikśu aḍyāpanaya navikaranaya hā pratisanviḍānaya kirīma; 4. bauddha vihārasthāna prādēshīya sanvardana maḍayasthāna lĕsa diyunu kirīma; 5. mĕhĕni sasuta sanvardhanaya kirīma; 6. duśkara tattva yaṭatē kaṭayutu karana bauddhayingē hā bauddha siddhasthāna sanvardhanaya kirīma; 7. dharma pravārya hā srī laṅkāvē kīrtiya gŏḍa nærīma; 8. bauddha sanvardanaya sandahā sahayōgaya dakvata sanviḍhāna gŏḍa nægīma hā jālagata kirīma; 9. bauddha sanvardāna sandahā aramudal sthāpanaya kirīma; 10. bauddha vyāpāra gŏḍanægīma hā; 11. bauddha purā vidyātmaka sthāna surukīma; 12. bauddha virōdhi abhiyōga valaṭa muhunaḍī ārakśāvīma sandahā piyavara gænīma.*
30 *nægĕnahira punch arābiya. varga kilomīṭar hayayi, muslim palli 47yi.* The phrase used here literally is "Muslim church" but the actual meaning is, of course, Mosque.
31 *mayiangana pūjā nagarayaṭat muslim palliyak. tavat bauddha pūjā nagarayak anathurē* (International Buddhist Council of Sri Lanka, July 2013).
32 *magē raṭa magē jāthiya magē gama / magē sat sirīth saha jāthika uruma / magē værayēnma nidahaskŏṭa tæbuma / magē yutukamayi salakavu hæmadĕnama.*
33 Rippin, 30.
34 *adhiṣṭhānayē punarāgamanaya. Gava ghātanaya epā.*
35 *ulamā raṭaṭama kŏkā pĕnvā ānduvē kanēn ringayi. nīti virōdhī halāl vĕnuvaṭa nī tyānukĕla halāl aragēna vĕna namakin ēyi.*
36 *muslimvaru lē dan dĕnnē næta. ehĕt, rōgī vū viṭa anungē lē ganiti. ehidī halāl dæyi balannē næta. muslimvaru gaman bimin yannē islām vatpiḷivĕt tahanam karana lada, vædima baṭahiraauṣadha bhāvitakarannē muslmvarunya. etæna halāl kramayak næta. emĕnma mædapĕradīga raṭavala da ihaḷa samajayaṭa matpæn, strīn, ūrumas piḷibanda tahanvī næti bava ē raṭavala jīvat vannō danita.*
37 *halal [English] gæna sataya matayak! apē muslim sahōdarayō halāl āhāra pamaṇak taman vaḷadana bava kiyanavā...hari eka api piligam.namut...muslim ayēkuṭa lē dĕnna avashaya vuva hŏt dĕnu labannē halāl lē pamaṇakda? dannā ayēku piliturak dĕnna* (Bokka, November 2013).
38 *sinhala bauddha janatāva anādimat kāḷayaka siṭa sahanashīlīnvaya, sahapīvanaya, karuṇāva, mētriya praguṇa kaḷa mitrishīlī jāthiyaki. bauddhayangē āhāra sanskrutiya tuḷa anaya jana kŏṭas samagada tamangē āhāra sanskrutiya tuḷa bēdāganī. ē anuva Sinhala alut avuruddaṭa sinhala bauddha janatāva tama asalvæsi hindu, kituṇu, islām janatāvaṭa kævum, kōkis pigānak yavayi. vĕsak pŏsŏn, æsaḷa utsava*

valadī dansalvala āgam bēdayĕn tŏrava kǣma bīma bĕdā dĕyi. ĕ thuḷin apa athara mithratvaya suhadatāvaya gŏḍanǣgĕnu ǣta. muslimvaru hajji utsavaya nimittĕn buriyāni, vaṭalappan, raṭaidi pigan asalvǣyiyanṭa bĕdā dĕyi. ĕ janavargavala hā jana kŏṭasvala āhāra sanskrutīn anuva mitrarvaya, sahayōgītāvaya gŏḍanǣgĕ. halāl kramaya thuḷin avishvāsaya, sǣkaya hā bĕdīma ǣtivĕ.

39 *srī lankāva tuḷa gava ghātanaya sampūrṇayĕnma tahanam kirīmaṭa janapati niyamayĕn nīti sǣkasē. gava ghātaka muslīm vyāpārikayin kŏṭi gaṇan mudal yŏdavā, avajātikavādīn lavā janapatiṭa maḍa gassavā, panata akulavā gǣnīmaṭa dǣḍi utsāhayaka…avadiyĕn siṭinna* (Sinhala Buddhist, 29 July 2013).

40 *kiri ammā varuti, obĕt mĕnĕk kal bivi kiri vala ṇaya gĕvimaṭa sinhala bauddha api sudānam* (ibid.).

41 *kŏḷamba varāyat muslim pātālaya atē. Jihādayaṭa aramudal ruskarana mahāparimāna jāvāramak!* (The Sword, 19 December 2013).

42 *vaturayi batuyi kǣvat halāl nam kannē nǣ. sinhala kaḍa ekak vat nǣti unat muslimkaḍavalaṭa nam yannē nǣ. mǣrunat jātiya āgama nam pāvā dĕnnē nǣ* (Sinhala Buddhist, 10 June 2014).

43 *muslim dahamaṭa anuvada apa asā ǣti ākārayaṭa satungē bĕlla kǣpīmaṭa kiyā ǣttēda itā rat pǣhǣgǣnvū rat vū yakaḍayak uḍa nǣnha bavaya. apa sitana ākārayaṭa eyada sattvayan kĕrĕhi ektarā ahinsāvak kriyāvaṭa nǣnvīmaṭa anubala dī maki. mahammad tumāda sathun nŏmarana lĕsa vyangayĕn hā kāvyamaya lesada pavasā ǣta. oba satĕku āhāraya piṇisa marannē nam ĕ satā gǣta gahagĕna, ǣdagĕna nŏā yutuya. maraṇayaṭa bhājanaya vana satā anĕk satun nŏdǣkiya yutuya. āyuḍayada nŏpĕnviya yutuya. yakaḍayak rat pǣhǣ gǣnvĕna sē giniyam kara pāvahan nŏmǣtiva ĕ mata siṭa satāva kǣpiya yutuya* (Virakōḍi, ibid., 5).

44 *kŏriyāvē balu mas itā praṇīta, nǣtuvama bǣri āhārayaki. katōlika ayavaluṇṭa ūru mas itā aganā āhārayaki. eya dĕviyan vahansē manuśya āhāraya sandahā mǣvuvaki. ehĕt muslim ayaṭa ĕvā vaha kaduruya. hindu āgamikayanṭa harakā dĕviyangē vāhanayayi. harak mas atishaya piḷikulya. apaṭa minī mas mĕnya. ehĕt harak mas muslimvaruṇṭa, kristiyāninṭa agra bhōjanayaki. chīnayē, tāyilantayē sarpayin, gĕmban, vishāla paṇuvan suvishēśa āhārayaki. mĕraṭa kukul gŏvipala mĕn ĕvāyĕ sarpa gŏvipalaval ǣti. apa ratē mānsha bhakśakayinṭa ĕvā imahat apriya janakaya. kukul, elu ādiya pamaṇak agra bhōjanaya* (ibid., 75).

45 *mē siyalla druśṭhinya. mē bhakśakayingĕn kavuda hari kavuda vǣradi yayi sitā balanna. apakśapātīva sitanna. dan ballana mē mānsha bakśakayin siyalu dĕnāma vǣradi nŏvĕdǣyi kiyā* (ibid., 75).

46 *muslim aya vikuṇana vaḍē pǣṭis vala sǣngavuṇu rahasak pravēsham vĕnna* (Sinhala Buddhist, 24 February 2014).

47 *e muslim kāntāvaṭa daruvĕk lǣbĕtta ittavā. ṭika vēlāvakin bas ekaṭa nǣggā vaḍē vĕḷĕndĕk. muslim vēḷĕndā vaḍē vikuṇata kŏṭa ara muslim gǣbiṇi mānāvaṭat vaḍē kanna uvamatā vuṇā. eka eyā tamangē svāmiyaṭa kivvā. e muslim manussayā ara vaḍē vēḷĕndāṭa katā kaḷā. vaḍē vēḷĕndā mē muslim yuvaḷa lagaṭa āvā. ǣvit ṭikak vēlā ovungē bhāśāvat katā kaḷā* (Sinhala Buddhist, 24 February 2014).

48 *hǣma nagarayakama tǣn tǣn vala muslim jātika vēḷĕndat vaḍē, pǣṭis vagē kǣma niyāgĕna punchi punchi karanna valin vēḷadām karanavā oya gŏllō dǣkalā ǣti. e hǣma muslim vēḷĕndĕkma vagē vēḷadāma karannē apē sinhala daruvan yana pāsǣl laga…panti laga…hŏḍaṭa balanna…e tǣn valin kĕṭi kǣma gattē sinhala kāntāvat… pāsǣl ḷamayit…mē hǣma dĕkama apē jātikya vada karana rasāṭatika duvyā mishrī karalā tiyana bava pahugiya kāḷĕdī oya hǣmōma kiyavalā ǣti nēda? e kaṭāva mama ara kalin kiyapu punchi kaṭāvĕnut oppu vĕnnē nǣdda?…muslim aya tamangē daruvanṭa, gǣbiṇi mūtāvaṭṭa, gǣhǣṇu ḷamaṭinṭa e kǣma kanṭta iḍa dĕnnē nǣttē ekayi. ittin…kĕṭi kǣmaka pēreta kamakaṭa paramparāvaka anāgataya nǣti kara gattē ǣyi? mē muslim vēḷĕndatgē vaḍē pǣṭis murukku vagē ganna epā…baḍagini nam kaḍĕkit biskaṭ pǣkaṭ ekak arat kanna…mē vēḷĕndō apē raṭa muslimkaraṇaya karata kumatthraṇayē pŏḍi pŏḍi kŏntrāt kārayō…e kumatthraṇa valaṭa ahu vĕnata epā* (ibid.).

49 'Island of Buddhism' here is a rendition of *dharamadvīpa* which is a common nationalist description of the island of Sri Lanka. It obviously echoes the exclusionary politics of the mythic texts.
50 (1) *mē dharamadvīpaye gava ghātnaya natara vēvā!* (2) *trastavāda turan vēvā!* (3) *balahatkārayēn āgamvalaṭa haravā gǎenīmaṭa erěhi paṇata pārlimentuve dī sammata vēvā!* (4) *bahujātika, bahuāhamka, sarva āgamka budu dahama vināsha karana pūṭṭu nǎeti vēvā!* (5) *baudda raṭaṭa gǎeḷapěna vyavasthāvak nirmāṇaya vēvā!* The letter and a clear rendition of the text can be found at http://thahanamwachana.blogspot.com.au/2013/05/thero-indarathana-and-us.html (accessed 9 April 2015).
51 See Lahiri (2014) for further details of Gandhi's use of fasting as a form of protest as well as the practice of self-immolation in South Asia.
52 See Keown (1996) for a detailed analysis of this issue.
53 *Lotus Sūtra*, 9. Also see James A. Benn's *Burning for the Buddha* for a detailed analysis of self immolation and sacrifice in Chinese Buddhism (2007).
54 Widger, 91–93.
55 Ibid., 107.

8 Conclusion

Buddhism has a reputation for vegetarianism and kindness towards animals. In the introduction we saw that historical figures such as Moncrief have even viewed this compassionate attitude towards animals as a flaw in the Buddhist religion. For Moncrief, Christianity rightly claims that human beings are superior to non-human animals and consequently of greater moral significance. On the other hand, we have also encountered modern scholars who seek to disabuse us of the notion that it is common in Therevāda Buddhism, at least as a lived tradition, for vegetarianism to be practiced. They make the valid point that sometimes Buddhists are just as cruel to animals as non-Buddhists elsewhere in the world.

What I hope is now clear that this tendency to either completely dismiss vegetarianism or incorrectly assume its common practice are both overly simplistic. In Mahāyāna countries like Taiwan, vegetarianism is ubiquitous. But in Sri Lanka, there is great debate over the doctrinal viability and practical necessity of vegetarianism. Within the Sinhala Buddhist community, a great many factors influence an individual's decision to undertake a vegetarian diet. Some of those factors are driven by religious motives, but other considerations are also important. In particular, the role of vegetarianism as a decision about one's health is an extremely influential factor.

The argument over the question of vegetarianism tends to also be split between lay proponents on one side and clergy who oppose it on the other. In accordance with the so-called Protestant Buddhist movement that so influences modern Sinhala Buddhism, proponents of vegetarianism tend to make greater doctrinal allowances than those who follow a more traditional interpretation of Buddhism. We have found that it is often monks who are especially distrustful of ethical vegetarianism, though there are also unique exceptions here too. Such exceptional monks are often renegades or otherwise hail from an unusual background that makes them stand out from the norm.

Protestant Buddhism is therefore not the exclusive domain of the laity, but can also appear within the ranks of the clergy. Vegetarianism, and the commensurate tendency to disregard or reinterpret the canonical texts, is one example of this desire for reformation. Such reforms appear to be innocent attempts to expand upon the principle of non-violence.

But such reforms can also manifest themselves in more violent ways. The *hālal* abolitionist movement, a movement most recently reinvigorated by disillusioned monks, is an obvious example of this. We have also seen this polemical aggressiveness even in the vegetarian health literature where there is a pattern of excluding foreign food sources in favour of a traditional Sinhala diet. This is sometimes even looked upon as a patriotic duty.

This matter constitutes a key tension in Buddhism, namely its peculiar relation between violence and non-violence.

In Chapter 1 I discussed the two animals of the lion and the cow. Both animals are important symbols of Sinhala Buddhist culture. The lion represents the aggressive and powerful aspect of Sinhala society while the cow represents its nurturing and non-violent tendencies. But this duality is a duality of Buddhism as a whole too. The principle of non-violence is a demanding maxim that has many behavioural implications. It is not always clear that this onerous principle can easily be carried out to its final conclusion. Buddhists the world over aspire to emulate the virtues of the Buddha but often fall back into moral error. This struggle between doing good and doing wrong, between violence and non-violence, is apparent in the origins of human society discussed in Chapter 1. In that tale, evil finds its genesis in the human need to kill and eat animals. The cosmological tale illustrates the fine line between moral transcendence and our ordinary tendency to fall prey to our baser urges.

We have also seen that tough moral decisions are sometimes transposed onto others. Sometimes these responsibilities are disregarded altogether. As we saw in Chapter 4, some monks view the issue of vegetarianism as not being locatable within the normal parameters of monastic responsibility. How and where food is sourced is, for these monks, ultimately a lay issue. The monastic responsibility here is discharged simply by diligently eating what is offered without question or judgement.

Still, this tendency to disregard the significance of vegetarianism is explainable by a number of factors. For one thing, the clergy are much more knowledgeable of, and influenced by, the *Vinaya Piṭaka* than the laity are. The *Vinaya*, of course, does not necessarily view animal killing as particularly serious. Though wrong, the *Vinaya* only views animal killing as an offence of expiation. Furthermore, the *Vinaya* and the *Sūtra Piṭaka* both report that the Buddha insisted that vegetarianism is not mandatory. Monks are therefore not alarmed by the possibility of eating meat and often view these allowances as precisely a doctrinal invitation to eat it.

Lay people, on the other hand, are primarily acquainted with the *Jātaka* stories and other entertaining texts in the *Sūtra Piṭaka*. These texts, and especially the *Jātaka* tales, take a much more sympathetic view of animals. It is no small surprise then, that a number of lay people in this study were quite open to commensurate animal welfare actions such as ethical vegetarianism. This sympathy for animals is bolstered by the voluminous Sinhala language materials that recount horrific stories of animal cruelty. This material is aimed squarely at ordinary lay Buddhists and primes them for the idea that animals matter and should be protected from harm.

History also plays a role in shaping views about animal welfarism and vegetarianism. The most obvious example of this is the special significance of the cow, which finds its origins in the Kiri Ammā cult. But these issues are also shaped by prior colonial influences. For example, during the colonial era Sinhala Buddhist propagandists sometimes used the issue of animal welfare as a way to muster support from Buddhists against foreign imperialists and missionaries. It is highly likely that these factors have influenced modern Sinhala animal welfare. Buddhist revivalism therefore has helped shape how the animal welfare and vegetarian movement has developed even today.

In light of these historical factors, and in light of the usefulness animal welfarism has proven as an instrument for division and political monopolisation, it is perhaps not surprising that some Sinhala Buddhists who are sympathetic to the moral ideal of animal welfarism and ethical vegetarianism, Buddhists who view such doctrines as an ultimate expression of the principle of non-violence, instead find themselves embracing violent action. Such violent actions, perversely, are sometimes done in the name of animal welfare. This is the case despite the fact that these very actions are purportedly justified on grounds of compassion, kindness and a desire to end suffering.

Bibliography

Sinhala language texts

Budda Putrayan Vahansē. *Pūjāvaliya* [*The Chronicle of Offerings*], (ed. Paṇḍita Kiriællē Gñāṇavīmala Nāhimi).

Dharmapāla, Anagārika. *Dænagata yutu karuṇu*, Boralæsgamuva: Visidunu Publishers, 2007(1930).

Galkissē Dhamamavansa Himi. *Tripiṭkāgat saukaya sanrañaṇa viḍi* [*A Compilation on the Preservation of Good Health in the Tripitaka*], Nugēgōdha: Muduṇaya koliṭi Printers, 2005.

Maḍihē Paññāsīha Mahā Nāyaka Māhimipāṇan Vahansē. *Buddāgama hā saukaya, saukaya hā āhāra* [*Buddhism and Health, Health and Food*], Maharagama: Siri Vajarañāṇa Dharmāyatanaya, 2004.

Pranāndu, Yĕlī. *Āhāra hā pōśaṇaya* [*Food and Nutrition*], Dankoṭuwa: Wasana Publishers, 2012.

Pūjaya Gñāṇapōnika Himi. *Jīvitayē āhāra varga sathara* [*The Four Foods of Life*] (trs. Vēdaya H.B. Jayasinha), Kandy: Buddhist Publication Society, 2008.

Pūjaya Kiribatgŏḍa Gñaṇānanda Svāmīn Vahansē. *Nirmānsha prashnaya: Buddimathunṭa visandā gænīma piṇisayi* [*The Question of Vegetarianism*], Colombo: Dayawansa Jayakody & Company, 2010.

Pujayapāda Vishvakīrti Sāhitayashūri Āchārya Buddagayāvē Sisilavaña mētriya Himipāṇō. *Nirmānsha prashnayaṭa: abhiyōgāthmaka piḷithurak (gavēśanāmaka kruthyaki)* [*The Question of Vegetarianism*], Dehiwala: Srīdēvi Publishers, 2011.

Ratnakāra, Shriyā. *Apaṭa jīvath věnna iḍa děnna* [*Give Us Space to Live*], Colombo: Baudda Sanskrutika Maḍayasṭhānaya [Buddhist Cultural Centre], 2009.

Sudasinha, G.D. *Nirmānsha āhārayakaṭa purudu věmu*, Rajagiriya: Harśaṇa Printers, 2012.

Sri Lankan Ministry of Education. *Health and Physical Education Teaching Guide and Manual: Grade 8 & 9 saukyya hā shārrika aḍyāpanaya guru mārgōpadesha sangrahaya: 8 vana sreṇiya*.

Virakkŏḍi, Vishvakīrti Dēshamānaya Sisirachandu. *Avihimsāvěn mētriyaṭa mētriyěn mētri budun dækmaṭa*, Dehiwala: Srīdēvi Publishers, 2012(2002).

Primary texts

Buddhaghosa, *The Expositor (Atthasālanī)*, (trs. Pe Maung Tin), vols I and II, London: Pali Text Society, 1976.

204 Bibliography

The Book of the Discipline (The Vinaya Piṭaka), (trs. Horner, I.B.), vols I, II, III, IV, V, and VI, Oxford: Pali Text Society, 2000.
The Book of the Gradual Sayings (Aṅguttara Nikāya), (trs. Hare, E.M.), Oxford: Pali Text Society, 2008.
The Connected Discourses of the Buddha (Saṃyutta Nikāya), (trs. Bhikkhu Bodhi), Boston, MA: Wisdom Publications, 2000.
The Group of Discourses (Sutta Nipāta), (trs. Norman, K.R.), Lancaster: Pali Text Society, 2006.
The Jātaka or the Stories of the Buddha's Former Births, (trs. Chalmers, R. (vols I and II), Francis, H.T. (vols III, V and VI), Neil, R.A. (vol III), & Rouse, W. H. D. (vol IV)), Oxford: Pali Text Society, 2005.
The Jaina Sutras Vol II (SūtraKritaṅga), (trs. Hermann Jacobi), Oxford: The Pali Text Society, 1968.
The Janavaṃsa, in the Taprobanian: A Dravidian Journal of Oriental Studies in and Around Ceylon, (trs. Hugh Neville), vol 1, 1886–1887.
The Laṅkāvatāra Sūtra: A Mahāyāna Text, (trs. D.T. Suzuki), Delhi: Munshiram Manoharlal Publishers, 1999.
The Long Discourses of the Buddha (Dīgha Nikāya), (trs. Maurice Walshe), Boston, MA: Wisdom Publications, 2009.
The Lotus Sūtra, (trs. Burton Watson), New York: Colombia University Press, 1993.
The Middle Length Discourses of the Buddha (Majjhima Nikāya), (trs. Bhikkhu Ñāṇamoli and Bhikkhu Bodhi), Boston, MA: Wisdom Publications, 2009.
The Minor Anthologies of the Pali Canon: Verses of Uplift (The Udāna) & As It Was Said (Itivuttaka), (trs. F.L. Woodward), Oxford: Pali Text Society, 2003.
The Mahāvaṃsa: The Great Chronicle of Sri Lanka, (trs. Douglas Bullis), Fremont, CA: Asian Humanities Press, 1999.
The Rajāvāliya: A Historical Narrative of Sinhalese Kings, (trs. Guṇasēkara, George J.A. Skeen), Colombo: Government Printer, 1954.

Secondary texts

Abeyeskere, Ananda. 'The Saffron Army, Violence, Terrorism: Buddhism, Identity and Difference in Sri Lanka', *Numen*, vol. 48, no. 1, 1–46, 2001.
Almond, Phillip C. *The British Discovery of Buddhism*, Cambridge: Cambridge University Press, 1988.
Alsdorf, Ludwig. *The History of Vegetarianism and Cow-veneration in India*, (trs. Bal Patil, ed. Willem Bollée), London: Routledge, 2010.
Aresculeratne, S.N. 'Interactions Between Traditional Medicine and "Western" Medicine in Sri Lanka', *Social Scientist*, vol. 30, no. 5/6, 4–17, 2002.
Bartholomeusz, Tessa J. *In Defense of Dharma: Just War ideology in Buddhist Sri Lanka*, London: Routledge, 2002.
Bastin, Rowan. *The Domain of Constant Excess: Plural Worship at the Munnesvaram Temple in Sri Lanka*, Oxford: Berghahn Books, 2002.
Benn, James. *Burning for the Buddha: Self-immolation in Chinese Buddhism*, Honolulu, HI: University of Hawaii Press, 2007.
Blaze, L.E. *History of Ceylon: A Classic History of Sri Lanka from the Ancient Times to the Modern*, Asian Educational Services, 1938.
Bodhipaksa. *Vegetarianism: A Buddhist View*, Cambridge: Windhorse Publications, 2009.

Bond, George. *The Buddhist Revival in Sri Lanka: Religious Tradition, Reinterpretation and Response*, Delhi: Motilal Banarsidass Publishers, 1992.

Bond, George. *Buddhism at Work: Community Development, Social Empowerment and the Sarvodaya Movement*, West Hartford, CT: Kumarian Press, 2004.

Bonnefoy, Yves and Donniger, Wendy. *Asian Mysthologies*, Chicago, IL: University of Chicago Press, 1993(1991).

Braun, Erik. *The Birth of Insight: Meditation, Modern Buddhism and the Burmese Monk Ledi Sayadaw*, Chicago, IL: University of Chicago Press, 2012.

Carrithers, Michael. *The Forest Monks of Sri Lanka: An Anthropological and Historical Study*, Oxford: Oxford University Press, 1983.

Chapple, Christopher Key. *Nonviolence to Animals, Earth, and Self in Asian Traditions*, New York: State University of New York Press, 1993.

Crooke, W. 'The Veneration of the Cow in India', *Folklore*, vol. 23, no. 2, 275–306, 1912.

Deegalle, Mahinda. 'Politics of the Jathika Hela Urumaya Monks: Buddhism and Ethnicity in Contemporary Sri Lanka', *Contemporary Buddhism*, vol. 5, no. 2, 83–103, 2004.

De Silva, K.M. *A History of Sri Lanka*, Sri Lanka, Colombo: Vijitha Yāpa Publications, 2005.

Dewaraja, Lorna. *The Muslims of Sri Lanka: One Thousand Years of Ethnic Harmony 900–1915*, Colombo: The Lanka Islamic Foundation, 1994.

DeVotta, Neil. *Blowback: Linguistic Nationalism, Institutional Decay and Ethnic Conflict in Sri Lanka*, Stanford, CA: Stanford University Press, 2004.

Dharmapāla, Anāgārika. *Return to Righteousness: A Collection of Speeches, Essays and Letters of the Anagarika Dharmapala*, Ceylon: Ministry of Education and Cultural Affairs, 1965.

Dixson, A.F., Halliwell, Gayle, East, Rebecca, Wignarajah, Praveen and Anderson, Matthew. 'Masculine Somatotype and Hirsuteness as Determinants of Sexual Attractiveness to Women,' *Archives of Sexual Behaviour*, vol. 32, no. 1, 29–39, 2003.

Douglas, Mary. *Purity and Danger: An Analysis of Concept of Pollution and Taboo*, London: Routledge, 1966(2002).

Feddema, J.P. 'The "Lesser" Violence of Animal Sacrifice: A Somehwat Hidden and Overlooked (Ignored?) Reality in Sinhala Buddhism', *Anthropos*, Bd. 90, H. 1/3, 133–148, 1995.

Ferro-Luzzi, Gabriella Eichinger. 'Hindu Rites in Modern Tamil Literature', *Anthrpos*, Bd. 98, H.2, 361–377, 2003.

Findly, Ellison Banks. 'Borderline Beings: Plant Possibilities in Early Buddhism', *Journal of the American Oriental Society*, vol. 122, no. 2, 252–263, 2002.

Freitag, Sandria B. 'Sacred Symbols as Mobilising Ideology: The North Indian Search for a "Hindu" Community', *Comparative Studies in Society and History*, vol. 22, no. 4, 597–625, 1980.

Fuller, C.J. *The Camphor Flame: Popular Hinduism and Society in India*, Princeton, NJ: Princeton University Press, 2004.

Gandhi, Leela. *Affective Communities: Anticolonial Thought, Fin-de-Siecle Radicalism and the Politics of Friendship*, Durham, NC: Duke University Press, 2006.

Geiger, Wilhelm. *An Etymological Glossary of the Sinhalese Language*, New Delhi: Asian Educational Services, 1997.

Gombrich, Richard. *Buddhist Precept and Practice: Traditional Buddhism in the Rural Highlands of Ceylon*, Delhi: Motilal Banarsidass Publisher, 1971(1991).

Gombrich, Richard. *Theravada Buddhism: Social History from Ancient Benares to Modern Colombo*, London: Routledge, 2008.

Gombrich, Richard and Obeyesekere, Gananath. *Buddhism Transformed*, Princeton, NJ: Princeton University Press, 1988.

Gough, Kathleen. *Rural Society in Southeast India*, Cambridge: Cambridge University Press, 2009(1981).

Gray David. 'Eating the Heart of the Brahmin: Representations of Alterity and the Formation of Identity in Tantric Buddhist Discourse', *History of Religions*, 45.1, 45–69, 2005.

Harvey, Peter. *An Introduction to Buddhist Ethics: Foundations, Values and Issues*, Cambridge: Cambridge University Press, 2000.

Hazra, Kanai Lal. *The Rise and Decline of Buddhism in India*, Delhi: Munshiram Manoharlal Publishers, 1995.

Horner, I.B. *Early Buddhism and the Taking of Life*, Kandy: Buddhist Publication Society, 1967.

Holt, John. *The Buddhist Visnu: Religious Transformation, Politics and Culture*, New York: Colombia University Press, 2004.

Holt, John. 'Protestant Buddhism?', *Religious Studies Review*, vol. 17, no. 4, 1991.

Hugh, Nevil and Deraniyagala, P.E.P. *Sinhala Verse, Vol. I*, Ceylon National Museum Manuscript Series, 1954.

Jayawardena, Kumari. 'Economic and Political Factors in the 1915 Riots', *the Journal of Asian Studies*, vol. 29, no. 2, 223–233, 1970.

Jha, D.N. *The Myth of the Holy Cow*, London: Verso Books, 2002.

Jones, Constance and Ryan, James. *Encyclopedia of Hinduism*, New York: Infobase Publishing, 2007.

Kannagara, A.P. 'The Riots of 1915 in Sri Lanka', *Past and Present*, vol. 102, no. 1, 130–164, 1984.

Kapferer, Bruce. *A Celebration of Demons*, Bloomington, IN: Indiana University Press, 1983(1991).

Kapferer, Bruce. *Feast of the Sorcerer: Practices of Consciousness and Power*, Chicago, IL: University of Chicago Press, 1997.

Kapferer, Bruce. *Legends of People, Myths and State: Violence, Intolerance and Political Culture in Sri Lanka and Australia*, New York: Bergham Books, 2011.

Kapleau, Roshi Philip. *To Cherish All Life: A Buddhist View of Animal Slaughter and Meat Eating*, Taipei: The Corporate Body of the Buddha Dharma Education Association, 1981.

Katulanda, P. et al. 'Pervalence and Projections of Diabetes and Pre-diabetes in Adults in Sri Lanka – Sri Lanka Diabetes', *Cardiovascular Study, Diabetic Medicine*, vol. 25, no. 9, 1062–1069, 2008.

Keown, Damien. 'Buddhism and Suicide: The Case of Channa', *The Journal of Buddhist Ethics*, vol. 3, 8–31, 1996.

Keown, Damien. *Buddhist Ethics: A Very Short Introduction*, Oxford: Oxford University Press, 2005.

Kemper, Stephen. *Buying and Believing: Sri Lankan Advertising and Consumers in a Transnational World*, Chicago, IL: University of Chicago Press, 2001.

Khare, R.S. 'A Case of Anomalous Values in Indian Civilisation: Meat Eating Among the Kanya-Kubja Brahmans of the Katyayan Gotra', *The Journal of Asian Studies*, vol. 25, no. 2, 229–240, 1966.

King, Richard. *Orientalism and Religion: Post-Colonial Theory, India and "The Mystic East"*, London: Routledge, 1999.
King, Winston. *In the Hope of Nibbana: An Essay on Theravada Buddhist Ethics*, La Salle, IL: Open Court, 1964.
Knox, Robert. *An Historical Relation of the Island Ceylon in the East Indies*, Dodo Press, 1958.
Lahiri, Simanti. *Suicide Protest in South Asia: Consumed by Commitment*, London: Routledge, 2014.
Liyanaratne, Jinadasa. *Buddhism and Traditional Medicine in Sri Lanka*, Colombo: Kelaniya University Press, 1999.
Locke, John. *Two Treatises of Government*, (ed. Laslett, P.), Cambridge: Cambridge University Press, 1988.
Malalgoda, Kitsiri. *Buddhism in Sinhalese Society, 1750–1900: A Study of Religious Revival and Change*, Oakland, CA: University of California Press, 1976.
McGetchin, Douglas. *Indology, Indomania and Orientalism: Ancient India's Rebirth in Modern Germany*, Fairleigh Dickenson, 2009.
McGilvray, Dennis. *Crucible of Conflict: Tamil and Muslim Society on the East Coast of Sri Lanka*, Durham, NC: Duke University Press, 2008.
MvGilvray, Dennis and Raheem, Mirak. 'Origins of the Sri Lankan Muslims and Varieties of the Muslim Identity', *The Sri Lanka Reader: History, Culture, Politics*, Durham, NC: Duke University Press, 2011.
Norman, K.M. 'Notes on Aśoka's Fifth Edict', *Royal Asiatic Society of Great Britain and Ireland*, April, no. 1/2, 1967.
Obeyeskere, Gananath. 'The Great and the Little in the Perspective of Sinhalese Buddhism', *The Journal of Asian Studies*, vol. 22, no. 2, 139–153, 1963.
Obeyeskere, Gananath. 'Religious Symbolism and Political Change in Ceylon,' *Modern Ceylon Studies*, vol. 1, 43–63, 1970.
Obeyeskere, Gananath. "The Impact of Āyurvedic Ides on the Culture and the Individual in Sri Lanka," in *Asian Medical Systems a Comparative Study* (ed. Charles M. Leslie), Ockland, CA: University of California Press, 1976.
Obeyeskere, Gananath. 'Social Change and the Deities: Rise of the Kataragama Cult in Modern Sri Lanka,' *Man*, vol. 12, no. 3/4, 377–396, 1977.
Obeyeskere, Gananath. *The Cult of the Goddess Pattini*, Delhi: Motilal Banarsidass Publishers, 1987(1984).
Obeyeskere, Gananath. 'Buddhism, Ethnicity and Identity: A Problem of Buddhist History,' *The Journal of Buddhist Ethics*, vol. 10, 192–242, 2003.
Ogden, Janes and Elder, Charlotte. 'The Role of Family Status and Ethnic Group on Body Image and Eating Behaviour', *Journal of Eating Disorders*, April, no. 3, 309–315, 1998.
Olcott, Henry Steel. *The Golden Rules of Buddhism*, available at: http://hpb.narod.ru/GoldenRulesBuddhismHSO.html,1887.
Orenstein, Henry. 'The Structure of Hindu Caste Values: A Preliminary Study of Hierarchy and Ritual Defilement', *Ethnology*, vol. 4, no. 1, 1–15, 1965.
Parker, Henry. *Ancient Ceylon*, New Delhi: Asian Educational Services, 1999 (1909).
Phelps, Norm. *The Great Compassion: Buddhism and Animal Rights.* New York: Lantern Books, 2004.
Pieris, P.E. *Ceylon and the Portuguese (1505–1658)*, Tellippalai: American Ceylon Mission Press, 1920.

Percival, Robert. *An Account of the Island of Ceylon: Its History, Geography, Natural History, with the Manners and Customs of its Various Inhabitants*, Blackfriars: C. and R. Baldwin, 1803.

Pfaffenberger, Bryan. 'The Kataragama Pilgramage: Hindu-Buddhist Interaction and Its Significance in Sri Lanka's Polyethnic Social System', *Journal of Asian Studies*, vol. 38, no. 2, 253–270, 1979.

Parmeshwaranand, Swami. *Encyclopedic Dictionary of Purāṇas Vol 1*, Delhi: Sarup and Sons, 2001.

Prothero, Stephen. 'Henry Steel Olcott and Protestant Buddhism', *Journal of the American Academy of Religion*, vol. 63, no. 2, 281–302, 1995.

Popkin, Barry M., Horton, Sue H. and Soowon Kim. 'The Nutrition Transition and Prevention of Diet Related Diseases in Asia and the Pacific', *Food and Nutrition Bulletin*, vol. 22, no. 4, 2001.

Powers, John. *A Bull of a Man: Images of Masculinity, Sex, and the Body in Indian Buddhism*, Cambridge, MA: Harvard University Press, 2009.

Raghavan, M.D. *The Kārava of Ceylon: Society and Culture*, Colombo: K.V.G. De Silva and Sons, 1961.

Ruegg, Seyfort D. 'Ahimsa and Vegetarianism in the History of Buddhism', *Buddhist Studies in Honour of Walpola Rahula*, London: Gordon Fraser, 1980.

Ray, Reginald. *Buddhist Saints of India: A Study in Buddhist Values and Orientations*, Oxford: Oxford University Press, 1999.

Rippin, Andrew. *Muslims: Their Religious Beliefs and Practices*, London: Routledge, 2011.

Ryan, Bryce. *Caste in Modern Ceylon: The Sinhalese System in Transition*, New Brunswick, NJ: Rutger University Press, 1953.

Sachs, Lisbeth. 'Misunderstanding as Therapy: Doctors, Patients and Medicines in a Rural Clinic in Sri Lanka', *Culture, Medicine and Psychiatry*, vol. 13, 335–349, 1989.

Sangharakshita. *Flame in Darkness: Life and Sayings of Anagarika Dharmapala*, Delhi: Tiratana Grantha Mala, 1980.

Sayers, Matthew. 'The Myth of the Holy Cow', *Journal of Asian Studies*, vol. 62, no. 1, 311–313, 2003.

Seneviratne, H.L. *Rituals of the Kandyan State*, Cambridge: Cambridge University Press, 1978.

Schmithausen, Lambert. 'The Early Buddhist Tradition and Ecological Ethics', *Journal of Buddhist Ethics*, vol. 4, 1–74, 1997.

Simoons, Fredrick J. *Not this Flesh: Food Avoidances and Prehistory to the Present*, Madison, WI: University of Wisconsin Press, 1994.

Spiro, Melford. *Buddhism and Society: A Great Tradition and its Burmese Vicissitudes*, Oakland, CA: University of California Press, 1982.

Stewart, James. 'The Question of Vegetarianism and Diet in Pali Buddhism', *Journal of Buddhist Ethics*, vol. 17, 2010.

Stewart, James. 'Cow Protectionism in Sinhala Buddhist Sri Lanka', *Journal of the Oriental Society of Australia*, vol. 45, 2013.

Stewart, James. 'Violence and Nonviolence in Buddhist Animal Ethics', *Journal of Buddhist Ethics*, vol. 21, 2014.

Stewart, James. 'Muslim-Buddhist Conflict in Contemporary Sri Lanka', *South Asia Research*, vol. 34, no. 3, 241–260, 2014.

Tambiah, Stanley J. *Buddhism Betrayed? Religion, Politics and Violence in Sri Lanka*, Chicago: University of Chicago Press, 1992.

Tambiah, Stanley J., *Sri Lanka: Ethnic Fratricide and the Dismantling of Democracy*, Chicago: University of Chicago Press, 1986.
Thomas, Edward. *The Life of the Buddha as Legend and History*, Whitefish, MT: Kessinger Reprints, 1927(2006).
Trainor, Kevin. *Relics, Rituals and Representations in Buddhism: Rematerialising the Sri Lankan Theravada Tradition*, Cambridge: Cambridge University Press, 1997.
Ulrich, Katherine, E. 'Food Fights: Buddhist, Hindu, and Jain Dietary Polemics in South India', *History of Religions*, vol. 46, no. 3, 228–261, 2007.
Waldau, Paul. *The Specter of Speciesism: Buddhist and Christian Views of Animals*, New York: Oxford University Press, 2001.
Wasson, G. and O'Flaherty, W.D. 'The Last Meal of the Buddha', *Journal of the American Oriental Society*, vol. 102, no. 4, 591–603, 1982.
Widger, Tom. 'Suicide and the Morality of Kinship in Sri Lanka', *Contributions to Indian Sociology*, vol. 46, 1–2, 2012.
Wijesinghe, Pushpa Ranjan. 'Obesity is a Wake Up Call for Developing World Too', *British Medical Journal (BMJ)*, 333, 809, 2006.
Wijeyeratna, Rohan de Silva. *Nation, Constitutionalism and Buddhism in Sri Lanka*, New York: Routledge, 2014.
Wickramasinghe V.P., Lamabadasuriya S.P., Ataputta N., Sathyadas G., Kuruparanantha, S., and Karunarathne, P. 'Nutritional Status of Schoolchildren in an Urban Area of Sri Lanka', *Ceylon Medical Journal*, vol. 49, no. 4, 114–118, 2004.
Williams, Duncan. "Animal Liberation, Death, and the State: Rites to Release Animals in Medieval Japan", in *Buddhism and Ecology* (eds Tucker, Mary and Williams, Duncan), Boston, MA: Harvard University Press, 1998.
Young, Richard Fox. 'The Carpenter Prēta: An Eighteenth-Century Sinhala-Buddhist Folktale about Jesus', *Asian Folklore Studies*, vol. 54, no. 1, 49–68, 1995.
Young, Richard and Senanayaka, G.S.B. *The Carpenter-Heretic: A Collection of Buddhist Stories about Christianity from 18th Century Sri Lanka*, Colombo: Karunaratne & Sons, 1998.

Index

āyurvedic medicines 148, 155, 157–8
Abeyesekere, Ananda 32
abstinence 43
An Account of the Island of Ceylon (Percival) 27–8
activism 119, 175–6
Adikāramitumā, E.W. 61
aggressive foods 35
All Ceylon Buddhist Congress 31, 128
All Ceylon Jamiyyathul Ulamā 185–6, 187
alms giving ceremony 82–6, 98–100
Alsdorf, Ludwig 16–17, 124
animal protectionism 15–17; all animals 78–9; big animals 47; medicine and 156–8; monks 110–12; in Sinhala myth 17–21
anti-vegetarianism 61–4
Arnold, Edwin 3
Aśoka, King 12–13, 15–17, 30
Atthasālinī (*The Expositor*) (Buddhaghosa) 2, 20–1

Basham 16
Bastin, Rowan 127
Bechert, Heinz 116
bestiality 19
Blatavsky, Madame 28–9
blood 134
Bŏdu Bala Sēna 182–6
Bodhipaksa 5
Bodhisattva 19, 58–9
body shape 149–51
Bokka 186
Bond, George 31, 166–7
Brahmadatta, King 44–5
Brahman tradition 13, 14
British period 27–30
Buddha: as a bodhisattva 44–5; on the destruction of life 1; eating habits problem 64–6; feeding 86–9; final meal 48; flawless body 145n52; food as fuel 105; meat-eating conditions 47–8, 102; starvation diet 152; as a vegetarian 49–50; wet nurses 135
buddhage 90–1
Buddhaghosa 2, 20–1, 41, 47, 54
buddhapūjā 73–7, 86–9, 91
Buddhism Transformed (Gombrich) 75
Buddhist Catechism (Prothero) 29
Buddhist Catechisms (Olcott) 118
Buddhist eggs 94–5
Buddhist Revivalist period 28
Burma 143n13

Cakkana 20–1
Carpenter Prēta Tale 22–3
Carrithers, Michael 85
castes 13–14, 21–2, 96n7
chaṇḍāla caste 30
Christianity *see also* Protestant Buddhism: castes 21; humans/animals 200; influence of 27; traitors 115; undermining of 23, 28, 29–30
civil disobedience 2
civil war 12
clinics 148–9
Colombo 9
compassion 41, 61, 63
consumption 99
contamination 87
cow products 126–7
cow protectionism *see also* halāl abolitionism; Organisation for the Preservation of Life: festivals 126; in India 124–5; in literature 131–5; in the media 128–31; in music 138–40; origins of 125–8; reasons for 123–4; social media 135–7; suicidal ideation 191–5

cows, veneration of 12, 122–3
cravings 77
critical religious spaces 89–92
Crooke, W. 124
cruel acts 50–5, 56, 129–30, 132, 201–2

dāna 73, 83–7
Daily Code for the Laity (Dharmapāla) 29–30
Daladā 91–2
Dayāratana, Akimýmana 175, 184
De Silva, K.M. 97n24
demons 32–3, 88
dependent origination 79
desire 54, 56, 83, 99
Devadatta 48, 105
Devol Deviyo 34–5
Dewaraja, Lorna 178–9
Dharma 16, 87, 110
Dharmapāla, Anāgārika 29–30, 179–80
diabetes 151
diet, twentieth century 30–2
Douglas, Mary 14

education 162–3
egg eating 93–5
Einstein, Albert 61
elephants 156
ethical vegetarianism: clergy/laity 119–20; defence of 50; doctrinally unsound 3, 102–8; as purview of the laity 108–10; reasons for 100–1; sincerity of 62; Western views 5
ethnic conflict 175–6, 178–82, 195–6
excess eating 94
exorcism 32–4
expiation 46
expulsion 46

factory farming 133
fast food 150
femininity 150
Fernando, Ishara 148–9, 167
Ferro-Luzzi, Gabriella Eichinger 124
first precept 63, 74–7, 111, 113–14
fishing 21–2, 46–7, 77
five precepts 43, 57, 62
Food and Nutrition (Pranāndu) 161–2
food contamination 190–1
food offerings 26, 73–4, 84
food sharing 82–6
food shops 78
From Non-violence to Maitreya (Virakŏdi) 188–9

fruit 151, 169
Fuller, Christopher 13, 14

Gandhi, Leela 4
Gandhi, Mohandas 13, 124, 193
Gangula Veda Medura 148
Gautama Buddha 58–9
germs 87
Give us Space to Live (Rathnakāra) 57–9, 133, 167–8
Gñanasāra 182–3
gods, dining with 34–6
Golden Rules of Buddhism (Olcott) 29
Gombrich, Richard: animal protectionism 133; egg eating 93, 94–5; first precept 75; Kataragama 35–6; meat offerings 33; modernist/traditional monk 119; Protestant Buddhism 116; translations 153; vegetarianism not practiced 30–1; violence towards animals 18
Gonçalves, Jacome 27
Gough, Kathleen 126
Gray, David 37n19

hālal 130–1
hālal abolitionism: activism 175–6; importance of 122–3; overview 185–9, 201; proponents of 136; *Stop Killing Cows* 137; suicidal ideation 191–5
Hajji 186–7
Harvey, Peter 47, 85
healing rites 140–1
healthy eating: health literature 161–3; history of 151–4; illness and diet 155; medical risks 149–51; vegetarianism for health 167–70; virtues of vegetarianism 158–60
Himipāṇo, Bhikkhu 133–4
Hinduism: cow protectionism 126–7; cows 124; deities 35; extent of vegetarianism 14; festivals 126; influence of 13, 92; undermining of 30, 55

A Historical Relation of Ceylon (Knox) 25

Holt, John 116, 118
The Holy Cow (Jha) 124–5
Horner, I.B. 15
horoscopes 19
hunting 17–18, 19–20, 25, 44–5, 63

Indaratane, Bowatte 191–5
India 12–15, 55, 124–5

212 Index

insects 43, 128
International Buddhist Council of Sri Lanka 136, 183–4
Isharo, Fernandos 158

Jātaka Tales 18, 44–5, 118, 201–2
Jainism 13, 63, 102
Janathā Vimukti Pĕramuṇa (JVP) 32
Janavaṃsa 21–2
Jesus 23
Jha, D.N. 124
Jīvaka Sūtta 102

Kāmadhenu 125, 132, 141–2
Kaha temple 73–4
Kali 33, 34
Kalinga campaign 15–16
Kandy 9
Kandyan Kingdom 24–7, 36
Kapferer, Bruce 33–4, 35, 87
Kapleau, Roshi 5, 49
karāva caste 21–2
karma 43–4, 51–5, 129–30
Kashyapa, King 11
Kataragama 35–6, 89–92, 155
Keḷaṇitissa, King. 20
Kegalle 9
Khare, R. S. 14–15
King, Richard 116
Kiri Ammā cult 125, 132, 136–7, 138, 140–2, 192
Knox, Robert 25, 30, 75, 127–8
Ksatriya caste 14
Kuvéṇi 20

Lankāvatāra Sūtra 167
Lankadīpa 50–5, 128–9
lay communities: detractors 80–1; ethical vegetarianism 108–10; first precept 74–7; food offerings 73–4; lay–monk social interactions 99; supporters 77–80
Let's all adopt a vegetarian diet (Sudasinha) 55–7
The Light of Asia (Arnold) 3
lions 11–12, 201
Locke, John 25

Māḷigāva 91, 98–100
Mahāvaṃsa 17–18, 177
Mahāyāna 167, 194
Mahavira 13, 49
Mahinda 17, 184
Maitreya 58–9, 188–9

Malalgoda, Kitsiri 116, 118
mandatory vegetarianism 105
material requisites 83, 100
McGetchin, Douglas 4
McGilvray, Dennis 145n47
meat-eating: body odour and 111; conditions for 47–8; countries 5; justifications for 14–15; meat produces illness 167–8; moral hierarchies 45–7; Orientalism and 4–5; permission for 103–8; restrictions 86; as treatment 156–8
medical risks 149–51
medicine 105–6, 148–9, 154–8
medieval period 179
meditation 74
merit 120n1, 149
middle way 63
milk: in ceremonies 127; importance of 82, 114, 140; mothers' milk 134–5, 136–7; powdered milk 135
minority groups 175–6
missionaries 117
Mōhinī 140
Moncrief, Robert 3–4, 200
monks: alms giving ceremony 82–6; animal welfarism 110–12; female clergy 183; flesh offerings 52; food offerings 26, 73–4; instruction manual 2, 19, 20; modernist/traditional monk 119; monastic responsibilities 108–10; motivations for vegetarianism 100–3; redisciplining 32; rulebook 45–7; suicidal ideation 191–5; views on vegetarianism 98–100
Morales, Father 24
mosquitos 163
mothers 124, 125, 161
mushrooms 64–5
music 138–40
Muslims 11 *see also hālal* abolitionism; animosity towards 115; ethnic conflict 175–6, 178–82, 195–6; food contamination 190–1; *hālal* 130–1; lions 11–12; slaughter houses 46–7

Nathaputha 63
nationalism: Buddhist groups 182–5; food contamination 190–1; and food practices 163–7, 175–6; history of 178–82; origins of 177–8
Nelson, Nihāl 138–9
New Year 127
nirvana 86–7

non-violence principle 1–3, 31 *see also* first precept
Norman, K. M. 16
not deserving 75–6
nursery rhymes 139–40

Obeyesekere, Gananath: egg eating 95; first precept 30–1, 75; food offerings 84; Kataragama 35–6; meat offerings 33; Pattini cult 140–1; Protestant Buddhism 116–17; translations 153
occupations 1–2
O'Flaherty, Wendy Doniger 65
Olcott, Henry Steel 4–5, 28–9, 116, 118
Orenstein, Henry 14
Organisation for the Preservation of Life 113–16, 123, 133, 134, 141–2
Orientalism 4–5, 29
obesity 150

Pāli texts: animal killing 1–2, 42–4; components 67n4; healthy eating 151–2; self-preservation 42; self-sacrifice 41; translations 153
pacificism 41–2
Parakramabahu IX 11
Parker, Henry 140
Pattini cult 140
Peiris, P.E. 127
Percival, Robert 27–8, 128
Phelps, Norm 5
philosophy, Buddhism as 5–6
physical activity 151, 162
Pieris, P. E. 24
plant life 43
politics, participation in 109–10
pollution 13–14, 168
Portuguese period 22–4, 127
poverty 151
poya 28, 67n6, 74, 78
Pranāndu, Yeḷ 161–2
prētas 23–4, 34
pregnancy 161
private property 2
pro-vegetarianism 55–9, 66
The Problem of Vegetarianism (Thēra) 62–4
processed foods 164
Protestant Buddhism 29, 116–19, 183, 196
protests 2, 178, 179–80
Prothero, Stephen 29
prudential vegetarianism 101, 106, 107–8
Pūjāvaliya 134–5

Pūjaya Gñānapōnika 153
Puṇṇa, 41, 193–4
purchasing meat 110–11
purification rituals 13–14
purity 78, 87

The Question of Vegetarianism (Himipāṇo) 133–4

Rājasiṃha, King 25, 27, 92
Rajāvāliya 18–20
Ratnakāra, Shriyā 57–9, 133, 167–8, 170–1
rebirth 44, 79–80, 86
relics 91–2
revenge literature 50–5
rice 164
rice paddies 136
riots 1915 178, 179–80
riots 1983 178
ritual killings 55
Ruegg, Seyfort D. 31, 75
Ryan, Bryce 21

sakuro caste 21–2
Sangharakshita 179
Sarvōdaya movement 166
Schmithausen, Lambert 43
self-defence 41
self-preservation 41–2
self-sacrifice 41
Seventh Day Adventists 55
Shabkar.org 5
sickness 140–1
siddha medicine 155
Simoons, Frederick J. 95
Sinhala Only Act 1956 177–8
Sinhala Rāvaya 175, 182, 184–5
slaughter *see also* fishing; *hālal*; hunting: boycott of slaughter houses 47; cruel acts 50–5, 56, 132, 201–2; hierarchy of animals 46–7; karma 50–5, 129–30; large animals 31; punishment for 44, 46, 47; revenge literature 50–5
social media 135–7
sons of the soil 166
Sri Lanka 6–7, 9
Stop Killing Cows – Sri Lanka 137
Sūtra Piṭaka 43, 118
Sudasinha, J.D. 55–7, 64–5
suicide 191–5
supernatural world 32–4
sweetmeats 34
Sīnigama temple 34–5

Tahanam Vachana (Censored Words) 79
Tamils 11, 126, 177–8
tantricism 14
Thai Pongal 126
Thra, Gñanananda 62–4, 65, 119–20
Theravāda 2, 5, 58–9, 193–4
Tibet 194
tigers 156

Virakkōdi, Vishvakīrti 132
Vedic tradition 13, 124
Vegetarian Society 60–1, 168, 169–70
vegetarianism: anti-vegetarianism 61–4; benefits of 57; detractors of 80–1; motivations for 100–3; non-mandatory 3; pro-vegetarianism 55–9, 66; reputation for 3–6; supporters of 77–80
Vijaya 19, 20
Vinaya 2, 45–7, 118, 201

Virakkōdi, Vishvakīrti 188–9
virtuous acts 43
vows 87

Waldau, Paul 5
Wasson, R. Gordon 65
wedding practices 36
Western diets 164–5, 169
Western medicine 154
Western products 163
Widger, Tom 194
Wijeysinghe, Pushpa 150–1
Wimalajōthi 182–3
wishes 97n16

xenophobia 175–6

Young Man's Buddhist Association 31
Young, Robert Fox 23, 24–7